Brandom

Key Contemporary Thinkers Series includes:

Brandom

Ronald Loeffler

polity

First published in 2018 by Polity Press

Polity Press
65 Bridge Street
Cambridge CB2 1UR, UK

Polity Press
101 Station Landing, Suite 300
Medford, MA 02155, USA

ISBN-13: 978-0-7456-6419-4
ISBN-13: 978-0-7456-6420-0(pb)

A catalogue record for this book is available from the British Library.

Typeset in 10.5 on 12pt Palatino by Toppan Best-set Premedia Limited
Printed and bound in the UK by CPI Group (UK) Ltd, Croydon

For further information on Polity, visit our website: politybooks.com

Für meine Mutter

Anneliese Löffler

Contents

Acknowledgments

This book is the fruit of intermittent extended periods of close study of Brandom's work over the course of the past two decades, starting with a graduate seminar on *Making it Explicit* at Northwestern University in the Fall of 1996, co-taught by Tom McCarthy and my dissertation adviser-to-be Michael Williams. Over the years, numerous teachers and colleagues have influenced my thinking about Brandom's work, and issues related to it. In addition to Michael Williams and Tom McCarthy, I am indebted to Cameron Bunker, Gary Ebbs, John Fennell, Chris Gauker, Michael Glanzberg, Sandy Goldberg, Jürgen Habermas, Steven Hendley, Cristina Lafont, Mark Lance, Chris Latiolais, Axel Mueller, Jay Rosenberg, Kevin Sharp, Jeremy Wanderer, and Meredith Williams.

Special thanks to my colleagues Jeff Byrnes, Andrew Spear, and Dwayne Tunstall at Grand Valley State University for doing a reading group together on the *Spirit of Trust* manuscript in the summer of 2014. The mix of Jeff's Heidegger-honed boundless creativity, Andrew's dogged neo-Cartesian brilliance, and Dwayne's living, breathing erudition about Hegel and classical American pragmatism, as it came alive in our discussions, has widened and deepened my interpretation and appreciation of Brandom's work considerably – and probably in more ways than I am aware of.

I am deeply grateful to two anonymous reviewers of an earlier draft of this manuscript for their generous, constructive, and helpful feedback, which has helped me to significantly improve this manuscript. Of course, I alone am responsible for any remaining mistakes and shortcomings.

Heartfelt thanks to Pascal Porcheron, the editor of this volume at Polity Press, and Ellen MacDonald-Kramer, the assistant editor, for all their work and kind assistance. Their encouragement, patience, flexibility, and helpfulness made working on this project much easier than it would otherwise have been. Many thanks also to Ann Klefstad for copy-editing the manuscript and to Rachel Moore for her work on the production of the book.

At last, thanks from the bottom of my heart to Carla Jackson for her loving patience and joyful, caring presence and companionship.

Abbreviations

The following abbreviations for works by Robert Brandom have been used in this text.

AR *Articulating Reasons: An Introduction to Inferentialism.* Cambridge, MA: Harvard University Press.

BSD *Between Saying and Doing: Towards an Analytic Pragmatism.* New York: Oxford University Press.

EE *From Empiricism to Expressivism: Brandom Reads Sellars.* Cambridge, MA: Harvard University Press.

MIE *Making It Explicit: Reasoning, Representing, and Discursive Commitment.* Cambridge, MA: Harvard University Press.

PP *Perspectives on Pragmatism: Classical, Recent, and Contemporary.* Cambridge, MA: Harvard University Press.

RP *Reason in Philosophy: Animating Ideas.* Cambridge, MA: Harvard University Press.

SOT *A Spirit of Trust: A Semantic Reading of Hegel's Phenomenology.* 2014 draft, http://www.pitt. edu/~brandom/spirit_of_trust_2014.html. Accessed 04/02/2014.

TMD *Tales of the Mighty Dead: Historical Essays in the Metaphysics of Intentionality.* Cambridge, MA: Harvard University Press.

Introduction

Robert B. Brandom is an American philosopher, influential on both sides of the Atlantic. Brandom was born on March 13, 1950. He received his BA degree *summa cum laude* in 1972 from Yale University, majoring in philosophy, and his Ph.D. degree in philosophy from Princeton University in 1977. In 1976 he joined the Philosophy Department at the University of Pittsburgh, where he has been a faculty member ever since and is currently a Distinguished Professor.

Brandom's most influential teachers at Princeton were Richard Rorty (his Ph.D. thesis supervisor) and David Lewis. In a 1999 interview, Brandom describes his relationship with his two mentors as follows:

> My aim in working with them was to address the sorts of problems that Rorty is concerned with, but to do so with the tools and methods of our day of which Lewis is the master. Rorty said of his own teacher Wilfrid Sellars that in him one finds the spirit of Hegel bound in the fetters of Carnap. If so, that is true of me as well. It might be said that I have aimed to present the spirit of Rorty – not so much bound in the fetters of Lewis, as expressed with the precision of his language.
>
> (1999: 1)

These reflections neatly characterize Brandom's central philosophical aspiration throughout his career to the present day. On the one hand, Brandom is inspired by Rorty's pragmatist vision that the key to understanding what makes us humans rational and capable of empirical knowledge is looking at our ability to communicate linguistically with each other. Brandom's work thus focuses squarely on the issues at the heart of theoretical modern Western philosophy: the nature of human reason and knowledge. And Brandom wants to tackle these issues in broadly Rortyan pragmatist terms – specifically, in terms of our ability to engage in linguistic, communicative social practices. On the other hand, Brandom's ambition is to pursue this pragmatist project with the clarity and rigor that David Lewis is famous for. Rather than merely glossing over the many philosophical and technical challenges his grand project poses, Brandom tends to tackle them at length and with an orientation to detail. This combination of a sweeping pragmatist vision about traditional modern Western philosophical themes and tenacious efforts to see through the details makes Brandom's work both exciting and difficult. Brandom's books tend to be long and dense, and the vocabulary in which he approaches these themes tends to be unfamiliar. The present book aspires to be a guide for the uninitiated through this thicket. It is no proper replacement for wrestling with Brandom's work oneself, but hopefully will provide inspiration and assistance.

In the quote above, Brandom also mentions the two philosophers who are most influential on his efforts to work out his Rorty-inspired project: G. W. F. Hegel and Wilfrid Sellars. Brandom sees his massive 1994 book *Making It Explicit* as an attempt to work out – without explicitly engaging with Hegel and in language palatable to a contemporary "analytic" philosophical audience – ideas at the heart of Hegel's philosophy, in particular Hegel's idea of the institution of reason and concepts through mutual social recognition and his understanding of reason and concepts as essentially holistic (1999: 2). The depth of Brandom's engagement with Hegel becomes more apparent in some of his subsequent work, which elaborates and refines the theory developed in *Making It Explicit* in the form of explicit interpretations of aspects of Hegel's work – culminating in the forthcoming *Spirit of Trust*, a commentary on Hegel's *Phenomenology of Spirit*. Moreover, Brandom's appropriations of Hegelian ideas are simultaneously appropriations and developments of themes of the work of Wilfrid Sellars (1912–1989), the great American critic of empiricist philosophy and, until his death, Brandom's colleague at Pittsburgh, in particular Sellars's neo-Kantian (and neo-Hegelian) conception of reason as essentially normative, his inferential role semantics, his theory of empirical knowledge, and his theory of logical and modal concepts as categorical in a broadly Kantian sense.

Of course, Sellars's work – not to mention Hegel's – is often seen as no less difficult and obscure as it is profound. While Brandom's work is not, I think, obscure, he shares with Hegel and Sellars a relish for a big, unified philosophical vision as well as a predilection for systematic thinking, in the sense that he tries to derive ambitious metaphysical or epistemological theses from a relatively small set of principles (principles of the workings of language in communication, for him) while aspiring to Lewisian standards of clarity and rigor. This is perhaps the reason why the reception of Brandom's work thus far has on the whole been keener and more energetic in continental Europe than in England and North America. Studying Brandom's work requires the patience to read through big, dense books, and the openness not only to look at old issues from a vantage point that is at once complex and unfamiliar but also to take a second (or first) look at some philosophers and ideas that – at least in mainstream Anglo-American "analytic" philosophical circles – are routinely dismissed as nebulous and (therefore) irrelevant. Such patience and openness tend to be more prevalent among philosophers trained in continental Europe, where philosophy in the "analytic" tradition, while influential, is not as dominant as it is on the other side of the Atlantic (or the Channel), where the vocabularies that academically trained students of philosophy are exposed to come from more varying philosophical traditions, where the legacy of German Idealism is entrenched and alive, where academic philosophy is perhaps still less professionalized, and where philosophy seminars tend to revolve around big, clunky books rather than short, elegant papers. If this diagnosis is accurate, my hope is that the present book may especially be of some assistance to Anglo-American analytic philosophers, in taking a crack at Brandom's work – though, again, this book cannot replace studying the work itself.

With Jeremy Wanderer's *Robert Brandom*, a terrific introductory monograph to Brandom's work already exists. The present volume is similar in aspiration and target audience, but, besides taking into account Brandom's most recent work – including the so-far-unpublished *Spirit of Trust* (the 2014 manuscript version of which has been available via Brandom's website for some time) – it naturally differs from Wanderer's book somewhat in focus and (some) interpretations. Our most important interpretive difference, I think, is that while Wanderer reads Brandom's pragmatism as a non-explanatory descriptive approach to reason and linguistic meaning – as an attempt to describe how reason and meaning are essentially tied to processes of linguistic communication – I read Brandom's pragmatism as an attempt to explain reason and meaning in terms of communication, which is how Brandom's pragmatism is more commonly interpreted. However, like Wanderer, I too treat *all* of Brandom's work, whether systematic or dedicated to the interpretation of historical texts and figures, as aimed at articulating and refining his pragmatist vision of language, reason, and knowledge. Brandom's work has developed significantly since the publication of *Making It Explicit*. However, later works are, I think, best seen as expansions and refinements of the comprehensive theory of linguistic communication first presented in that landmark book, and I feel, accordingly, free throughout to cite freewheelingly from Brandom's oeuvre in its entirety, without worrying much about its chronological order (unless indicated otherwise).

Chapters 1 and 2 introduce Brandom's fundamental theoretical commitments – his pragmatism, his inferential role semantics, his conception of reason as irreducibly normative and instituted through a process of mutual social recognition – by, respectively, placing his project in the context of more mainstream approaches to language and linguistic communication and introducing Brandom's appropriation of the German Idealist tradition. Chapters 3 through 8 then gradually add more detail to these fundamentals: his normative pragmatics, that is, his scorekeeping model of linguistic communication (chapter 3); his key semantic notions of inference and substitution and his theory of anaphora (chapter 4); his account of empirical knowledge (chapter 5); his theory of logical vocabulary (chapter 6); his theory of representation and communicative success (chapter 7); and his theories of objectivity and of the sociohistorical process of instituting conceptual norms through discursive practice (chapter 8).

1

Meaning and Communication

In a popular lecture, Brandom made the following meta-philosophical remark:

> Philosophy is a reflexive enterprise: understanding is not only the *goal* of philosophical inquiry, but its *topic* as well. *We* are its topic; but it is us specifically as *understanding* creatures: *discursive* beings, makers and takers of *reasons*, seekers and speakers of *truth*.
>
> (RP 113)

This remark indicates what Brandom sees as the first goal of philosophy and the proper method for pursuing this goal. Brandom embraces the large legacy of the eighteenth-century German philosopher Immanuel Kant, according to which a critique of reason is the proper foundation for any other philosophical inquiry, and hence the first goal of all philosophy. The right understanding of the principles, powers, and limitations of our ability to reason – to conceptualize, comprehend, interpret, examine, evaluate, draw inferences, argue, and explain – not only yields answers to the big philosophical questions *concerned with* reasoning, cognition, meaning, and logic (questions within epistemology and the philosophy of mind/psychology/language/logic) but also constrains the right answers to the big philosophical questions concerned with the fundamental constitution of reality and our status as free and responsible beings (questions within metaphysics and ethics). Moreover, Brandom embraces the linguistic turn in philosophy, associated with developments in twentieth-century

Anglo-American philosophy, in the sense that, according to him, the right understanding of linguistic meaning and linguistic communication – the right understanding of us as social beings who communicate with each other using meaningful speech – is in turn the key to a proper understanding of our ability to reason (e.g. PP 21–6). Let us begin by introducing, in this chapter, Brandom's approach to language and linguistic communication and, in the next, Brandom's appropriation of the Kantian legacy.

The Received View

Brandom's theory of linguistic meaning and linguistic communication is a dramatic inversion of a certain influential picture of the matter, variations of which are widely accepted today. Let's call this influential picture the *Received View*[1] and let's introduce its core features in this section before outlining, in the remaining chapter, Brandom's contrasting picture.

A prominent theory of meaning and communication falling under the Received View is what Jay Rosenberg calls "agent semantics" (Rosenberg 1975, chap. 2). I shall illustrate the Received View by developing agent semantics a bit. In Brandom's words, according to agent semantics,

> linguistic meaning is explained in terms of a prior capacity to engage in practical reasoning. ... Agent semantics treats the contentfulness of utterances as derivative from that of intentional states. The content of an assertion derives from the content of the belief it is the expression of, and from the content of the intention that it be understood as expressing that belief. It follows that it must be possible to make sense of the contents of beliefs and intentions prior to and independently of telling this sort of story about the use of linguistic expressions.
>
> (MIE 147)

According to agent semantics, a linguistic utterance by a speaker in a particular context of linguistic communication – an assertion, question, request, command, overt assumption, guess, or some such – is, literally, a kind of rational, intentional action. Specifically, it is an action carried out by the speaker with the intention to overtly give her interlocutors a reason to change their minds and/or to behave in certain ways. For example, an English speaker's assertion "It will rain" is, in the agent semantic view, a rational action carried out by the speaker with the intention to get her interlocutors to believe that it will rain, and thus to change their minds in this particular way.[2] And the speaker aims to achieve this goal, according to agent semantics, by also intending her interlocutors to recognize her former intention and to use such recognition as a reason for forming the belief that it will rain (Strawson 1964; Grice 1989a, 1989b). In short, according to agent semantics, a linguistic utterance in communication is, literally, a speech act: a rational action carried out by the speaker with a set of specific, complex intentions to overtly give her interlocutors reasons to change their mind and/or to behave in certain ways. Linguistic communication is successful, in this view, to the extent that the interlocutors recognize the speaker's intentions; that is, that they recognize her as openly giving them a reason to change their minds and/or to behave in a specific way.

This is a metaphysical thesis about speech, according to which speech is a species of intentional action. Along with it, agent semantics comes with a semantic thesis, according to which a speech act inherits its overall linguistic significance, that is, its conceptually structured propositional meaning that p and its illocutionary force (assertive, interrogative, imperative, optative, commissive, declarative, etc.), on the occasion of utterance from the specific intentions with which the speaker performed the act, and in particular from the propositional content of these intentions. For example, in the scenario described above, the speaker's utterance "It will rain" is an assertion that it will rain because it was carried out with the specific set of intentions described. Had the speaker performed that same utterance with different intentions – for example, intentions to overtly provide reasons for the interlocutors to believe that the sun will shine, or to express *their* opinions about what the weather will be like, or to close the window, etc. – that same utterance would, on that occasion, not have been an assertion that it will rain, but rather an assertion that the sun will shine, a question what the weather will be like, or a request or command that the door be shut.

A cottage industry of literature is devoted to developing this approach to linguistic meaning and communication. Fortunately, we do not need to walk into this thicket. For our purposes, it suffices to identify two central theses of agent semantics that are also essential theses of the Received View. First, according to agent semantics (and the Received View in general), speakers are rational beings independently of, and prior to, their ability to communicate linguistically, and their ability to communicate is explained in terms of their antecedent ability to reason. Prior to their ability to speak, rational beings are endowed with propositionally contentful mental states – cognitive attitudes such as beliefs, desires, intentions, assumptions, suppositions, etc. with propositional (hence conceptual) contents that p, that q, that r, etc. In Brandom's terminology, they are endowed with *discursively intentional* mental states prior to their ability to speak. Since reasoning is the cognitive activity of forming and maintaining a system of such discursively intentional mental states in accordance with standards of good evidence, logic, coherence, relevance, comprehensiveness, etc., rational beings are thus able to form and maintain such systems, in at least rudimentary forms, in accordance with such standards independently of, and prior to, developing the ability to speak with each other. Indeed, according to agent semantics and the Received View in general, rational beings are able to reason, prior to being speakers, not only about the inanimate world (about the weather, food, tools, etc.) by forming beliefs, desires, intentions, etc. with contents containing concepts such as rain, sunshine, fruit, door, etc., but also about their own and each other's psychological states (about each other's beliefs, desires, perceptions, memories, feelings, etc.). That is, they are able, prior to being speakers, to form higher-order beliefs, desires, intentions, etc. with contents containing, among other concepts, psychological concepts such as beliefs that, desires that, intends that, feels that, remembers that, perceives that, etc., about the minds of other rational beings. Proponents of the Received View do not deny that the ability to communicate linguistically dramatically increases a speaker's conceptual repertoire and dramatically enhances her ability to reason – both concerning the inanimate world and concerning each other's minds and our shared social world – but they deny emphatically that the ability to communicate linguistically is essential for being a rational, concept-using thinker and agent at all. We are concept-using rational creatures first and creatures who communicate with each other using a natural language only afterwards, and the Received View explains the ability to communicate in terms of this antecedent ability to reason in the medium of concepts.

Second, according to agent semantics (and the Received View in general), language inherits its significance, and in particular its conceptually structured propositional meaning, from the discursively intentional mental states, and in particular their conceptually structured propositional contents, which speakers posess prior to their ability to communicate linguistically. Linguistic meaning is, in this sense, derivative while the contentfulness of discursively intentional mental states is original.

A third thesis of the Received View concerns the semantic nature of propositional mental contents and concepts, and hence derivatively of sentence meaning and word meaning. Most people agree that discursively intentional states are *qua* propositionaly contentful states representational, that is, that they are *about* possible states of affairs in the world. Relatedly, they agree that – setting aside logical concepts such as <u>and</u>, <u>if … then</u>, <u>something</u>, <u>necessarily</u>, etc. – the concepts constituting these propositional contents are representational too, in the sense that, due to the kinds of concepts they involve, these propositional contents are *about* individuals, kinds, properties, relations, etc., in the world. For example, looking at children playing in a lake, I currently believe <u>that the water out there is warm</u> and <u>that Thabo is playing with Nora</u>, I desire <u>that I am in that lake myself</u> and intend <u>that we shall have lunch shortly</u>. In virtue of their propositional contents, my beliefs represent, respectively, the actual states of affairs that the water out there is fairly warm and that Thabo is playing with Nora, my desire represents the possible state of affairs that I am in that lake myself, and my intention represents the future actual state of affairs that we will have lunch shortly. Moreover, among the concepts deployed, the singular concepts <u>Thabo</u> and <u>Nora</u> represent, respectively, the individuals Thabo and Nora, the one-place predicative concept <u>being warm</u> represents the property BEING WARM (or, perhaps, the class of warm things), the natural kind concept <u>water</u> represents the kind WATER, and the two-place predicative concept <u>is playing with</u> represents the relation PLAYING WITH – the relation in which any two individuals stand to each other just in case the first one plays with the second. The third thesis of the Received View is that the representational dimension of these propositional contents, and of the concepts deployed in them, *constitutes them* at least in part *as* the contents and concepts they are. More generally, the third thesis of the Received View is that the semantic significance of any propositional contents and any (non-logical) concepts consists at least in part in their specific representational dimension. Being a propositional content or a (non-logical) concept in general consists at least partially in being a mental representation, and being a specific propositional content and (non-logical) concept in particular consists at least partially in representing a specific item of the proper category (a certain state of affairs, individual, property, kind, relation, etc.).

Since the meaning of language and speech derives from the conceptually structured propositional contents of discursively intentional states, according to the Received View, the third thesis thus implies a philosophical view about the nature of linguistic meaning. The meaning of English sentences such as "The water out there is warm" and "Thabo is playing with Nora," and of the corresponding assertions, consists at least partially in their representational dimensions: the fact that they represent the states of affairs that the water out there is warm and that Thabo is playing with Nora. And the meaning of non-logical words such as "Thabo," "water," "is warm," or "is playing with" involved in these sentences and assertions consists at least partially in *their* representational dimensions: the fact that they represent the individual Thabo, the kind WATER, the property BEING WARM, and the relation PLAYING WITH.

This representationalist approach to the nature of propositional content and non-logical concepts saddles proponents of the Received View with the challenge to explain how creatures get to be in propositionally contentful representational, discursively intentional states – hence how they get to be reasoning creatures – in the first place, independently of, and prior to, their ability to communicate linguistically. Commonly, proponents of the Received View pursue this explanatory task by attempting to reduce the representational dimension of propositional contents and non-logical concepts to some natural physical or biological relation between the rational subject (or her brain) and her environment. For example, proponents of the Received View might say that my concept dog represents the kind DOG, and thus is the concept that it is, because the perceptual presence of dogs tends to cause me to employ that concept, that is, because the concept is causally related to dogs in suitable ways (Stampe 1977). Or they may say, similarly, that my concept dog represents the kind DOG because it carries information (in the information-theoretic sense) of dogs (Dretske 1981; Fodor 1987), or because it is an evolutionary adaptation whose phylogenetic development enhanced the fitness of our ancestors in environments where dogs are present (Dretske 1988; Millikan 1984, 1989; Papineau 1984, 1998).

Note that none of these explanations presupposes that those who possess the concept dog need to be able to communicate with others using a natural language and, indeed, that they even need to have a sense that there are *other* concept-using rational beings besides themselves. Rather, standing in the suitable causal, information-theoretic, or adaptive relation to dogs, together with other purely intrapersonal cognitive abilities, suffices to be able to conceptually represent dogs and hence to reason about them. Moreover, note that these explanations of the representational dimension of propositional contents and non-logical concepts are *naturalistic* in the sense that they reduce this representational dimension to certain purely non-normative relations between the concept user and aspects of her environment. BEING CAUSED BY, CARRYING INFORMATION OF, or BEING ADAPTED TO are all relations that can obtain, and have in the natural historic past obtained, in a purely natural, non-normative, non-social world, that is, in a world void of norms, obligations, entitlements, correctness, right or wrong. Accordingly, proponents of the Received View typically combine their commitment to representationalism about propositional mental content and concepts with a commitment to a semantic naturalism that reduces the representational dimension of content and concepts and, indeed, the ability to reason to per se non-normative features of the world. (I should stress, however, that this commitment to naturalism, while widely accepted among proponents of the Received View, is not essential to the Received View, by contrast to the three theses outlined above.)

Brandom's alternative

Brandom rejects the Received View and envisions a dramatic inversion of its strategy to explain linguistic meaning and communication:

> The explanatory strategy pursued here is to begin with an account of social practices, identify the particular structure they must exhibit in order to qualify as specifically *linguistic* practices, and then consider what different sorts of semantic contents those practices can confer on states, performances, and expressions caught up in them in suitable ways. The result is a new kind of conceptual role semantics. It is at once firmly rooted in actual practices of producing and consuming speech acts, and sufficiently finely articulated to make clear how those practices are capable of conferring the rich variety of kinds of content that philosophers of language have revealed and reveled in.
>
> (MIE xii)

Brandom's ambitions, like those of proponents of the Received View, are not only descriptive but also explanatory. He wishes not only to describe the central features of linguistic communication and linguistic meaning and their relations to our abilities to reason and to use concepts, but also to explain how communication and meaning obtain in the world. However, his explanatory strategy is a dramatic inversion of the Received View. Rather than beginning with an independent account of conceptual mental representations and explaining, in terms of it, linguistic meaning and linguistic communication, Brandom begins with an independent account of social practices in general, understood as exchanges of socially significant performances between at least two participants – "independent" in that, Brandom contends, this account presupposes none of the semantic, epistemic, and cognitive notions or features of central concern in the philosophy of language and mind (notions and features such as meaning, propositional attitudes, propositional content, speech act, illocutionary force, reasoning, inference, concepts, representation, truth, etc.). He then aims to explain linguistic communication as a species of such social practices – *discursive* social practice – distinguished from non-discursive varieties by a specific structure. The description of this structure does again not presuppose any of the semantic, epistemic, and cognitive features and notions of interest. With this account of specifically discursive social practices provided, Brandom then aims to show that features of discursive practices and the participants in them, so described, deserve to be identified with the various semantic, epistemic, and cognitive features of interest, or that the latter features are in some other sense "instituted" or "conferred" by discursive practices so conceived. Since the description of specifically linguistic social practices does not presuppose any of these semantic, epistemic, and cognitive features, recovering them in this way from discursive social practices thus described amounts to an explanation of them.

On the semantic side, Brandom's fundamental notion is inferential role ("conceptual role"), which he will identify with an aspect of the overall role that performances may legitimately play in discursive social practices. The propositional meaningfulness of performances in discursive practices, according to Brandom, is their inferential role. Brandom will identify the ability of specifically discursive practitioners to trace and honor in practice the inferential roles of the performances exchanged with the most fundamental form of reasoning, and certain states and attitudes of such practitioners, caught up in such tracing and honoring, with discursively intentional mental states (beliefs, intentions, etc.). Thus, while the fundamental semantic notion of the Received View is the notion of a conceptual mental representation, and while the Received View aims to explain reasoning itself at least in part in such representational terms, Brandom's fundamental semantic notion is the notion of inferential role, which he identifies with an aspect of the overall role of linguistic performances in discourse, and he explains reasoning itself in terms of discursive practitioners' ability to trace and honor the inferential roles of the performances exchanged in discursive social practices.

Inferential role semantics

In the remainder of this chapter, let's say a bit more about the central aspects of Brandom's alternative, beginning with inferential role semantics. In general, the sentences of a language stand in multifarious inferential, compatibility, and incompatibility relations to each other, which competent speakers trace more or less accurately when they reason in the medium of the language. For example, the English sentence "LBJ was US President on 08/06/1966" has "LBJ won the previous presidential election" and "LBJ was US President" as consequences. The sentence is compatible with "LBJ wore a blue necktie on 08/06/1966" and "JFK was previously US President," and is incompatible with "Lyndon B. Johnson was Speaker of the Senate on 08/06/1966" and "LBJ passed away in 1963." Speakers of English, reasoning about Lyndon B. Johnson's US Presidency in the medium of English sentences, trace such inferential, compatibility, and incompatibility relations between the sentences involved – both among each other and between them and further sentences – more or less accurately and completely. Everybody agrees that the web of inferential, compatibility, and incompatibility relations between these sentences, among each other, and to other sentences, is intimately related both to the meaning of each of these sentences and (what seems to be a different thing) to a thick background of factual information about LBJ, the institutions of the US Presidency and Speaker of the Senate, the wearing of neckties, the history of the US, etc. – information that could be explicated by yet further sentences. Thus "LBJ was US President on 08/06/1966" implies "LBJ won the previous presidential election," is incompatible with "Lyndon B. Johnson was Speaker of the Senate on 08/06/1966," but compatible with "LBJ wore a blue necktie on 08/06/1966," both because of what each of these sentences means and because in fact by 08/06/1966 LBJ had become the President in the usual way (through an election, rather than because his predecessor died in office while LBJ was Vice President), in fact LBJ and Lyndon B. Johnson are the same person, in fact the President cannot simultaneously be Speaker of the Senate, and he may in fact wear a blue necktie whenever he wants.

The distinct *inferential role* of each of these sentences S then, is determined by the sum of S's inferential, compatibility, and incompatibility relations to other sentences, and these relations are in turn determined both by S's meaning and (what seems to be a different thing) collateral factual information, as well as by how variances in this collateral factual information would affect these relations. For example, given its meaning, the sentence "LBJ was US President on 08/06/1966" would have remained incompatible with "Lyndon B. Johnson was Speaker of the Senate on 08/06/1966" and compatible with "LBJ wore a blue necktie on 08/06/1966" if, counterfactually, Lady Bird Johnson had divorced LBJ by 08/08/1966. However, given their meaning, the first two sentences would have been compatible if, counterfactually, the American Constitution had allowed the President to be simultaneously the Speaker of the Senate while the first and third sentence would have been incompatible if, counterfactually, US presidents had not been allowed to wear neckties. That is, the distinct inferential role of "LBJ was US President on 08/06/1966" consists in the sum of its inferential, compatibility, and incompatibility relations to other English sentences, and this inferential role is determined both by the meaning of the sentence and (what seems to be a different thing) by collateral factual information, as well as by the ways in which changes in collateral information would affect these relations.

This much is uncontroversial. Inferential role *semantics* is more controversial. This is the view that the meaning of a sentence (the propositional content it expresses) *consists*, at least in part, *in* its inferential role. A sentence's meaning does, on this view, not merely determine, relative to a background of collateral information, its inferential, compatibility, and incompatibility relations to other sentences, but rather consists, at least in part, in these inferential relations. Relatedly, a speaker's linguistic understanding of a sentence does, in this view, not merely determine, relative to a background of collateral information, what she takes the sentence's inferential role to be, but rather *consists*, at least in part, *in* what she takes its inferential role to be. To understand a certain sentence S *is*, in this view, at least in part, to more or less accurately trace and honor the inferential, compatibility, and incompatibility relations in which S stands to other sentences, relative to actual or counter-factual collateral information.

Yet while a commitment to inferential role semantics, so characterized, would be controversial, it would per se neither be particularly new nor particularly bold. Indeed, if combined with two further commitments, inferential role semantics, so characterized, may be integrated into the Received View. First, a proponent of the Received View might hold that the linguistic meaning of a sentence does not consist in its representational dimension alone, but rather in its representational dimension *combined with* its inferential role. That is, he may advocate a hybrid view about the nature of meaning according to which meaning essentially comprises both a representational and an inferential dimension, neither of which is reducible to, or explainable in terms of, the other (Kremer 2010, McDowell 2008). Such a view would be a version of what Brandom calls *weak inferentialism* (AR 28): the view that inference is necessary but insufficient for constituting conceptually structured linguistic meaning. Second, the proponent of the Received View may hold that linguistic meaning may be derived from the ability of speakers to reason in the medium of discursively intentional mental states independently of, and prior to, their ability to speak, treating the original propositional contents <u>that p</u> of discursively intentional states *themselves* in this hybrid way, that is, as consisting in the combination of mutually irreducible representational and inferential elements. Thus, when combined with these two steps, a commitment to inferential role semantics may be integrated into the Received View.

Brandom rejects these two steps, however, and his specific version of inferential role semantics is, accordingly, outside the Received View. First, Brandom's semantic inferentialism is *strong* in the sense that, according to it, the inferential role of a sentence is necessary *and sufficient* for constituting the meaning of the sentence (AR 28). Brandom thus rejects the hybrid view. According to him, the inferential role of any sentence S alone constitutes its propositional meaning. Second, as alluded to above, according to Brandom, sentence meaning *qua* inferential role does not derive from a speaker's ability to reason independently of, and prior to, her ability to speak. There is no such independent ability to reason, according to Brandom. Rather, it emerges as an aspect of specifically discursive social practices themselves, where these practices are antecedently fully described in terms that do not presuppose that the participants are able to reason independently of, and prior to, their ability to participate in such practices. In this sense, specifically *discursive* reasoning – reasoning as part of one's ability to engage in specifically discursive practices, that is, one's ability to trace and honor the inferential roles of linguistic performances exchanged – is original, and a speakers' ability to reason in solitude, that is, in abstraction from her participation in discourse, is derived from her ability to reason discursively.

What turns this explanatory strategy into a full-scale inversion of the Received View is that Brandom wishes to explain the representational dimension of propositionally contentful talk and thought – which Brandom does not deny talk and thought to have – in terms of its inferential role.

> The idea of inference without representation *turns out* to be unintelligible. But we show that by talking about propositional content to begin with in purely inferential terms, [we] come to see that in doing so we have assembled all the raw materials needed to make sense not only of the expressive dimension of such content. ... but also the representational dimension.
>
> (Brandom 2010b: 352)

While a sentence's or linguistic performance's inferential role alone constitutes its meaning (its propositional content), Brandom agrees with proponents of the Received View that every propositionally contentful item *has* a representational dimension. However, contra those proponents he maintains that this representational dimension, rather than playing any part in constituting the item's propositional contentfulness, is a non-semantic and, as it were, epiphenomenal add-on to the item's inferential role, which alone constitutes its meaning. For Brandom, representation is non-semantic; it is philosophically explained in terms of meaning *qua* inferential role (together with other per se non-semantic, structural features of discursive practices), rather than vice versa (MIE 75; Brandom 2010b: 352; PP 214).

Pragmatism

Just as proponents of the Received View usually do not treat its *semantically* fundamental notion of a conceptual representation as primitive overall, but rather explain it in, usually, naturalistic causal, information-theoretic, or evolutionary biological terms, so

Brandom does not treat his *semantically* fundamental notion of inferential role as primitive overall, but seeks to explain it in terms of less problematic notions. However, whereas explanations within the Received View of conceptual representation are couched in terms unspecific to linguistic communication – causation, information, evolutionary adaptation, etc. – Brandom's explanation of inferential role is couched in terms of the very item that is last in the Received View's overall explanatory strategy: linguistic communication (discursive practice). Seemingly paradoxically, Brandom starts his *semantic* explanation with a theory of linguistic practice – a theory that, on pain of circularity, must not be couched in terms of any of the traditional central semantic, epistemic, and cognitive notions of his interest (inference, reasoning, meaning, propositional contentfulness, propositional attitude, concept, representation, reference, truth, etc.) – and he aims to explain all these semantic, epistemic, and cognitive features in terms of this theory. He calls any theory that favors such an order of explanation *pragmatist*.

> "Pragmatism" ... is a generic expression that picks out a family of views asserting various senses in which practice and the practical may be taken to deserve explanatory pride of place. One more determinate class of such views concerns the relation between pragmatics and semantics. In this more specific sense, a view deserves the appellation "pragmatism" insofar as it insists that semantic theory must answer in various ways to pragmatic theory – for instance by asserting some sort of explanatory priority of pragmatics over semantics.
>
> (PP 58)

Pragmatism in general maintains an explanatory priority of tangible human practices and human copings with the natural or social environment over more abstract items of philosophical concern, such as the categories of metaphysics, epistemology, the philosophy of language, or philosophical psychology. Pragmatism in the philosophy of language in particular is characterized by the slogan, "semantics must answer to pragmatics." *Pragmatics*, according to Brandom, is the study of the use of language in communication or, more generally, the study of the things speakers do and the skills they employ when they talk to each other (PP 57). Brandom's pragmatist thesis is that semantic theorizing about propositional content and linguistic meaning in abstraction from pragmatics, while feasible and useful for various limited purposes, is bound to yield an incomplete and distorted view of meaning, propositions, concepts, and so on. A complete and undistorting semantic theory "answers to pragmatics," in the sense that it reveals the semantic features of thought and talk – their propositional contentfulness *qua* inferential role – as in various senses grounded in the use of language in communication. We can thus regard Brandom's pragmatism as a systematic attempt to make sense of, and to provide a qualified theoretical justification for, Ludwig Wittgenstein's famous dictum that "the meaning of a word is its use in the language" (Wittgenstein 2001, § 42).

How is such grounding of meaning in use to be understood, according to Brandom? Intuitively, some conversations are semantically more complex than others. Thus, compare conversations in which the interlocutors simply describe the shapes and colors of simple geometric objects with conversations in which they engage in counterfactual thinking and explicitly take into account different viewpoints. Intuitively, the propositions expressed in the latter conversations are more complex than the propositions expressed in the former. Accordingly, Brandom advocates a "layer cake picture" (MIE 206), according to which types of conversation are ordered hierarchically in accordance with their degrees of semantic complexity. Some conversations are also pragmatically more complex than others, in the sense that the pragmatic skills speakers must employ to participate in the more complex conversations – the set of know-how they need in order to use language skillfully in these conversations – involves the skills they need to employ in order to participate in simpler conversations, but not vice versa. For example, the pragmatic skills employed in conversations that involve counterfactual thinking and that explicitly take into account different viewpoints also involve the sorts of pragmatic skills employed in simple conversations about, say, the shapes and colors of plain geometric objects – but not vice versa. Brandom maintains that to the ordering of conversations in accordance with their degree of semantic complexity – the degree of complexity of the propositional contents articulated in these conversations – corresponds an ordering of them in accordance with their degree of pragmatic complexity. Participation in the semantically simplest possible conversations requires the smallest possible set of pragmatic skills needed to participate in any conversation at all. Brandom calls such maximally simple yet genuine conversations *autonomous* discursive practices. Using Wittgenstein's characterization of conversations as language games, Brandom calls them "language games one could play though one played no other" (BSD 27).

(We shall deal with autonomous discursive practices in chapters 3 to 5.) Participation in non-autonomous conversations of increasing semantic complexity – increasing complexity of the propositions expressed – requires a corresponding increase in the pragmatic skills needed to participate. Someone may have all the pragmatic skills required for participation in autonomous discursive practices, yet lack the pragmatic skills for participating in semantically more complex ones. But everyone able to participate in any semantically more complex, non-autonomous conversation also has the pragmatic skills to participate in autonomous discursive practices. Chapters 6 and 7 will discuss how such incremental increases in semantic and pragmatic complexity are to be understood.

Given this correspondence between degrees of semantic complexity and the sizes of the pragmatic skillsets required to participate, Brandom envisions the following pragmatist explanatory strategy:

> For any vocabulary (any kind of saying-*that*) there are some practical abilities (some bits of know-*how*) that are ... *necessary* to count as deploying it, and ... there are some practices-or-abilities that are ... *sufficient* to confer those contents or count as deploying that vocabulary. Together [such necessity and sufficiency] ... articulate[s] the sense in which pragmatists take practices-or-abilities to be privileged with respect to ... the capacity to say, mean, or believe (hence to know) anything discursively.
>
> (BSD 40–41)

First, for any autonomous discursive practice, the pragmatic know-how required for participation in it is necessary and sufficient for that practice to have its semantic features, that is, for the sentences in it to have maximally simple propositional meanings (inferential roles). Second, for any of the increasingly more involving non-autonomous discursive practices, reached by adding increasingly sophisticated non-autonomous pragmatic know-how to the original autonomous one, the application of this increased set of pragmatic know-how is necessary and sufficient for that non-autonomous practice to have its semantic features, that is, for at least some of the sentences in it to have increasingly complex propositional meanings (inferential roles).

Brandom calls the view that the pragmatically skillful use of language in communication is necessary for the language in use to be meaningful and for the participants to be in propositionally contentful cognitive states *linguistic pragmatism* (PP 67), and the view that it is sufficient for the language and the speakers to exhibit these semantic features *semantic pragmatism* (e.g. BSD 40–1, PP 61–3). Linguistic and semantic pragmatism combined thus assert a very strong dependency of the semantic features of thought and talk – inferential role – on the pragmatically skillful use of language in communication.[3] According to it, necessarily, language is meaningful and creatures are rational, that is, in propositionally contentful mental states and able to trace inferential roles, if and only if the language is used in communication and the creatures are discoursing, linguistically communicating creatures.

Few are currently prepared to accept such a strong dependency of meaning and reasoning on pragmatic features of conversations, and certainly no proponent of the Received View is. Accordingly, it is important to see what this dependency thesis does, and does not, commit Brandom to. It commits him to the view that the *discursively intentional* features of thought and talk – propositional meaning and conceptual content – strongly depend upon the skillful use of language in communication. It does not commit him to deny that much sophisticated non-conceptual cognition may take place in speakers as well as non-linguistic organisms and even certain artifacts. Indeed, Brandom agrees that non-discursive organisms and many artifacts exhibit much intelligence, despite their inability to reason in the medium of concepts, such as the ability to pursue goals by perceiving, skillfully tracking, approaching, or pursuing environing objects. As we shall see beginning in chapter 5, the presence of such pre-discursive *practically intentional* skills in humans is a prerequisite for them to learn to speak a natural language. Brandom concedes that it is both natural and appropriate to characterize these non-discursive practically intentional cognitive abilities as representational and, indeed, in a sense even inferential (PP 202 Fn. 16 and PP 216). Thus, while Brandom's thesis that only speakers of natural languages may reason, genuinely infer, and represent in the medium of concepts is still ambitious, it is not the over-ambitious, implausible thesis that only speakers of natural languages may represent and be intelligent in any good senses of these words at all.

Normative pragmatics

Let's turn to discursive practices themselves. How should we think of them and the pragmatic know-how involved in participating in them? Conversations are in multifarious respects governed by an enormously complicated system of norms. For example, norms govern the phonetic, morphological, syntactic, aesthetic, cultural, and moral aspects of conversations. Any minimally competent participant in a conversation must exhibit a great deal of sensitivity to these norms. She is responsible to comply with these norms, and, accordingly, subject to critical appraisal, challenge, approval, or disapproval by her peers, depending on the degree of her compliance with these norms. Brandom identifies the core pragmatic skills needed to participate in a conversation with the participants' skills to be sensitive to, and to follow, the norms governing the conversation. Accordingly, Brandom thinks that the pragmatic theory describing discourse and speakers' pragmatic know-how and (if all goes well) explaining the semantic features of thought and talk must therefore describe discourse and the speakers' pragmatic know-how as norm-governed in various ways. That is, it must be a *normative* pragmatics.

Brandom places important constraints on this normative pragmatic theory:

> One of the overarching methodological commitments that orients this project is to explain the meanings of linguistic expressions in terms of their use. ... Claims about the relations between meaning and use have a clear sense only in the context of a specification of the vocabulary in which that use is described or ascribed. ... The specification of use here is neither so generous as to permit semantic or intentional vocabulary nor so parsimonious as to insist on purely naturalistic vocabulary. Instead it makes essential use of normative vocabulary.
>
> (MIE xii–xiii)

Setting aside the more complicated case of non-autonomous discourse, the pragmatic theory in terms of which the envisioned pragmatist explanation of the semantic features of autonomous discourse is to be given must obviously not describe the participants as already in propositionally contentful states and the performances exchanged as already propositionally meaningful, for the obvious reason that the envisioned pragmatist explanation would otherwise be circular. Thus, this pragmatic account of an autonomous speaker's pragmatic know-how in particular must be free from attributions of such semantic states or capacities to him. It must, Brandom says, in this sense be a *fundamental pragmatist theory* of pragmatic know-how, that is, a theory that rejects a "platonistic intellectualism that seeks to explain practical abilities in terms of some sort of grasp of *principles:* some sort of knowing that behind each bit of know how" (PP 65, BSD 40–1).

Accordingly, this fundamental pragmatist theory must in particular avoid displaying the pragmatic ability of autonomous discursive practitioners to *follow the norms* of their conversation as consisting in, or as mediated by, explicit, propositional knowledge of these norms. Brandom motivates such a fundamental pragmatism about the ability to follow the norms of an autonomous conversation by arguing against the contrary intellectualist position, according to which the ability to follow any norm must be grounded in a conceptualization of this norm, that is, in the norm-follower's propositional knowledge as to what that norm is. Such an intellectualist position belongs to a family of views about norm-following that Brandom calls *regulism* (a term of art invoking the German word *Regel,* or rule). A *rule,* in Brandom's terminology, is a norm as made explicit in the form of a sentence or a proposition. Regulism says that all norms are rules and that following a norm or assessing someone else's performance in light of the norm essentially involves having explicit, propositional knowledge of that norm: knowledge of the corresponding rule (MIE 19–20).

Yet Brandom, relying on similar arguments by Wittgenstein and Sellars, holds that regulism in general, and the envisioned intellectualist position about the pragmatic know-how to follow a norm in particular, face a vicious infinite regress.[4] Thus, according to Wittgenstein, a rule R can be correctly or incorrectly applied under particular circumstances, that is, its proper application under particular circumstances is *itself* norm-governed. Yet the norms governing the application of R, Wittgenstein argues, are not contained in R itself but must be norms other than R. For example, the rule expressed by a stop sign is "Stop here," and an approaching driver applies this rule by following the different (though related) norm "When seeing a sign of this sort, employ the brakes and bring the car to a full stop near the sign." According to regulism, someone who knows how to apply R under given circumstances must thus explicitly know further rules R', R", etc. governing the proper application of R. Yet R', R", etc. may *themselves* be properly or improperly applied under given circumstances; that is, their application is governed by yet further norms, which, according to regulism, must thus be explicitly known by the one following R. In short, regulism implies that, absurdly, following any norm requires an infinite regress of explicit knowledge of ever-different rules.

Brandom thinks that this regress problem shows that

> there is a need for a *pragmatist* conception of norms – a notion of primitive correctnesses of performances *implicit* in *practice* that precede and are presupposed by their *explicit* formulation in *rules* and *principles*.
>
> (MIE 21)

The regress argument does not, of course, show that no norm can be made explicit as a rule, but rather that anyone who has explicit knowledge of a rule, and knows how to apply it, must be able to follow some norms *implicitly* or *in practice*, that is, follow them without having explicit knowledge of them.

Brandom must assume that, at least in autonomous discursive practices, the participants follow *all* the norms of the practice merely implicitly, so as to avoid the implication that the envisioned pragmatist explanation of semantics in terms of pragmatics is circular, in the sense of invoking unexplained explicit, propositional knowledge of some of these norms from the start. The argument against regulism does not strictly speaking prove that discursive practices where all the norms are followed merely implicitly are possible, since it does not refute the middle-ground position that, while explicit knowledge of any rules requires the ability to follow some norms implicitly in practice, the ability to follow any norms implicitly in practice also requires explicit knowledge of some rules. Without discussing this middle-ground position, however, Brandom seems to think that the regress argument against regulism supports the view that this middle-ground position is at best optional, and that he is therefore entitled to his preferred conception of all-around implicit norm-following in, at least, autonomous discursive practices.

How should we think of a speaker's ability to follow norms implicitly in practice? One option is to think of it naturalistically and, in effect, behavioristically, in terms of the accord or discord of a speaker's discursive behavior with a certain regular pattern of behavior in the speaker's linguistic community. Brandom calls theories of norms and norm-following along this line *regularist*. A simple version of regularism has it that the past behavior of members of the community falls into certain regular patterns, and stipulates that these patterns constitute standards of correctness –

norms – against which the future behavior of individual community members is assessed. An individual's behavior is correct,
according to such simple regularism, so far as it accords with the
patterns of past behavior among community members (MIE 26–7).
Like any version of regularism, the simple regularity theory is
naturalistic in the sense that, since behaviors and their patterns are
in principle fully describable in purely non-normative, descriptive,
statistical language and since, according to the simple regularity
theory under consideration, norms reduce to such patterns, norms
are not, metaphysically speaking, over and above the natural,
descriptive, statistical features of reality but reduce to such features. Furthermore, the simple regularity theory would account for
a speaker's ability to follow norms implicitly in practice. After all,
following a norm of discourse, according to it, is simply a matter
of linguistic behavior according with a pattern of past linguistic
behavior. It neither requires that the speaker explicitly knows the
norm/the pattern, nor even that she has any implicit, non-propo-
sitional sensitivity to the fact that she is bound by these or other
norms. Behaving in accordance with the pattern suffices for her to
follow the norm.

Relying yet again on an argument by Wittgenstein, however,
Brandom argues that the problem with simple regularity theories
is that any finite pattern of (past) behavior can be gerrymandered
so as to accord with infinitely many mutually incompatible regular
patterns of behavior, and thus does not determine a single pattern
of behavior at all. For example, the act of counting (in the past) 2,
4, 6, 8, 10 accords with the regular counting pattern captured by
the function $n + 2$ as well as the different regular counting pattern
captured by the function $n + 2$ if $n < 1000$ and $n + 4$ otherwise, as
well as with infinitely many other regular counting patterns. Thus,
someone who counts 2, 4, 6, 8, 10 does not thereby determine
whether the continuation … 998, 1000, 1002, 1004, … or the continuation … 998, 1000, 1004, 1008, … , or any other continuation
that accords with 2, 4, 6, 8, 10 is correct. Thus, no finite stretch of
behavior determines just one regular pattern of behavior, and
hence cannot determine a single standard of correctness for future
behavior. This gerrymandering problem dooms the simple regularity theory (MIE 27–8).[5]

Dispositional versions of regularism avoid this problem. According to them, the *dispositions* of members of a community to behave
in certain ways under certain circumstances, rather than actual
behaviors, determine the standards of correctness in light of which

further behavior is to be assessed. Possibly, these members may be the majority in the community, or a minority of experts identified via dispositions to defer to them among the other community members. The point is that, by contrast to actual past behavior, a disposition to behave *does* determine a single pattern of future, or counterfactual, behavior that accords with it – to wit, the behavior manifesting the disposition under future, or counterfactual, circumstances – rather than an infinity of mutually exclusive, gerrymandered patterns. In this regard, such dispositional theories are an improvement over simple regularity theories. Moreover, such theories make, yet again, sense of the idea of following norms "implicitly in practice" since, according to them, following a norm is a matter of being disposed to behave in certain ways, and being disposed to behave in certain ways need not involve any explicit knowledge, neither of norms nor of anything else. After all, stones, water, or tectonic plates are disposed to behave in certain ways, but they clearly lack propositional knowledge.

Yet however someone may elaborate such a dispositional regularist approach to discursive practices, Brandom argues that the result fails in principle.[6] His punch line is that "if whatever one is disposed to do counts for that reason as right, then the distinction of right and wrong, and so all normative force, has been lost" (MIE 29; cf. also MIE 40–41). Brandom's complaint is that, according to dispositionalist regularity theories, *any* manifestation of the dispositions to behave among those members of a linguistic community who set the standard of correctness – perhaps the majority of community members, or a minority of experts – is by definition correct. After all, in the view under consideration, to be correct is to accord behaviorally with the pattern of behavior that sets the standard, which is determined by those members' dispositions to behave. Yet surely the question whether someone's behavior accords with the majority's, or the experts', dispositions to behave needs to be distinguished from the question whether that behavior is correct (MIE 41, 593–4). For example, the behavior of those members of the community whose dispositions set the standard obviously accords with their dispositions to behave, but sometimes such behavior can be mistaken. Thus even the most expert scientists frequently get things wrong in their areas of expertise. Yet it is hard to see how the dispositional regularity theorists can make room for the possibility that those community members whose dispositions set the standard can sometimes be wrong, without illicitly appealing to normative standards that are not explained in dispositional terms. That is, the dispositional regularity theory, Brandom claims, is caught in a dilemma. "It can go wrong [in two ways]: by failing to produce a genuinely normative product or by employing some already normative raw materials." (MIE 41).

The lesson Brandom draws from his discussion of regularism is that all attempts to naturalize norms face mighty (and, as he clearly suspects, insuperable) difficulties. Accordingly, rather than making such an attempt, Brandom accepts a commitment to *non-naturalism* about norms and, consequentially, opts for a genuinely *normative* pragmatic theory of discourse. In other words, the pragmatic theory in terms of which Brandom wishes to describe discursive practices and the participants' pragmatic know-how and in terms of which he wishes to offer his pragmatist explanation of the semantic features of such practices, while not employing any semantic or discursively intentional vocabulary from the start, "makes essential use of normative vocabulary" (MIE xiii). That is, while this pragmatic theory will describe these discursive practices as normative, it will not offer any naturalistic explanation of their normative features, but will rather treat these features as *sui generis* normative.

This commitment to non-naturalism about norms does not mean, however, that Brandom thinks that nothing elucidating can be said about the origin of norms. As we shall see in the next chapter, and in chapter 8, Brandom has a great deal to say about where norms are coming from. However, nothing naturalistic can be said about the origin of norms, he claims. The correct account of the origin of discursive norms in particular, according to Brandom, already employs normative vocabulary.

Why Brandom's pragmatist alternative?

Not much of Brandom's work to date is dedicated to arguing directly against the Received View, and to motivating his pragmatist alternative in this way. Rather, Brandom is largely content to situate his pragmatist approach to linguistic communication and linguistic meaning within what he identifies as distinct and overlapping "rationalist" (inferentialist) and "pragmatist" (use-based) traditions within Western philosophy – spanning from Leibniz and Spinoza, via Kant and Hegel, to late nineteenth- and twentieth-century thinkers such as Frege, the later Wittgenstein, Heidegger, Dewey, Quine, Davidson, Dummett, Sellars, and Rorty

(TMD chaps. 1 and 2; AR 22–6) – and focuses all his efforts on working out his distinct pragmatist position within these traditions, apparently satisfied with the direct arguments that fellow members of those traditions have provided against the Received View. Indeed, Brandom clearly admires the nuance and technical rigor with which the Received View has been elaborated in the twentieth century (MIE 6), and plainly one of his chief ambitions is to show that his own pragmatism allows for an equally satisfying nuanced, rigorous, and refined treatment of every philosophically interesting detail of language, reasoning, and logic. Brandom's argumentative strategy against the Received View is thus largely indirect: place his own refined and elaborate finished pragmatist product alongside the best versions of the Received View and let people decide for themselves which of the two approaches looks, on the whole and in the details, on balance more attractive.

Yet Brandom's pragmatist inferentialism is also intended to provide principled alternatives to certain foundational features of the Received View that are widely regarded as the Received View's Achilles heels – even among its proponents. Thus, to get their project off the ground, proponents of the Received View must provide a satisfying theory of conceptual mental representations. This theory must make plausible not only how certain items in the subject's mind or brain can have determinate representational content but also how, reasoning in the medium of mental representations, *the subject herself ipso facto* implicitly *takes or treats* herself to be directed toward the represented, worldly items (what Brandom calls "representational purport") (MIE 6–7) – and it must do so, of course, without appealing to the subject's ability to engage in discourse with others. Even many proponents of the Received View agree that their camp has so far not succeeded in providing satisfying theories of either aspect of mental representations,[7] and Brandom seems to share the deep skepticism of many fellow rationalists and pragmatists that any such theory can succeed.[8] Thus, Brandom sees much more promise in sidestepping entirely the burden of offering such a theory of representation, by treating *inference* rather than representation as semantically fundamental, motivated by the conviction that an account of inferential relations and of what it is for a subject to treat certain items as inferentially related (which we could call "inferential purport") is not equally problematic – especially since this account is to be given in discursive, normative pragmatic terms – and by explaining the representational dimension of thought and talk (which, again, Brandom does not deny) in the context of this normative pragmatic, discursive account of inference.

Relatedly, since the Received View regards social interactions in general and linguistic communication in particular as species of rational action, to be explained in terms of an antecedently given ability to reason, its proponents are virtually committed to regard the most basic forms of genuine reasoning as fundamentally private and solipsistic. That is, they are virtually committed to hold that genuine reasoning about the natural, non-psychological world is possible antecedently to any ability to engage in social exchanges and, indeed, antecedently to the subject's having any sense that there might be any other reasoning creatures besides herself. To be sure, the Received View explains the ability to engage in social interactions in general and linguistic communication in particular in terms of the ability not only to engage in first-order reasoning about the non-psychological world but also to engage in higher-order reasoning about the beliefs, desires, and intentions of those with whom one interacts and, in this sense, in terms of the ability to recognize *others*. However, proponents of the Received View tend to regard the specific ability to engage in higher-order reasoning about other minds as an optional add-on to the general ability to engage in first-order reasoning about the natural, non-psychological world, and inessential for the ability to reason at all. To the extent that they do that, they are thus committed to a conception of reasoning as a fundamentally private, solipsistic affair.

Yet starting perhaps with Wittgenstein's arguments against the possibility of a private language and continued with Davidson's arguments that rational activity can emerge only in the context of interpersonal, interpretive activity,[9] many twentieth-century thinkers have found the idea of reasoning as a fundamentally private, solipsistic affair deeply problematic. Everyone agrees that reasoning is an essentially norm-governed affair, in the sense that it can be more or less proper, and that rational beings have to be sensitive to this normative dimension of their rational activity. Yet norms in general appear to be essentially public in the sense that one's efforts to follow them involves sensitivity to the fact that others might assess these efforts. Plausibly, it is part and parcel of my efforts to rationally solve a problem, to reason toward a certain conclusion, or to plan a course of action, that I regard these efforts as the subjects of potential critique, acceptance, reproach, rejection, or praise by others. If this line of thought is correct, as Brandom clearly thinks it is, the Received View's conception of reason as fundamentally private and solipsistic is deeply problematic. Accordingly, rather than offering convoluted arguments from within the Received View that, after all, the fundamentally private, solipsistic character of reasoning is unproblematic, or that despite first impressions to the contrary reasoning turns out to be essentially public, Brandom finds it more promising to step outside the Received View altogether, to take the fundamentally public, non-solipsistic character of reasoning at face value, and to accommodate this character in natural, straightforward fashion by explaining the most fundamental form of reasoning as a feature of specifically discursive norm-governed social practices – practices that are essentially non-solipsistic and mutually interpretive.

Summary

Brandom's central concern is to offer a comprehensive theory of linguistic communication and linguistic meaning, as well as of related features of core interest in the philosophy of language and mind and in epistemology: propositional attitudes, propositional contentfulness, concepts, rationality, inference, representation, reference, logic, truth, and so on. He is committed to a *pragmatist* order of explanation, in the sense that he wishes to account for all these features of thought and talk *in terms of* the use of language in communication. The heart and foundation of Brandom's enterprise is a *normative pragmatic* theory of linguistic communication, that is, a theory of the skillful, norm-governed use of language in communication by at least two speakers. This envisioned normative pragmatic theory of communication is non-naturalistic, in the sense that it does not include a reductive explanation of the norms of discourse in purely non-normative terms. Yet since this theory is supposed to explain all the semantic, epistemic, and cognitive features of thought and talk listed above, the normative pragmatic vocabulary in terms of which this theory is couched must not presuppose or imply the existence of any of these features from the start. Brandom wishes to respect this constraint by treating discourse, understood in normative pragmatic terms, as a structurally distinct species of norm-governed social practice, and by regarding norm-governed social practices in general as exchanges of socially significant performances that do not presuppose any of the listed semantic, epistemic, and cognitive features. In particular, he wishes to respect this constraint by defending the view that participants in norm-governed social practices in general need not have any explicit propositional knowledge of the norms governing the practice, but that they may be sensitive, and be able to follow, these norms merely implicitly, or in practice – that is, unmediated by explicit knowledge of the norms.

Brandom's central and fundamental semantic notion is *inference*. Disavowing standard approaches to linguistic meaning and propositional contentfulness in representational terms – reference, satisfaction, truth-conditions, etc. – Brandom treats the meaningfulness (propositional contentfulness) of linguistic performances (speech acts) and of sentences in the abstract as consisting solely in the sum of their inferential, compatibility, and incompatibility relations to other such performances and sentences and, in this sense, as their inferential role. A speaker's *reasoning* within the medium of her language – which Brandom regards as the most basic form of reasoning – in turn consists in the speaker's efforts to trace and honor the inferential roles of sentences and linguistic performances in practice. Thus, the primary semantic target of Brandom's pragmatist explanation is an account, in normative pragmatic terms, of the inferential roles of linguistic performances exchanged in discourse – that is, their role in discursive reasoning. With this normative pragmatic theory of discursive reasoning in place, Brandom envisions gradual identification of all the other semantic, epistemic, and cognitive features of thought and talk listed above with various aspects of discursive reasoning so understood, or gradual explanation of them in terms of this theory.

2

Mighty Dead: Kant and Hegel

In the last chapter, we saw that Brandom has two overarching theoretical aspirations. First, he wants to account for the semantic features of language and cognitive mental states – conceptually structured propositional linguistic meaning and mental content – exclusively in terms of inferential role, that is, in terms of the inferential, compatibility, and incompatibility relations in which sentences and cognitive mental states stand to each other. Second, he wants to explain linguistic meaning and mental content in turn in normative pragmatic terms: that is, in terms of the norm-governed use of a public language in communication by at least two interlocutors. Pursuing this twofold aspiration is a minority position in the landscape of contemporary analytic philosophy. Yet Brandom sees it in continuity with two overlapping "rationalist" and "pragmatist" traditions within modern Western philosophy, ranging from strands in the philosophies of Spinoza and Leibniz via central aspects of German Idealist thought broadly speaking (in particular Kant's and Hegel's work) to threads in the works of twentieth-century figures as diverse as Frege, Heidegger, the late Wittgenstein, Sellars, Quine, Davidson, and Dummett. Brandom devotes much of his writing to interpretations of aspects of these thinkers' works, motivated by the goal of finding precedence, inspiration, and legitimization for his own systematic philosophical enterprise.

The bulk of Brandom's writings in the history of pre-twentieth-century philosophy to date concerns Kant's and Hegel's contributions to these rationalist and pragmatist traditions. This focus should be unsurprising. As mentioned at the outset, for Brandom the central task of philosophy is to provide a critique of reason, that is, the right account of us as reasoning creatures. This is, of course, Kant's and Hegel's enterprise and, accordingly, Brandom at some point goes so far as *defining* philosophy simply as "the kind of thing that Kant and Hegel did" (RP 126). Yet even more important for Brandom than these meta-philosophical affinities with Kant and Hegel are the substantial philosophical innovations ushered in by the German Idealist tradition, in particular Kant's idea to treat reason and reasoning as essentially normative and autonomous, and Hegel's approach to reason and reasoning so understood as essentially socio-historical, and as instituted and maintained via a process of specifically discursive mutual social recognition. This chapter introduces Brandom's interpretations of Kant and Hegel. In keeping with Brandom's main motives for these interpretive efforts, I shall abstain from assessing these efforts in light of existing Kant and Hegel scholarship and instead introduce Brandom's interpretations entirely with an eye on his own systematic philosophical ambitions.

The methodology of Brandom's historical writings

Brandom's engagement with the history of philosophy is unified in focus and methodology. He firmly focuses his interpretations of historical texts and figures on topics and notions that are central to his own systematic philosophy – representation, reasoning, logic, normativity, meaning, understanding, discourse, knowledge – leaving on one side aspects of those historical works that, no matter how central they may have been to the concerns of their authors and their contemporaries, are secondary for Brandom's own systematic concerns. Moreover, Brandom's interpretive method is consistently and avowedly "critical" and "reconstructive," in the sense that it does not so much place the topics and notions it focuses on into the context of the interpreted author's own specific, more or less idiosyncratic historical background, commitments, and concerns, but rather into the context of much larger historical traditions and developments – traditions and developments in which Brandom situates his own systematic philosophical convictions and commitments. Accordingly, these interpretations do not aspire to offer a charitable reconstruction of the interpreted author's (or his or her contemporaries) *own* interpretation of the significance of these works. His readings are, accordingly, of lesser value to someone interested in a close, historically faithful reading of these works. They are, in Brandom's technical terminology (the meaning of which will become clearer in chapter 7), not interpretations *de dicto*. Instead, by unabashedly and purposefully placing the author's work in the context of *our* contemporary philosophical concerns and commitments, some of the author's claims are set aside as false, unjustified, or irrelevant while others are distilled and magnified as true, important, and path-breaking to us. Thus, by interpreting the author's work in this, as Brandom calls it, *de re* fashion, ideas embedded in an otherwise more or less obscure, exotic historical text and context appear as truly instructive and, indeed, path-breaking in light of our own present philosophical concerns: they become "Animating Ideas."

Brandom himself compares this method of interpretation with improvisation in bebop, "in which a melody is treated as an occasion for improvisation on its chord structure" (TMD 117). The melody is the familiar idea or element of the historical work that is the focus of Brandom's attention, while the re-contextualized *de re* interpretation of that idea is the improvisation. On the one hand, the interpretation leaves the distinct, familiar contour of a historical figure's contributions recognizable to any student of Western philosophy. On the other hand, the interpretation freely elaborates and assesses these contributions in light of later developments and present concerns and, indeed, freely recasts these contributions in contemporary terminology (which from a historicist perspective may seem anachronistic), and thus aims to demonstrate that they offer important lessons for philosophy today.

This way of engaging with the history of philosophy has a twofold advantage. First, given Brandom's ambitions as a systematic philosopher, it makes the case that Brandom's own systematic work is situated in a larger historical tradition. This effort is designed to counter the impression that his work is simply a solitary individual's historically unmotivated rebellion against what, in chapter 1, we called the Received View. Second, by offering critical, reconstructive interpretations of figures as widely ignored, if not maligned, among contemporary analytic philosophers as Hegel and Heidegger, Brandom presents core elements of their works in rigorous and systematic terms that should be understandable to, and critically appraisable by, this analytic mainstream, thus potentially rekindling interest in these figures themselves and, indeed,

rekindling interest in the history of philosophy as a source of inspiration for contemporary systematic philosophers.

The normative nature of reason

Brandom's interest in Kant largely focuses on central aspects of
what Kant calls his theories of the understanding – the faculty
enabling us, constrained by the pure concepts of the understanding, to form empirical judgments and to gain empirical knowledge
– and practical reasoning. Brandom is not interested in what Kant
calls reason narrowly conceived (the faculty producing what Kant
calls regulative ideas), nor in what Kant calls intuition (sense experience per se, as structured by its "pure forms," space and time, in
abstraction from the role the understanding plays in structuring
experience). Accordingly, unless indicated otherwise, talk about
reason is in the following to be understood as talk about the understanding and practical reason in Kant's sense and about the trans-
formation of Kant's theories of the understanding and practical
reason in Hegel's hands, as interpreted by Brandom.

Kant's "deepest and most original idea" (RP 32), according to
Brandom, is this:

> What distinguishes judgment and intentional doing from the activi-
> ties of non-sapient creatures is ... that they are things knowers and
> agents are in a distinctive way *responsible* for. Judging and acting
> involve *commitments*. They are *endorsements*, exercises of *authority*.
> Responsibility, commitment, endorsement, authority – these are all
> *normative* notions.
>
> (RP 32)

Kant's central idea is to draw the distinction between reason and
nature in normative terms. Nature is the realm of what happens in
fact, in accordance with deterministic causal laws or (according to
certain post-Kantian developments) statistical regularities. Natural
entities and processes as such are unconstrained by, and insensitive
to, norms and standards determining what ought to happen, what
rightfully may happen, or what should not happen. Accordingly,
they are not bearers of responsibilities, authorities, commitments,
entitlements, and prohibitions nor, therefore, the proper subjects of
critical appraisal, praise, or blame. By contrast, rational beings as
such are just such bearers and subjects. *Qua* theoretically rational,

epistemic beings, we are responsible for forming judgments based on good evidence and in light of standards of good probabilistic thinking, to draw the right conclusions from our judgments, and to keep our system of theoretical judgments coherent. *Qua* practically rational beings, we are responsible for setting the right goals for ourselves, both morally and (relative to our beliefs, desires, and personal maxims) prudentially, to make proper decisions and to form proper intentions in light of these goals and to weed out incompatible maxims, goals, or intentions. In general, *qua* rational beings we are responsible for justifying our theoretical judgments and practical commitments properly (justificatory responsibility), to draw the right theoretical or practical consequences from them (amplative responsibility), and to weed out incompatibilities from our system of theoretical judgments and practical commitments (critical responsibility) (RP 36). Thus, theoretical and practical reasoning is evaluable in light of a vast, complicated system of norms and standards of reasoning. *Qua* rational beings we are responsible and authorized to follow these norms, and accordingly the proper subjects of critical appraisal in light of them.

Kant is not the first one to see this contrast between the non-normative character of nature and the normative character of reason. But what distinguishes him from earlier thinkers is that he *defines* the contrast between nature and reason in terms of the contrast between the non-normative and the normative. A good reason is defined as what is justified responsibly, what justifies amplatively, and what withstands critical scrutiny, in accordance with the norms of reasoning. Theoretical and practical judgments are defined as states that are more or less properly adopted in light of these norms. And a rational being as such itself is nothing more nor less than a being bound by these norms, that is, a being capable, and bound, to perpetually form theoretical and practical judgments in justificatorily, amplatively, and critically responsible ways based on the norms of reasoning, and, in this sense, nothing more nor less than a "unit of account" for critical appraisal and instruction depending on the degree of its adherence to these norms (BSD 193). To be sure, we humans are citizens of two worlds, according to Kant (1997: 74). *Qua* embodied and empirical psychological beings, we are natural beings and subject to all the laws and statistical regularities of nature, including psychological ones. Seen as natural beings we are under no obligations, permissions, and prohibitions – just like the rest of nature. Yet *qua* rational beings we are nothing but subjects to the norms of reason and, in this regard, nothing but bearers of responsibilities and entitlements to form theoretical and practical judgments based on these norms.

A rational being's characteristic task responsibility then is to perpetually update its system of theoretical and practical judgments into an integrated, unified, holistic system, in accordance with the norms of justificatory, amplative, and critical reasoning: to accommodate new information (coming in from the senses or from testimony) by forming new judgments, to see the amplative and justificatory connections between new and old judgments, to weed out incompatible judgments or to repel claims incompatible with our judgments, and so on. Brandom maintains that the unity of such a system, which these connections provide, is what Kant means by what he calls the *original synthetic unity of apperception*, and that a rational being's characteristic cognitive activity of integrating, weeding out, and expanding its system of judgments is what Kant calls *synthesizing:*

> What is produced, sustained, and developed by practically acknowledging these critical, amplative, and justificatory integrative task responsibilities is a *unity* precisely in the sense of being governed by, subject to assessment according to, those norms of integration. It is a *synthetic* unity in that it is produced by the activity of synthesis that is integrating disparate commitments into such a unity. ... It is an *original* synthetic unity of *apperception* because what makes an act or episode a *judging* in the first place is just its being subject to the normative demand that it be integrated into such a systematically unified whole
>
> (RP 37; cf. SOT chap. 1: 9).

We must disambiguate a wider and a narrower conception of reason here. The wider conception is in play when we characterize the contrast between reason and nature in terms of the normative vs. the non-normative. On this conception, *any* norm is a norm of reason, and any norm-governed creature is *ipso facto* rational. The narrower conception is in play when we characterize a rational being as one capable of forming theoretical and practical judgments, and as bound by the corresponding norms of theoretical and practical reasoning. Judgments are propositionally contentful states, and creatures bound by the corresponding norms are, accordingly, concept-using creatures. On this conception, only norms governing the use of concepts are norms of reason, and only concept-using creatures are, accordingly, rational beings. Of course, in principle the wider and the narrower conceptions of reason may in the end collapse. All norms may in the end turn out to be norms governing the use of concepts, and all norm-governed creatures may, accordingly, be concept-using, judging creatures. However, the issue should not be prejudged, and Brandom does in fact not share this view – although Kant and Hegel have apparently held it (TMD 223). He holds that a creature may be *deontic*, or norm-governed, without being *discursive*, or capable of propositionally contentful thought and talk (more on this in the next chapter). Indeed, for all that Brandom says, the fellows on the title page, hanging out on that cliff, may just be such merely deontic, non-discursive creatures, despite the fact that they can be trained to behave in ways that, to us, seem discursive. They may well engage in norm-governed behavior, for all that Brandom says, but they are incapable, he thinks, to develop sensitivity to the specific norms governing propositionally contentful thought and talk, concepts and so on, and they are thus not rational creatures in the narrow sense (MIE 89; 1995a 897). Which conception of reason, then, is Brandom's? Although he frequently casually uses the wider conception of reason, the narrow conception reflects his views more properly. Only concept-using creatures are rational, according to Brandom, and only norms governing the use of concepts are, accordingly, norms of reason. In the following, I shall accordingly use "reason" in this narrow sense.

"Judgment" is ambiguous too in the considerations above, allowing for the distinction between the cognitive activity or state of judg*ing* and the content judg*ed*, that is, between "what one is *doing* in making oneself responsible" as a rational being and "what one makes oneself responsible *for*" by doing it (RP 35). To form a judgment in the first sense is to take a certain cognitive attitude toward a content that p – paradigmatically, to believe or intend that p. Judging that p is governed by norms of reasoning, of course. The norms of reasoning (in the narrow sense) just are the norms of justificatory, amplative, and critical reasoning dictating what theoretical or practical judgments we should form. A judgment that p (in the sense of activity or state) is proper just in case it has the right kind of rational support or license, derived from various other theoretical or practical judgments that q, r, etc., from observations of one's environment, or from someone else's say-so (justificatory responsibility). And it rationally requires or allows the subject to form further judgments that s, t, etc. and to act in certain ways (amplative responsibility), as well as *not* to form yet further incompatible judgments that u, v, etc. and *not* to carry out certain incompatible actions (critical responsibility). In short, a judgment that p occupies a particular location in what Wilfrid Sellars calls the "space of reasons" – the space of norms relating the judgment that p to multifarious other actual or potential judgments that q, r, s, t, u, v (those that support it, follow from it, or are incompatible with it), including theoretical judgments formed in response to perceptual input, and practical judgments (intentions) to act in certain ways (Sellars 1997: 76. Cf. MIE 234–5; RP 3–4; AR 28–9).

How about the propositional content that p, in abstraction from whether or not someone forms a judgment (in the first sense) with that content? In which sense is it normative too – as it presumably must be if propositional content is the medium in which we reason and reason is wholly and constitutively normative? As seen in the last chapter, Brandom identifies a propositional content with its inferential role, that is, with the inferential and incompatibility relations it bears to other contents that q, r, s, t, u, v, etc. Naturally enough, Brandom (like Sellars) regards the norms of justificatory, amplative, and critical reasoning structuring the space of reasons as norms of inference and incompatibility. Accordingly, Brandom identifies the inferential role constituting the content that p, given his commitment to inferential role semantics, with the norms of reasoning connecting actual or potential theoretical or practical judgments that p justificatorily, amplatively, or critically, with other actual or potential theoretical or practical judgments that q, r, s, t, u, v, etc. The content that p is thus itself normative through and through. The norms determining the location of actual or potential judgments that p in the space of reason *are* the content that p. It follows that, on Brandom's view, the cognitive state or activity of judging that p and the content that p, in abstraction from the state or the activity, cannot be philosophically characterized except in terms of each other. Any state or activity of judging has a role in reasoning, hence a particular location in the space of reasons, hence a content that p. And any content that p is a set of norms constraining a subject's justificatory, amplative, and critical reasoning, that is, her activity of maintaining and updating her system of theoretical or practical judgments that p – her system of states of judging (BSD 42).

Concepts are the sub-propositional semantic components of propositional contents that p. They cannot be contents of judgment on their own, but only in combination with certain other concepts, forming propositional contents. Concepts are norms of reasoning

too, according to Brandom, in accordance with Kant's characterization of concepts as *rules*.[1] Brandom's central claim regarding concepts is that their semantic dimension consists in nothing but the
contribution they make to the roles in reasoning of all the propositional contents in which they may figure. That is, a concept $\underline{C}$ is
semantically nothing but an item that helps determining the positions in the space of reasons of any actual or potential judgment in
the content of which $\underline{C}$ figures. In this sense, $\underline{C}$ itself consists in
nothing but norms of reasoning. Concepts have no semantic life
apart from their contributions to determining the positions in the
space of reasons of any judgments in the content of which they
figure. We will see in chapter 4 how Brandom thinks this works.

The space of reasons includes observation judgments, formed in
immediate response to the perception of aspects of one's environment, and intentions to act, in more or less immediate response to
which the subject performs certain actions – what Sellars calls
"language entry moves" and "language exit moves" (1991: 327–30)
– and I should say a few words about them here, though only
chapter 5 will discuss them in detail. Observation judgments are
formed more or less reliably in response to the observed non-linguistic circumstances, and non-linguistic actions are performed
more or less reliably in response to one's intentions and, more
broadly, to one's system of theoretical and practical judgments. As
we shall see in chapter 5, Brandom thinks of the more or less reliable processes of forming observation judgments and performing
actions as irreducibly norm-governed processes, yet he denies that
they are *inferential* processes, since inferential processes can only
connect sentences to other sentences (or judgments to other judgments), and neither observed circumstance nor actions are sentences or judgments. On the other hand, Brandom will argue that
the noninferential processes leading to observation judgments and
intentional actions nonetheless make a crucial semantic contribution. Due to them, judgments and intentions can be *empirically*
contentful, in the sense that these noninferential processes make a
crucial contribution to determining the inferential roles of specifically empirical judgments and intentions. The inferential role of
these judgments and intentions carries information about the
largely non-normative, non-linguistic, non-reasoning world. Given
his view that the noninferential processes leading to observation
judgments and intentional actions help in determining the inferential role of empirical judgments and intentions, Brandom calls his
semantic inferentialism "broad" (AR 21, 28; 2007: 164–5).

Note that this broad inferentialism is compatible with Brandom's commitment to strong inferentialism – the view that inferential relations alone constitute propositional meaning and content. Specifically, broad inferentialism does not imply that the noninferential processes leading to observation judgments and intentional actions amount to a representational dimension that partially constitutes the propositional content of empirical judgements and intentions. That is, broad inferentialism does not imply a hybrid semantic view, according to which mutually irreducible inferential and representational components constitute the semantic dimension of specifically empirical talk and thought. Although noninferential processes contribute to the determination of the inferential role of empirically contentful judgments and intentions, *that role alone* constitutes the content of these judgments and intentions, according to Brandom, as we shall see more clearly in chapter 5.

Given Brandom's identification of content with norms of reasoning, reasoning turns out to be simultaneously an epistemic and a semantic activity. Reasoning is the more or less successful epistemic effort to minimize the presence of unjustified judgments in one's system of judgments and to maximize the presence of (relevant) justified ones, that is, to live up to one's epistemic responsibilities. And it is simultaneously the semantic effort to clarify the content of one's judgments for oneself, by tracing their broadly inferential connections, that is, by determining their locations in the space of reasons. Philosophical semantics and epistemology are, accordingly, largely overlapping enterprises, on Brandom's approach. Moreover, since he identifies concepts and propositional contents with norms of reasoning, Brandom regards his semantic theory as a version of rationalism, as indicated previously (AR 25). However, Brandom's rationalism is far from the views of the classical proponents of rationalism, such as Plato, Descartes, Leibniz, or Spinoza. Brandom holds neither that all concepts are innate nor that all knowledge is *a priori*. First, noninferential processes of forming observation judgments and performing intentional actions play an essential role in determining the norms of empirical reasoning, as just said. Second, as we shall see throughout the remainder of the book, judgments and their content cannot be formed, sustained, and developed except through the ability to engage in, and actual engagement in, norm-governed discursive social practices, according to Brandom, and in this regard too his rationalism differs starkly from the one advocated by its classical proponents.

Autonomy

Much Enlightenment political thought revolves around the idea that a political community must constitute itself through a social contract, into which each subject uncoercedly agrees to enter. Subjects may have political rights and obligations, laws may have authority, and political institutions may be legitimate, on this view, only to the extent that such rights, obligations, authority, and legitimacy flow directly or indirectly from this contract. An usurping individual or group may non-normatively coerce individuals and enforce a set of rules, but can in principle not through such coercive force institute rights, obligations, authority, and legitimacy. Rather, the power to institute or confer rights, obligations, etc., depends on being authorized to do so, and such authority must flow from the social contract. The creation of political rights, obligations, and legitimate authorities and institutions is thus essentially *attitude-dependent*, according to the social contract tradition, in the sense that it depends on the subjects' attitude of agreement to the social contract; political subjects are free to the extent that they are self-legislating (autonomous), that is, to the extent that their lives are normatively constrained by norms, rights, duties, and authorities that are directly or indirectly self-imposed, via their agreement to the social contract (RP 61; TMD 218–19).

Kant's views on the source of the norms of reason are an expansion, internalization, and radicalization of this Enlightenment account of the source of political rights and obligations. Rational beings as such are autonomous, according to Kant, in that the norms of reason governing them do not flow immediately from some independent source outside the rational subject – Platonic Forms, a deity's divine command, or the mind-independent natural world – but rather essentially depend on the subjects' attitudes of acknowledging or recognizing their authority. In this sense, rational beings are only bound by norms they give to themselves:

> The ... autonomy idea is that we, as subjects, are genuinely *normatively* constrained only by rules we constrain *ourselves* by, those that we adopt and acknowledge *as* binding on us. ... The difference between non-normative *compulsion* and normative *authority* is that we are genuinely *normatively* responsible only to what we *acknowledge as* authoritative. In this sense, only we can bind ourselves, in the sense that we are only *normatively* bound by the results of

exercises of our freedom: (self-constitutive) *self*-bindings, commitments we have undertaken by acknowledging them.

(RP 63)

One of Brandom's big theoretical commitments is to this Kantian idea of the autonomy of reason. The norms binding rational beings as such and constituting them and the concepts they use are instituted by the reasoning subjects themselves. Brandom undertakes enormous efforts to refine this idea into something defensible.

How should we think of the autonomy of reason? Being bound by certain norms implies being responsible to follow these norms and hence being the proper subject of appraisal, instruction, and critique. And that in turn implies being sensitive to the fact that one is bound by certain norms. Creatures incapable of regarding themselves as constrained by norms are incapable of being constrained by norms, hence not the proper subjects of critical appraisal. Kant aims to capture this internal connection between being bound by norms and being sensitive to being bound by norms when he defines the rational will as the capacity to determine actions not so much in accordance with laws (rules) but rather *"in accordance with the representation of* laws" (Kant 1998: 24). Brandom comments:

> The point he is making is that we act according to our *grasp* or *understanding* of rules. The rules do not immediately compel us, as natural ones [i.e., laws of nature] do. Their compulsion is rather mediated by our *attitude* towards those rules. What makes us act as we do is not the rule or norm itself but our *acknowledgement* of it. It is the possibility of this intervening attitude that is missing in the relation between merely natural objects and the rules [i.e., laws] that govern them
>
> (MIE 31; cf. also AR 94, Stout 2010: 145–8).

Qua rational beings we are bound by a vast array of norms. Accordingly, each rational being is, in Brandom's terminology (which will be ubiquitous henceforth), at any time the bearer of a vast array of *commitments* and *entitlements* corresponding to these norms. These commitments and entitlements, that is, these *normative statuses*, determine how the subject having them must, may, and must not reason at the time. Yet the subject's being so committed and entitled at the time depends on her sensitivity to the fact that she is bound by norms of reasoning, that is, in Brandom's terminology, on the subject's *acknowledging* a certain array of commitments and entitlements at the time. Acknowledged commitments and entitlements are the *normative attitudes* in which our sensitivity to the norms binding us consists.

Indeed, since rational beings are nothing but beings constrained by norms of reason, Brandom thinks of a subject's system of theoretical and practical judgments simply *as* a system of acknowledged commitments and entitlements. A judgment that p is an acknowledged theoretical or practical commitment to a content that p. Moreover, the subject's sensitivity to the fact that certain norms of justificatory, amplative, and critical reasoning relate her actual and potential judgments to each other in certain ways consists in the subject's acknowledgment of a vast array of commitments to certain norms of justificatory, amplative, and critical reasoning relating these judgments to each other, that is, to norms of inference and incompatibility constituting the propositional content of these judgments. And the subject's synthesizing activity over time, according to Brandom, consists in her going through a sequence of constellations of acknowledged commitments and entitlements over time: a sequence of, on the one hand, constellations of acknowledged theoretical or practical commitments to certain contents that p, q, r, etc. (a constellation of judgments) and, on the other hand, constellations of acknowledged commitments to certain norms of justificatory, amplative, and critical reasoning *relating* these judgments to each other and to certain further potential judgments (deemed incompatible with the actual ones, or deemed justified in light of them but not yet formed).

We will begin to see in detail how this works, according to Brandom, in the next chapter. Currently, what matters is that the commitments and entitlements a subject acknowledges do not usually track perfectly the commitments and entitlements she really has. The former attitudes constitute the subject's more or less accurate *takes* on her rational obligations and permissions in her given situation, whereas the latter statuses are her de facto rational obligations and permissions in the situation. A subject can presumably not be mistaken in every respect about the commitments and entitlements she really has. After all, being capable of critique and instruction requires having insight into at least some of one's own true commitments and entitlements, as a basis for potentially gaining more insight into them. Still, a subject's set of acknowledged commitments and entitlements at any given time usually corresponds to the set of commitments and entitlements she really has only imperfectly. We routinely are committed and entitled to things that we do not (yet) acknowledge and we routinely acknowledge commitments or entitlements to things that we are in fact not committed or entitled to.

Inspired by German Idealist thinking, Brandom aspires to exploit this contrast between normative attitudes and normative statuses for an ambitious account of reason's autonomy:

> norms are in an important sense in the eye of the beholder, so that one cannot address the question of what ... norms are, independently of the question of what it is to acknowledge them in practice. The direction of explanation to be pursued here first offers an account of the practical attitude of *taking* something to be correct according-to-a-practice, and then explains the status of *being* correct-according-to-a-practice by appeal to those attitudes.
>
> (MIE 25. Cf. also e.g. MIE 280, 627; RP 61, 69–70)

Reason is autonomous, Brandom wishes to argue, in that subjects' reasoning activity – the activity of successively acknowledging constellations of commitments and entitlements – is essentially involved in "determining," "instituting," "conferring," or "creating" (terms in which Brandom frequently describes the matter) the very norms and normative statuses constraining and governing this activity. The successive constellations of normative attitudes reasoning subjects form when they are active are not only efforts to follow the norms of reasoning in practice but are also the factors that bring these norms into being. Indeed, because Kant thinks of the rational activity of using concepts as what institutes the norms of reasoning themselves, and hence the very concepts in use, Brandom considers Kant to be a pragmatist (RP 41, TMD 212).

In MIE, Brandom calls this approach to reason's autonomy *phenomenalism about norms* (MIE 627). The approach is phenomenalist in that, according to it, what the norms *appear* to be to reason when it synthesizes – reason's successively going through constellations of acknowledged commitments and entitlements – somehow creates, institutes, confers, or determines the very norms governing reason's synthesizing efforts. Pursuing such an approach to norms is, to be sure, a most delicate undertaking. The envisioned phenomenalism must obviously not imply that whatever seems right to the reasoning subject *ipso facto* is right (MIE 52, RP 64), but must allow for the possibility that the normative attitudes the reasoning subject forms when it synthesizes can be mistaken in light of the norms of reason. It will thus be critical that phenomenalism about norms balances the claim of the attitude-dependence of the norms of reason, that is, the claim that the norms of reason are instituted through the normative attitudes subjects form when they reason, with a sense in which these norms are attitude-independent, so as to not imply that everything that seems right to the reasoning subject when it synthesizes is *ipso facto* right (RP 64).

Indeed, at least in MIE Brandom thinks that this sense of attitude-independence needs to be rather robust:

> the primary explanatory challenge [for phenomenalism] ... is to show how ... genuine, and therefore *objective*, conceptual norms can be elaborated. These bind the community of concept-users in such a way that it is possible not only for individuals but for the whole community to be mistaken in its assessments of what they require in particular cases.
>
> (MIE 54. Cf. also MIE 592–607.)

At least in MIE, Brandom thinks that the norms of reason are objective in the rather Kantian sense that not only the reasoning of individual subjects but also the reasoning of the whole community of rational beings – past, present, and future – may be mistaken in certain respects. There may be cases in which the whole community reasons one way, and yet such reasoning is erroneous. (As we shall discuss in chapter 8, compared to his approach to the matter in MIE, Brandom has in more recent writings refined and, perhaps, partially revised this position.)

Mutual recognition

Squaring the autonomy of reason – the attitude-dependence of the norms of reason claimed by phenomenalism about norms – with the attitude-independence of the norms of reason, hence the sense in which not only individuals but also the entire community may reason in erroneous ways, may seem like an impossible task. Here, I shall only outline Brandom's strategy for pursuing this task. Only in chapter 8, with the relevant technical details introduced, will we be able to see how he tries to reconcile these two demands.

Brandom's strategy to reconcile the attitude-dependence and the attitude-independence of norms of reasoning is yet again deeply influenced by German Idealist thinking about autonomy, this time Hegel's. Brandom thinks that Kant's theory of autonomy falls short of carrying the explanatory burdens assigned to it.

Very roughly, Kant sees experience, the application of concepts, as beginning with the *selection* of concepts. The potential knower has available a myriad of different possible determinate rules of synthesis of representation. Experience requires picking one, and trying it out as the rule for combining the manifold of presented intuitions. If it doesn't quite "fit," or permits the synthesis only of some of the intuitions that present themselves, then a mistake has been made and a related, overlapping, but different determinate concept is tried in its place. Thus although it is up to the knower what concept to try out, the *success* of the attempted synthesis according to that rule is not up to the knower. The exercise of spontaneity is constrained by the deliverances of receptivity.

                    (TMD 213; cf. also RP 65–6; SOT chap. 6: 73–7)

According to Brandom's Kant, reason's synthesizing activity has a two-phase structure. First, reason selects, from an antecedently given stock of fully determinate possible norms of reasoning, the ones that seem most suitable for the task at hand. Second, reason then applies the selected norms and thereby binds itself to them, by forming judgments whose content is determined by the selected norms.

This two-phase model arguably succeeds in reconciling the demands of the attitude-dependence and the attitude-independence of the norms of reasoning. The norms are attitude-dependent in the sense that reason selects the norms it binds itself to. True, reason has no say regarding which candidate norms "fit" the task at hand best; the determinate nature of the candidate norms themselves, over which reason has no influence, settles that matter. Still, which candidate norms are to have authority over reason depends on reason's granting such authority by selecting them. And the norms of reason are attitude-independent in the sense that the determinate nature of the selected norms then determines what reason, by binding itself to these norms, has truly committed and entitled itself to. Since reason has no influence over that determinate nature, it is thus not up to reason to influence the commitments and entitlements it truly adopts by having selected these norms. Reason may be at least partially ignorant or mistaken about what it really has committed or entitled itself to. For example, I may judge that the coin in my pocket is made of pure gold, thus selecting the concept <u>gold</u>, rather than some gerrymandered concept that applies to gold as well as to other metals that superficially resemble gold, and applying it to the coin in my pocket. I thereby have bound myself to whatever the norms constituting the concept <u>gold</u> are, rather than to the different norms constituting the gerrymandered concept. My having bound myself this way depends on my attitude – my forming *this* judgment, containing the concept <u>gold</u>, rather than a similar judgment involving the gerrymandered concept. Yet, not being very knowledgeable about chemistry, I may fail to form the consequential judgment that the coin in my pocket has a density of 19.3 g/cm^3, that is, I may fail to *acknowledge* a commitment to the corresponding norm of amplative reasoning from <u>being gold</u> to <u>having a density of 19.3 g/cm3</u>. Nonetheless, I *am* so committed, as a matter of having applied the concept <u>gold</u>, which this norm of amplative reasoning partially constitutes. Since my attitudes have no influence over the content of this concept and this norm, my being so committed is thus, in this sense, independent of my attitudes.

Hegel's main complaint about this two-phase model, according to Brandom, is that it does not address the question of where the determinate nature of the candidate norms, from which reason selects, comes from. The model simply takes such determinateness for granted, and it thus is, in a pejorative sense, merely "formal," "abstract," "empty," and "uncritical" (Brandom 1976: 193; RP 66). One would think that the autonomy of reason means that reason itself, in the process of synthesizing, generates the very determinate nature of the norms binding it too – creates those very norms – rather than merely selecting these norms from an antecedently and mysteriously given heaven of possible, determinate norms. At least Hegel thinks so, and Hegel's chief contribution to the Kantian legacy, according to Brandom, is a theory of autonomy that accounts in detail for how the synthesizing activity of reason creates, rather than merely selects, the determinate norms governing that very activity. This theory is also at the heart of Brandom's own overall project.

The core thesis of this theory is that norms and normative statuses are essentially social achievements. They are gradually determined by our ongoing, ordinary rational activity in the context of mutual social recognition. Hegel's account thus combines two key moves, according to Brandom. First, Hegel replaces Kant's two-phase model with a one-phase model, according to which

> conceptual content arises out of the process of applying concepts – the *determinate* content of concepts is unintelligible apart from the *determination* of that content, the process of determin*ing* it. Concepts are not fixed or static items. Their content is altered

by every particular case in which they are applied or not applied in experience.

(TMD 215)

The synthesizing activity of rational beings, Hegel wants to say, is simultaneously a process of applying determinate concepts, that is, of following determinate norms of reasoning, and a process of further determining these very norms. The determinateness of the norms itself is now attitude-dependent, by contrast to the Kantian model, in the sense that the synthesizing processes of adopting successive constellations of judgments, hence successive constellations of normative attitudes of acknowledging commitments and entitlements, successively and gradually determines the conceptual content of those judgments, hence the norms of reasoning constituting that content. The shift to this one-phase model thus includes the introduction of a historical notion of the determinateness of norms. Whereas according to Kant's two-phase model, the content of possible norms of reason is eternal and unchanging, and in particular unaffected by reason's activity of selecting and applying them, it is historical and evolving according to Hegel's one-phase model. Successive usages of a concept in the ongoing synthesizing process simultaneously successively apply the norms constituting the concept and successively further determine the content of those very norms.

Second, the attitude-independence of norms and normative statuses from normative attitudes is, on this Hegelian approach, a matter of the social contrast between a reasoner's *acknowledgments* of commitments and entitlements at a given time, or successively over time, and his or her *attributions* of commitments and entitlements to *another* reasoner at that time, or successively over time:

> Taking someone to be responsible or authoritative, attributing a normative deontic status to someone, is the attitude-kind that Hegel ... calls "recognition" (Anerkennung). Hegel's view is what you get if you take the attitudes of *both* recognizer and recognized, both those who are authoritative and those who are responsible, to be essential *necessary* conditions of the institution of genuine normative statuses, and require in addition that those attitudes be symmetric or reciprocal (*gegenseitig*). In a certain sense ... Hegel also takes it that those *individually necessary* normative attitudes are *jointly sufficient* to institute normative statuses. What institutes normative statuses is *reciprocal* recognition. ... The reciprocal recognition model he recommends to resolve this incompatibility balances moments of normative

independence or authority of attitudes over statuses, on the part of
both recognizer and recognized, with corresponding moments of
normative *dependence* or responsibility to the attitudes of others,
by reading both of these aspects as individually only necessary,
and only jointly sufficient to institute normative statuses in the
sense of giving them binding force.

(RP 70–72)

Hegel's idea is that rational beings are essentially non-private,
social beings, in the sense that they essentially do not only take
themselves as authorized and responsible to faithfully follow the
norms of reasoning, but also treat others as bound by these same
norms. Insofar as rational beings mutually recognize each other in
this way, they treat each other as equal and worthy of respect and
esteem (connotations that the German "Anerkennung," by contrast
to the English "recognition," carries). Still, what you and I regard
as my and your respective normative statuses under any given
circumstance may differ. You may attribute commitments and entitlements to me that I do not yet acknowledge and I may acknowledge commitments and entitlements that you do not attribute to
me – and similarly for your acknowledgments of commitments and
entitlements and my attributions of commitments and entitlements
to you. That is, although different people regard themselves and
each other as bound by the same set of norms of reason, whatever
those are, different people diverge to some extent in what exactly
they take those norms to be, hence they diverge in various respects
and to varying degrees in their assessments as to which normative statuses any one of them adopts under given circumstances.
For example, I (a tradesman) may sincerely judge the coin in my
pocket to be made of pure gold. While I do not thereby acknowledge a consequential judgment to my coin's having a density of
$19.3 \, \text{g/cm}^3$, you (a chemist) will attribute a commitment to form
this consequential judgment to me, in the sense that, according
to you, I am bound to form the latter judgment, given that I have
formed the former one. Similarly, being oblivious about the current
market value of pure gold, you may attribute an entitlement to
me to sell the coin at no more than $500 on the current market
– an entitlement that I, knowing more about the matter, do not
acknowledge. (On the other hand, I presumably also acknowledge
a consequential commitment to my coin's being made of a precious
metal, and that is also a commitment you attribute to me. That is,
from your viewpoint, my acknowledgment of this commitment
is correct.)

In general, our assessments of what any one of us is committed and entitled to under given circumstances converge and contrast in various ways, and such convergence and contrast mimics the attitude-independence of content in the following sense. Just as someone's application of a concept under given circumstances may commit or entitle her to things she does not yet acknowledge, and not commit or entitle her to things she does acknowledge, so others may *hold her* to commitments and entitlements that she does not acknowledge, and *fail to hold her* to commitments and entitlements that she does acknowledge. Hegel's idea – and, following him, Brandom's – is that the contrast between what the norms of reason and someone's commitments and entitlements really are vs. what that person takes these norms to be and which commitments and entitlements she acknowledges results from this social contrast between what *one* rational being takes the norms of reason to be (the commitments and entitlements *she* acknowledges and the commitments and entitlements *she* attributes as *to be* acknowledged to another person under any given circumstances) vs. what *that other* rational being takes the norms of reason to be (the commitments and entitlements *he* acknowledges and the commitments and entitlements *he* attributes to the former person as *to be* acknowledged by her under these circumstances). That is, the constellations of acknowledgments and attributions of commitments and entitlements, distributed over socially interacting rational beings and changing in systematic interaction with the course of the social exchange, somehow institute, determine, or create the very norms of reason governing the exchange and binding the participants.

Note that this social strategy of accounting for the attitude-independence of norms still defends a version of phenomenalism about norms. Attributions of commitments and entitlements to others are normative attitudes just as much as acknowledgments of commitments and entitlements are, though normative attitudes of a different kind. Acknowledged commitments and entitlements are intrapersonal, reflecting a subject's take on what her own commitments and entitlements are, whereas attributions of commitments and entitlements to others are interpersonal, reflecting a subject's take on what another subject's commitments and entitlements are. Social interactions between rational beings are shot through with normative attitudes of both types. At each stage of a social interaction, each participant acknowledges a system of commitments and entitlements and attributes a system of commitments and entitlements to any other participant, and each participant's acknowledgments and attributions of commitments and entitlements change in systematic dependence with the development of the interaction. The presence of both kinds of normative attitudes in each participant is the mark of mutual social recognition, and mutual social recognition so understood somehow institutes and determines the very norms of reason governing the participants, in accordance with phenomenalism about norms, which claims that normative attitudes institute and determine the norms.

Note also that this mutual social recognition model still defends a version of the autonomy of reason. The model rejects the naïve claim that each rational creature is autonomous in the sense that the intrapersonal normative attitudes constituting *her own* reasoning (her acknowledgments of commitments and entitlements), in abstraction from her assessments of the reasoning of others (her attributions of commitments and entitlements to them) and from the assessments by others of her reasoning (their attributions of commitments and entitlements to her), can institute the norms of reason binding her. That is, the mutual social recognition model rejects the view that a rational being could through her own private, isolated synthesizing efforts of forming such intrapersonal normative attitudes alone somehow wind up instituting the same public norms of reason that bind all rational beings. But the model still accommodates the autonomy of reason in an extended sense. Although, according to it, my autonomy as a rational being constitutively requires affirmation and constraint by others – "*my* freedom [my self-legislation] ... depends on *others*" (TMD 220), those others, insofar as they so affirm and constrain my reasoning, are creatures I recognize as rational beings like myself – as belonging to "us." That is, they are creatures I recognize as authorized by, and responsible to, the same norms that bind myself, and as creatures recognizing me as authorized by, and responsible to, those same norms. According to the mutual recognition model, norms are neither laid down somewhere external to rational activity (such as mind-independent nature, a Platonic Realm, or divine command), nor laid down in asymmetric social relations of repression and submission, or mutual instrumentalization and manipulation. Rather, they are laid down in symmetric relations of mutual social recognition, where anyone's acknowledgments and attributions of commitments and entitlements potentially carry as much weight as anyone else's in the institution and determination of the norms of reason that equally bind every participant.

The game of giving and asking for reasons

Unsurprisingly, in light of the discussion in chapter 1, the kind of
mutual social interaction that is solely responsible for the institution of conceptual norms, according to Brandom (though perhaps
not according to Hegel), is linguistic communication (RP 72) – what
Brandom often calls the "game of giving and asking for reasons."
Discourse is the paradigm of a social interaction in which reasoning
takes place in the context of mutual social recognition. Through
speech, speakers express propositions and hence concepts, and, if
they are sincere, propositional attitudes (paradigmatically, beliefs
and intentions). Moreover, each participant acknowledges and
attributes in practice commitments and entitlements reflecting
what she takes to be the norms of justificatory, amplative, and critical reasoning pertaining to the linguistic performances exchanged
and the beliefs and intentions expressed. Accordingly, each participant acknowledges and attributes in practice commitments and
entitlements to certain further judgments and further linguistic
performances, that is, she treats in practice herself and every other
participant as committed or entitled to actually form these further
judgments and to actually (be prepared to) perform these further
linguistic performances, in accordance with what she takes to be
these norms of justificatory, amplative, and critical reasoning. And
her acknowledgments and attributions of commitments and entitlements change in systematic interaction with the linguistic performances exchanged, constrained, on the one hand, by what she
takes to be the norms of justificatory, amplative, and critical reason
and, on the other hand, by how her own system of theoretical and
practical judgments has changed in response to the last performance as well as by how she takes the various other participants
to have changed their various systems of theoretical and practical
judgments in response to it.

Through this mutual social recognition involved in it, discursive
activity, when conducted non-manipulatively and non-coercively,
is a collective effort to find out not only what to believe and intend
but also what the norms of reasoning are that bind us, in the uncontroversial epistemic sense that, by engaging in such non-manipula-
tive, non-coercive discourse, we assist and prod each other as best
we can not only to see what we should, may, or must not believe
and intend but also, as part and parcel of that same activity, to see
the norms of justificatory, amplative, and critical reasoning connect-

ing these beliefs and intentions to each other, to further potential beliefs and intentions, and to the statements exchanged. Moreover, according to Brandom's way of thinking of the autonomy of reason – his phenomenalism about norms – this mutual social recognition involved in discursive practice at the same time also determines the norms of justificatory, amplative, and critical reasoning in the much more ambitious and controversial semantic (or metaphysical) sense that it creates and institutes those very norms.

The next chapter will introduce the basic abstract framework of Brandom's theory of the game of giving and asking for reasons – his theory of scorekeeping. Chapters 4 through 7 will add details and expansions to this theory, thus making this basic framework look more and more like a theory capable of accounting for our actual discursive practices with all their nuances and in all their variety. Only in the last chapter, with those details and expansions on the table, will we revisit Brandom's thesis of phenomenalism about norms, and only there will we discuss how he tries to vindicate this thesis.

Summary

This chapter outlined Brandom's approach to the nature of reason and reasoning, which is heavily influenced by Kant's and Hegel's thinking about the matter. From Kant, Brandom adopts the idea that reason is constitutively normative. In Brandom's adaptation of this idea, a theoretical or practical judgment that p is essentially a position in the normative space of reasons, relating that judgment via norms of good reasoning to further actual or potential judgments that q, that r, that s, etc. – judgments from which the judgment that p follows inferentially (justificatory reasoning), judgments that follow inferentially from the judgment that p (amplative reasoning), and judgments that are incompatible with the judgment that p (critical reasoning). Its position in this space – or web – of norms of reasoning thus determines the inferential role of the judgment that p and hence constitutes, given Brandom's commitment to inferential role semantics, in particular its content that p. Metaphysically speaking, a content that p is nothing but a *relatum* of a bundle of norms of reasoning, relating that *relatum* to other such *relata* – other contents that q, that r, that s.

Rational subjects are no more and no less than beings bound by these norms of reasoning, and rational activity is no more and no less than such a subject's effort to follow these norms. In judging that p, a subject takes up a constellation of commitments, entitlements, and prohibitions (normative statuses) to form certain further judgments that q, that r, that s, etc., in accordance with the norms of reasoning, and the subject's rational activity is her more or less successful effort to recognize and honor these normative statuses, by *acknowledging* a constellation of commitments, entitlements, and prohibitions (normative attitudes) to form certain further judgments – more or less in accordance with the actual commitments, entitlements, and prohibitions (normative statuses) she has adopted. A subject's system of judgments at any given time, according to Brandom, is nothing but a system of acknowledged commitments, entitlements, and prohibitions to, on the one hand, certain contents that p, that q, that r, etc. (actual and potential judgments) and, on the other hand, certain inferential and incompatibility relations between these acknowledged commitments, entitlements, and prohibitions (rational relations between these actual and potential judgments).

Brandom also adopts from Kant the idea that reason is autonomous – the idea that reason somehow freely gives to itself the norms binding itself. In Brandom's hands, this Kantian idea becomes the thesis of phenomenalism about norms, according to which the normative attitudes that subjects form when they reason somehow create or institute the very norms governing such reasoning and binding the subjects. In order to allow for the possibility of mistaken reasoning, this sense in which the norms of reason depend on the reasoning subjects' normative attitudes must be balanced with a sense in which these norms are attitude-independent. Brandom aspires to account for this attitude-independence – for the fact that not everything the subject takes to be right is *ipso facto* right – by giving his phenomenalism about norms a Hegelian twist. According to Hegel's mutual social recognition model, rational activity essentially has an interpersonal, social, mutually interpretive dimension. Reasoning for oneself, on this model, essentially depends on the interpersonal social abilities to assess, in the context of social interaction, the reasoning of those with whom one interacts; it depends on the ability to recognize those with whom one interacts as other subjects who also assess one's own reasoning. In this sense, rational beings are essentially public, interpersonal, social creatures: they not only *acknowledge* commitments, entitlements, and prohibitions but also *attribute* commitments, entitlements, and prohibitions to other rational subjects in

the context of socially interacting with them. Apropos phenomenalism about norms, the norms of reason themselves are, on this
Hegelian view, somehow instituted or created by the interplay
between constellations of normative attitudes of both types, distributed equally over the participants in the context of their social
interactions. Somehow, the interplay of these two attitude-types
within and *between* the individual participants institutes the norms
themselves governing the interaction, and in particular the norms
of reasoning. And the contrast between taking oneself to be right
and being right in particular somehow falls out, according to the
mutual social recognition model, from the social contrast between
what one subject vs. another subject takes to be right in the context
of their social interaction. (Chapter 8 will discuss how Brandom
thinks this works.)

3

Scorekeeping

We saw in chapter 1 that Brandom wishes to offer a pragmatist explanation of the central semantic features of thought and talk – conceptually structured propositional mental content and linguistic meaning – and all the related epistemic, cognitive, and logical features of thought and talk (inference, representation, reasoning, justification, formal validity, etc.) in terms of a normative pragmatic description of linguistic communication, that is, in terms of a description of speakers' norm-governed skillful use of language in communication. In effect, we saw at the end of chapter 2 the key idea behind Brandom's normative pragmatic description of linguistic communication. Linguistic practice, normative pragmatically characterized, is the norm-governed exchange of linguistic performances between at least two participants. At each stage of a conversation, every participant has a constellation of commitments and entitlements (normative statuses), paradigmatically to certain linguistic performances, in accordance with the norms governing the conversation. Moreover, at each stage of the conversation, every participant tracks in practice these normative statuses as best as she can, in accordance with what she takes to be the norms governing the exchange: she *acknowledges* a constellation of commitments and entitlements herself, paradigmatically to certain performances, and she *attributes* constellations of commitments and entitlements, paradigmatically to certain performances, to every other interlocutor. Every participant's normative statuses change in systematic ways in response to each new linguistic performance in accordance with the norms governing the practice, and every participant tracks these changes in practice as best as she can by changing her normative attitudes accordingly, in accordance with what she takes the norms to be.

The primary semantic target of Brandom's pragmatist explanation is the propositional meaning of the linguistic performances exchanged. We saw in chapter 1 that Brandom identifies the meaning or propositional contentfulness of a statement or thought with its inferential role, that is, its role in reasoning. And we saw in chapter 2 that a statement's or thought's inferential role, hence its meaning or content, is itself normative, according to Brandom's Kantian conception of reasoning, consisting in the norms determining how the statement or thought must or may be used in reasoning relative to other statements and thoughts (and their inferential roles); that is, consisting in the norms determining what counts as a reason for (or against) endorsing the statement or thought and what the statement or thought counts as a reason for (or against). In short, according to Brandom, a statement's or thought's propositional content (its inferential role) is a location in the space of reasons. Thus, the primary target of Brandom's pragmatist explanation is an account, in terms of his normative pragmatic vocabulary of commitments and entitlements and their acknowledgments and attributions in discursive practice, of the inferential role, so conceived, of the linguistic performances exchanged.

Importantly, Brandom's pragmatism must be distinguished from his phenomenalism about norms (his Hegelian attempt, rehearsed in the last chapter, to explain or otherwise elucidate the obtainment of the norms governing discursive practices in terms of mutual social recognition). The normative pragmatic description of discursive practices at the heart of Brandom's pragmatism takes the norms governing social practices in general for granted – it is an irreducibly *normative* pragmatic description, as seen in chapter 1. Brandom's pragmatism ventures to explain specifically discursive practices and the norms of inference/reasoning governing it in terms of normative pragmatic descriptions of social practices in general. (The next sections will elaborate on this.) On the other hand, Brandom's phenomenalism about norms proposes to explain the norms governing discursive practices *themselves*, in terms of the normative attitudes of acknowledging and attributing commitments and entitlements, which the participants adopt in practice and in which their mutual social recognition consists.

In this and the next four chapters we shall focus in depth on Brandom's pragmatism, taking norms for granted. A deeper engagement with Brandom's phenomenalist project will be the topic of chapter 8.

Deontic scorekeeping

The foundation of Brandom's pragmatism is a general notion of norm-governed social practices – *deontic* practices – understood as the norm-governed exchanges of types of performances (types of vocalizations, gestures, bodily movements, moves of figures on a board, or some such) between at least two participants. We may think of deontic practices in general as norm-governed social games and of each type of performance as a type of move a participant may make in the game. At each stage of the game, every participant has various commitments and entitlements to certain moves, in accordance with the norms governing the game. That is, each participant has certain deontic statuses (normative statuses). The constellations of commitments and entitlements, distributed over the participants at a given stage, is the *score* of the game at that stage. A legitimate move usually alters the score in certain ways, depending on the previous score, the type of move made, and who made the move. That is, at least some players usually acquire some new deontic statuses, or cease to have some old ones, in response to a legitimate move. Furthermore, each competent participant is sensitive to the norms governing the game, and exhibits such sensitivity not only by contributing to the exchange more or less appropriately but also by *keeping score* implicitly in practice, that is, by tracking the various participants' deontic statuses throughout the exchange. Scorekeeping is done by adopting certain kinds of *deontic attitudes* (normative attitudes) at each stage. A scorekeeper *acknowledges* multifarious commitments and entitlements to certain moves herself at any stage of the game (reflecting what she takes her own deontic statuses to be at that stage), and *attributes* multifarious commitments and entitlements to certain moves to each of her fellow practitioners at that stage (reflecting the deontic statuses she takes others to have at that stage). Score is thus kept by each participant for each participant. The score kept by a participant at a given stage is the participant's perspective on the real score of the game at that stage. That kept score will by and large agree with the real score, but it will also usually deviate from it here and there. The participant's scorekeeping attitudes may be mistaken in some respects, given the norms of the game (MIE 182–6).

Now, a performance of some arbitrary type P by some participant is proper in the context of many different (though not all) scores, and when performed under these circumstances, it will alter the score in certain ways, determined by the previous score and the norms of the practice. Call the sum total of ways in which proper performances of P may thus interact with the score – the sum total of ways in which a proper performance of P may alter any given score into the new score – P's *pragmatic significance* (MIE 182–3). P's pragmatic significance thus determines under which circumstances a participant is committed or entitled to P, and how a proper performance of P alters the commitments and entitlements of at least some players. (This is a generalization of the sense of "pragmatic" introduced in chapter 1, since P need not be a linguistic performance. Still, since the "pragmatic significance" of P constraints proprieties of performing P, and since pragmatics proper concerns the proprieties of specifically linguistic performances, it is natural and benign to label the feature in question P's "pragmatic significance".)

Brandom insists that none of the core semantic, epistemic, and logical notions in the philosophy of language and mind, epistemology, and logic (propositional content, meaning, concepts, truth, inference, representation, reference, speech act, belief, intention, epistemic justification, reasoning, negation, etc.) are applied or presupposed in this abstract, normative pragmatic characterization of deontic social practices. The characterization is couched in the vocabulary of having, of acknowledging, and of attributing commitments and entitlements to certain performances in accordance with certain norms. And while, in light of the problems with regularism we discussed in chapter 1, the norms and the participants' normative attitudes cannot be naturalized, neither need the performances exchanged themselves be propositionally contentful, epistemically justified, true, etc., nor need the players be rational beings endowed with propositionally contentful mental states. In light of the regress problems with regulism discussed in chapter 1, the players' sensitivity to the norms cannot consist exclusively in explicit, propositionally contentful knowledge of the norms. Yet on the other hand such sensitivity to the norms may be entirely implicit, according to Brandom, in the sense that the players may display it solely by making, or being prepared to make, the appropriate moves at any given stage of the exchange, unmediated by any propositional knowledge of the norms (rules) governing their interaction. Similarly, Brandom thinks that a player's ability to attribute commitments and entitlements to peers may be entirely implicit, in the sense that these attributions may be unmediated by any explicit, propositional knowledge on the player's part about the peer's psychology, his normative attitudes, his score, etc. and may manifest themselves solely in the player's preparedness to sanction the peer, depending on the peer's compliance with what the player implicitly takes to be the norms governing the practice (MIE 42–6, 161–5). That is, a player's sensitivity to the norms and her ability to keep score may, Brandom thinks, in principle entirely consist in practical know-how in the sense of fundamental pragmatism encountered in chapter 1: an ability that does not depend on any propositional knowledge of rules, principles, or facts. (See conclusion for discussion.)

Assuming that this is so, Brandom ventures to explain, on the basis of this normative pragmatic conception of deontic practices, specifically linguistic practices – *discursive* practices – with all their semantic, epistemic, and logical core features. First, he describes in the normative pragmatic terms available to him deontic practices that exhibit the specific *structure* of linguistic practices. Second, he argues – boldly – that deontic practices with this specific structure, because they have this structure, literally *are* discursive practices (instances of linguistic communication) and, in particular, that they literally have all the characteristic semantic, epistemic, cognitive, and logical features of discursive practices. This is a reductive explanatory strategy, not in the naturalistic sense that linguistic practices and their semantic, epistemic, and logical core features reduce to non-normative, naturalistic features of the natural and social world, but in the non-naturalistic sense that they reduce to species of deontic social practices that can be antecedently fully described in normative pragmatic terms, free from any unexplained semantic, epistemic, and logical core notions.[1]

Brandom develops this explanatory strategy in two steps. First, he describes, in the normative pragmatic terms available to him, deontic practices that have the structure of *autonomous* discursive practices – "language games one could play though one played no other" (BSD 27). These are the simplest possible genuinely discursive practices. And he argues that, due to the presence of this structure, certain aspects of the described practices deserve to be identified with the semantic, epistemic, and cognitive features of autonomous discursive practices. This means that the described deontic practices themselves literally are autonomous discursive practices. Second, he then accounts for ever more complex, non-autonomous discursive practices in terms of the less complex and, ultimately, autonomous discursive practices already accounted for, by equipping the original autonomous discursive practitioners with ever more additional normative pragmatic know-how – know-how that enables them, and their discursive practices, to exhibit ever more complex semantic, epistemic, and cognitive features and abilities – and ultimately the semantic, epistemic, and cognitive features and abilities that *we*, and *our* discursive practices, exhibit. In this and the next two chapters, we shall focus exclusively on Brandom's account of autonomous discursive practices. Chapters 6 and 7 will focus on his theory of non-autonomous discourse.

Autonomous discursive practices

Brandom claims that

> the absolutely minimal condition on a practice deploying proposi-tional contents (being a practice in which something can be said, so thought), [is one where] the one and only speech act that *must* be present is asserting.
>
> (Brandom 2010d: 316; cf. also MIE 172)

Assertion is indispensable in discourse, thinks Brandom, because the core of discourse is the game of giving and asking for reasons, and the speech act through which reasons are paradigmatically given and asked for is assertion. Reasons can be given for asser-tions, and giving reasons for them or for other kinds of speech acts usually consists in making further assertions – or, anyway, depends upon the ability to make further assertions (MIE 167, 171). Thus, Brandom concludes that discursive practices where the only speech acts made are assertions – *assertional practices* – are strictly speaking the only autonomous discursive practices.[2] The initial task for Brandom is thus to describe in purely normative pragmatic terms deontic practices that exhibit the specific structure of assertional practices, and to make the case that various features of deontic practices with this structure deserve to be identified with the semantic, cognitive, and epistemic core features of assertional prac-tices – hence that the described practices themselves *are* assertional practices.

The official normative pragmatic description of these practices, to which the next few sections are devoted, will be quite abstract, given the sparse vocabulary in which it is couched. It will also be preliminary. The following two chapters will add complexity to this description, making it more plausible that what we are describing here are indeed genuinely discursive practices. Ultimately, "the proof" will be "in the pudding" (Brandom 2008b: 218, 220). In light of this abstract and preliminary character, the uninitiated reader may want to do a relatively swift and cursory first read of the rest of this chapter, so as to get the general gist of Brandom's take at assertional practice, and then return for a more thorough second read after having read some of the subsequent chapters.

Commitments

The envisioned deontic practices are not necessarily engaged in for any purpose beyond engaging in them. In particular, unless very specific, optional qualifications are added, engaging in them will not determine winners and losers. (Think of playing catch or singing together.) Let tokenings of an arbitrarily large but finite number of types of vocalizations V1, V2, ... , Vn be the moves in our practices. (Alternatively, the moves may instead be hand-signals, moves of counters on a board, scribbles on pieces of paper, etc., or any combination thereof.) Of course, Brandom will identify these types of vocalizations with declarative sentences and their performances with assertions. Each player is able to reliably produce and identify vocalizations of these types as well as to reliably track in practice who has vocalized which type at what stage of the game. If a player vocalizes the type Vx at some stage – *avows* Vx – she is thereby *committed to* Vx. That is, the norms of our practices are such that vocalizing a type is one way, though not the only way, of becoming committed to that type. This corresponds to the intuitive sense in which making an assertion commits the speaker to the assertion and to the corresponding statement. Relatedly, through vocalizing Vx a player also *acknowledges commitment* to Vx. That is, vocalizing a type Vx is one way, though not the only way, of acknowledging commitment to Vx, corresponding to the intuitive sense in which by making an assertion the speaker overtly acknowledges a commitment to the assertion. Being committed to a type Vx and acknowledging commitment to it are intimately related, and avowing Vx achieves both. However, they are not the same. As we shall see, a player may acknowledge commitments she doesn't have, and she may have commitments she doesn't acknowledge.

Ordinary English distinguishes between acknowledging commitments *to* something (say, a relationship or a political idea) vs. acknowledging commitments *to do* something (say, go to the cinema). Like the latter, the former imposes on the committed person various consequential obligations, permissions, and prohibitions *to do* certain things. But in the former case, these consequential deontic statuses tend to be more varied, complex, and indirect, and they also tend to include normative constraints on *others* as well. For example, if someone is committed to a friendship, he himself is thereby obligated and permitted to do many varied things under different circumstances, and prohibited from doing others. This commitment *also*, however, imposes obligations, permissions, and prohibitions on others – both the friend and third persons. In our practices, a player's acknowledged commitment to a type Vx is an acknowledged commitment *to* that type (MacFarlane 2010: 90–91). It is a complex, norm-governed state of mind that obliges, permits, and prohibits the player *to do* many things under many different circumstances – only one of which will be the obligation to re-avow Vx under certain circumstances. This state of mind also imposes multifarious normative statuses on others who attribute this commitment to Vx to her.

In our practices, being committed to a type of vocalization leads to certain consequential deontic statuses for the player. In particular, being committed to Vx *commits* the player *consequentially* to certain other types of vocalizations $Vc1, Vc2, \ldots, Vcm$ – often conditionally upon having certain collateral commitments to other types. These are *committive consequences* of her commitment to Vx, and they correspond to the intuitive sense in which making a certain assertion commits the speaker consequentially to certain further assertions. In our practices, the player who is committed to Vx should be prepared to avow the types $Vc1, Vc2, \ldots, Vcm$ to which she is consequentially committed, just as someone who has made an assertion should be prepared to make the assertions she is consequentially committed to. There are thus so far two ways for a player to become committed to a type of vocalization: by avowing it and by inheriting it in consequence of being committed to certain other types.

Players often fail to acknowledge the committive consequences of commitments they acknowledge, but they nonetheless *undertake* these committive consequences, that is, they have these unacknowledged consequential commitments – just as speakers often fail to make assertions that they are in fact committed to in light of other assertions they have made. The notion of undertaking a commitment to a type is thus more normative than the notion of acknowledging one. Undertaken commitments are commitments a player is *bound* to acknowledge – whether he does so or not – given the commitments he does acknowledge.

Others will keep score on our player. Think of the score a scorekeeper K keeps on a player P as what K writes on a whiteboard (entitled "P's score"); think of the commitment-score K keeps on P as what K writes on one half of that whiteboard (entitled "P's commitments"), subdivided into an "undertaken" and an "acknowledged" section. K keeps track of the commitments to types that K takes P to undertake and to acknowledge by writing the corresponding types into, or by erasing them from, the relevant sections of the whiteboard. If P tokens Vx, K will immediately add Vx to both the "undertaken" and the "acknowledged" section of the commitment-half of P's score, and into the "undertaken" section, *all* the types Vci, Vcii … , Vcn which K *takes to be* committive consequences of P's tokening of Vx (given, perhaps, various collateral commitments that K takes P also to undertake independently). Moreover, in light of various clues, K will add many of these undertaken committive consequences also into the "acknowledged" section of the commitment-half of P's score – the committive consequences that K takes P to also acknowledge, given these clues. Finally, K may also add to the "acknowledged" section certain committive consequences that K (in light of these clues) takes P to acknowledge, given P's acknowledged commitment to Vx, even though, according to K, P does not really undertake these committive consequences.

Of course, the committive consequence relation between certain types of vocalizations is determined by certain norms governing the practice. Deontic statuses of a special type correspond to these norms: *inferential commitments*. Inferential commitments concern consequence relations *between* types of vocalizations, by contrast to commitments to types of vocalizations themselves, which concern individual types. The contrast reflects the fact that in discourse we need to distinguish between commitments to assertions and commitments to consequence relations between assertions. For example, we need to distinguish between a speaker's commitments to "Fluffy is a dog" and "Fluffy is mammalian" on the one hand, and her commitment to the fact that the latter statement is a consequence of the former. The distinction between commitments to types and inferential commitments between types in the deontic practices we are modeling is intended to capture this feature. Thus if, given the norms of our practice, Vy is a committive consequence of Vx (perhaps relative to certain collateral commitments to other types) – if commitment to Vx commits consequentially to Vy – then a player has an inferential commitment from Vx to Vy. Let's call it a *c-inferential commitment* from Vx to Vy, reflecting committive consequence (as opposed to permissive consequence, about which more below). Importantly, P has this c-inferential commitment regardless whether P undertakes or acknowledges a commitment to Vx itself, just as in discourse a speaker has an inferential commitment from "Fluffy is a dog" to "Fluffy is mammalian," regardless whether he undertakes or acknowledges a commitment to "Fluffy is a dog."

Brandom insists that having inferential commitments does not require having any *concept* of inference or being able to reason explicitly about inference – formally or informally. Rather, having a c-inferential commitment, from Vx to Vy, only means being capable to follow the corresponding norm of inference *implicitly* or *in practice*, by committing to Vy in consequence of committing to Vx as well as by treating others in practice as bound by this norm – unmediated by any explicit, propositional thoughts about the validity of the inference or the corresponding norm of inference.

The contrast between being bound to acknowledge vs. acknowledging in fact applies to inferential commitments as well – corresponding to contrast, in discourse, between a speaker's being bound by a norm of inference between two statements vs. his treating in practice the two statements as inferentially related. Thus, P is bound to acknowledge certain c-inferential commitments between Vx and various committive consequences Vy1, ..., Vyn (relative, perhaps, to certain collateral commitments to other types), given the norms of the practice: P has these c-inferential commitments whether or not P acknowledges them. These c-inferential commitments map P's commitment to Vx – given that P has avowed Vx – onto P's *undertaken* consequential commitments to Vy1, ... , Vyn. Moreover, P acknowledges certain c-inferential commitments regarding Vx in fact, and these acknowledgments constitute what P *takes to be* the committive consequences of Vx (relative, perhaps, to collateral commitments to certain other types). That is, they map P's commitment to Vx onto commitments to certain types that P *acknowledges* as committive consequences of Vx. Since P is not infallible, these may include acknowledged commitments to some types other than Vy1, ... , Vyn, and they may exclude acknowledgments of commitments to some of the Vy1, ... , Vyn themselves.

Of course, the scorekeeper K draws in practice a corresponding contrast between what K takes to *be* the c-inferential commitments P has regarding Vx vs. the ones K takes P to *acknowledge* regarding Vx. What K takes to be the c-inferential commitments P has determines what K writes into the "undertaken" subdivision in response to P's tokening of Vx. Roughly, these correspond to what K *himself* regards as committive consequences of Vx; that is, they reflect K's *own acknowledged* c-inferential commitments regarding Vx. Since K too is not infallible, what K writes into the "undertaken" subdivision in response to P's tokening of Vx may also include some types other than Vy1, ... , Vyn (types that K falsely treats as committive consequences of Vx), and excludes some of the Vy1, ... , Vyn themselves (K may miss some of the real committive consequences of Vx). And what K takes to be P's acknowledged c-inferential commitments regarding Vx determines what K writes into the "acknowledged" subdivision in response to P's tokening of Vx. No extra portion of whiteboard needs to be reserved for tracking P's inferential commitments per se. Rather, we can think of K as tracking the c-inferential commitments that P has vs. the ones P acknowledges by connecting types of vocalizations on the scoreboard accordingly with, say, light blue vs. dark blue arrows. Thus, if K takes P to have a c-inferential commitment from, say, Vx to Vy7, K will draw a light blue arrow from every Vx sign on the scoreboard (in any subdivision) to every Vy7 sign (in any subdivision), and if K takes P to acknowledge a c-inferential commitment from, say, Vx to Vy5, K will draw a dark blue arrow from every Vx sign to every Vy5 sign.

If at any stage of the game K wishes to check whether P acknowledges a commitment to a type of vocalization, K may *query* P by (let's evocatively assume) vocalizing that type with a raised pitch at the end. By issuing such a query regarding, say, Vz, K himself does not acknowledge or undertake a commitment to Vz, but rather puts P on the spot. If P acknowledges a commitment to Vz she must avow Vz in response, whereas if she doesn't she must *disavow* acknowledgment to Vz by (let's say) vocalizing Vz while shaking her head. Such a disavowal does not express anything like logical negation. That is, disavowing Vz is not the same as avowing Not-Vz; in autonomous discursive practices no type of vocalization is the logical negation of another type of vocalization. Rather, someone who disavows Vz thereby expresses non-acknowledgment of commitment to Vz. Since we are at it, let's also stipulate that through disavowals, perhaps in response to queries, a player may not only express non-acknowledgment of commitments to types to which she never acknowledged commitment in the first place, but also *withdrawals* of hitherto acknowledged commitments to types and, indeed, withdrawals of previous avowals of types. If a player successfully withdraws acknowledgment of commitment to Vx, she thereby ceases to undertake the committive consequences Vy1, ... , Vyn – *except* the ones that the player has independently avowed and the ones that are committive consequences of other types the player is independently committed to. A player's attempt to disavow Vz is thus unsuccessful if Vz is a committive consequence of a commitment to a type the player continues to have. Of course, when P disavows commitment to a certain type, K will keep score accordingly as best as he can.

Brandom calls queries and disavowals *auxiliary* moves (MIE 192). He thinks that autonomous discursive practices need not strictly speaking include such moves – assertion is the only speech act that is (strictly speaking) needed to pass the threshold from the merely deontic to the genuinely discursive. He concedes, however, that it is useful to include auxiliaries in the family of games we are envisioning, since this makes it easier to model the discursive practices *we* are familiar with.

Entitlements

Entitlements (licenses, authorizations, permissions) to types of vocalizations are a second fundamental deontic status in the practices we are modeling. Being committed to a type does not imply being entitled to it, nor vice versa, although very often players are both committed and entitled to a type. In particular, by contrast to commitment to a type, entitlement to a type cannot be earned through simply avowing the type, nor can it be earned through simply avowing something else to which the player is not entitled and of which the type in question is a committive consequence. After all, we are trying to model practices that have the structure of the game of giving and asking for reasons, and in games of giving and asking for reasons the act of just saying something usually provides neither a reason for saying it nor a reason for what is said, nor does it provide, in one important sense of "reason," a reason for the consequences of it. What's missing is the dimension of justification for what is said, and entitlement to a type is the deontic status in terms of which Brandom will seek to capture this dimension of justification in games of giving and asking for reasons. In the practices we are modeling, avowing a type is proper in *every* respect only if the player is entitled to it – although doing so is still proper in *some* respect, if the player is committed to the avowed type in consequence of being committed to some other types and unless avowal of that type is not prohibited by other deontic statuses the player already has (the next section will cover this).

Brandom frequently assimilates commitments and entitlements to, respectively, obligations and permissions (MIE 160). This assimilation highlights the normative nature of commitments and entitlements. Still, in our games, commitments and entitlements to types work in some important ways differently from obligations and permissions, and they should thus be considered as technical terms whose content is filled by the stipulated norms governing our games rather than by assimilation to the more intuitive deontic notions of obligation and permission. For example, an obligation to do something implies permission to do it, yet as just seen, being committed to a type does not imply being entitled to it. Moreover, if someone is obliged to do something then he is in a position to do it – "ought" implies "can" – yet as we shall see, players routinely cannot acknowledge, let alone avow, *all* the commitments to types they undertake, simply because there are too many of them.

Entitlements to types, like commitments to them, have consequences. Someone who is entitled to Vx is (usually given certain collateral entitlements to other types) consequentially *entitled* to various further types Vz1, … , Vzn. These are Vx's *permissive consequences*. All of Vx's committive consequences are among Vx's permissive ones, but not vice versa. That is, commitment and entitlement to Vx entitles consequentially to types to which it does not commit – types that the player may avow, but is not bound to avow, when queried (AR 195; Brandom 2010f: 29). Brandom frequently indicates that the contrast between committive and non-committive permissive consequence is modeled on the contrast between deductive and inductive inference (Brandom 2010f: 21) and, indeed, that the former contrast is a "generalization" of the latter contrast (Brandom 2010f: 21), that is, that deductive and inductive consequences are specific, discursive kinds of (respectively) committive and permissive consequences in deontic practices. Thus, the inference from "Pittsburgh is west of Philadelphia" to "Philadelphia is east of Pittsburgh" is deductive, and commitment to the former claim commits consequentially to the latter (and vice versa). And the inference from "This match is well struck" to "It will light" is inductive, and entitlement to the former claim entitles, but does not commit, consequentially to the latter. A speaker may have strong evidence that the match is well struck, and thus be entitled to the corresponding claim, but she may be ignorant about the further circumstances (Is the match dry? Is enough oxygen present?) and, if so, is not obligated to assert that the match will light, when queried, but is still permitted to assert it.

However, whether the contrast between deductive and inductive inference is a species of the contrast between committive and permissive consequence raises many thorny issues, and it seems safer to regard the assimilation merely as an illuminating analogy. For example, if a speaker both knows that the match is struck well *and* has good evidence that the circumstances are normal (match dry, oxygen present) she seems to be not merely entitled but also committed to assert that the match will light. Withholding the latter claim under these circumstances seems improper, and the most natural diagnosis of the impropriety is that under the circumstances she is also committed to it. Yet even if that is so the latter claim remains an inductive consequence of the former.[3]

Corresponding to the norms determining permissive consequences, the players yet again acquire inferential commitments. If Vz is a permissive consequence of Vx, then each player has, we shall say, a *p-inferential commitment* from Vx to Vz – by contrast to the c-inferential commitments corresponding to committive consequences. Whether or not the player is entitled to Vx, she should acknowledge the entitlement-preserving inference from Vx to Vz. P-inferential commitments are indeed commitments, not entitlements. If Vz is a permissive consequence of Vx, then every player is *committed* to acknowledge in practice the corresponding p-inference from Vx to Vz (relative to collateral commitments and entitlements to types, and whether or not she is entitled to Vx itself). She not only may but must acknowledge in practice the p-inference from Vx to Vz. To illustrate, every competent English-speaking reasoner must (not merely may) acknowledge in practice the p-inference from "This match is well struck" to "It will light" (relative to collateral entitlements to claims indicating normal conditions). Doing so is not optional. In general, although there is a contrast between commitment and entitlement *to* types, there does not seem to be a contrast between commitments and entitlements to inferential relations *between* types. Every player is committed to acknowledge them (relative to collateral commitments and entitlements to types) and, of course, also entitled to do that, since doing so is licensed by the norms of inference governing the practice.

Entitlements to types are yet again undertaken vs. acknowledged and, similarly, players are bound to acknowledge vs. acknowledge in fact p-inferential commitments. Someone who undertakes entitlement to Vx undertakes (relative to collateral commitments and entitlements to types) entitlements to all its permissive consequences Vz1, ... , Vzn, though she may not acknowledge some of these permissive consequences (in which case she does not acknowledge the corresponding p-inferential commitments) – indeed, she may not acknowledge entitlement to Vx itself. A scorekeeper K will again track player P's acknowledged and undertaken entitlements to types and p-inferential commitments as best as she can, by utilizing the half of the whiteboard for P entitled "P's entitlements" and subdivided into "undertaken" vs. "acknowledged" sections. Thus, if K attributes in practice to P as both undertaken and as acknowledged entitlement to Vx, K will add Vx to both the "undertaken" and the "acknowledged" sections of the entitlement half of the whiteboard for P. Moreover, K will write into the "undertaken" subsection every type that K *takes to be* the real permissive consequences of P's undertaken entitlement to Vx (relative to collateral commitments and entitlements to types that K takes P to undertake), and into the "acknowledged" subsection all the types K takes P to acknowledge as permissive consequences of P's entitlement to Vx. Obviously, many of these types will show up in both subsections, and many of them will be among the Vz1, ... , Vzi. Finally, K will mark the p-inferential commitments that she takes P to have vs. acknowledge by connecting types of vocalizations within and across *every* subsection of the scoreboard accordingly with, say, light green arrows vs. dark green arrows for the p-inferential commitments that K takes P to, respectively, have vs. acknowledge. (Similarly, K will mark c-inferential commitments across the "commitment" and "entitlement" half of the whiteboard, which K takes P to have vs. acknowledge, by drawing yet again light vs. dark blue arrows accordingly.)

Incompatibility

The committive consequence relation links commitments to types to other such commitments; the permissive consequence relation links entitlements to types to other such entitlements. Our games are characterized by a further normative relation between types, which links commitment to types to entitlements to types: the *incompatibility relation*. This further relation is supposed to capture the fact that, in discursive practices, every assertion is incompatible with certain other declarative sentences and (potential) assertions. Accordingly, in our practices, any commitment to a type *precludes* (relative, perhaps, to certain collateral commitments and entitlements to types) entitlement to certain other types and, similarly, commitment to any of these other types precludes both entitlement to the former type and to certain further types. The norms of the game thus determine, for any type Vx (and given certain collateral commitments and entitlements), two sets of types Vue1, ... , Vuem and Vuc1, ... , Vucn, such that, first, if a player is committed to Vx then she is prohibited from acknowledging entitlement to any of the Vue1, ... , Vuem and, second, if she is entitled to Vx then she is prohibited from acknowledging commitment to any of the Vuc1, ... , Vucn. Of course, the two sets of types are overlapping, so as to accommodate the fact that, in discursive practices, not only does commitment to, say, "Fluffy is a dog" preclude entitlement to "Fluffy is a reptile" but also does entitlement to "Fluffy is a dog" preclude commitment to "Fluffy is a reptile." As with the two consequence relations, the incompatibility relation is normative, not psychological. It is psychologically possible for a player to simultaneously acknowledge commitment and entitlement to incompatible types, just as it is psychologically possible to draw mistaken consequences, or to fail to draw right ones. Someone who acknowledges commitment and entitlement to incompatible types commits a mistake, but making such a mistake is certainly psychologically possible and, indeed, unfortunately quite common.

Brandom regards the incompatibility relation as fundamental; that is, he does not try to define it in terms of the other two (equally fundamental) consequence relations (Brandom 2010f: 21–2; MIE 169). All three relations between types of performances characterize autonomous discursive practices, and neither relation is reducible to, or definable in terms of, the other two. Moreover, he insists that the incompatibility relation is yet again not formal: a player's sensitivity to the corresponding norms of incompatibility does not require possession of the logical concept of negation. *We* theoreticians use the concept of negation in the meta-language in terms of which we explicitly characterize these norms, yet our players display sensitivity to these norms merely implicitly in practice by keeping score more or less in accordance with them, and by applying sanctions to others in light of implicitly attributed apparent violations of these norms. To the norms determining incompatibilities correspond again certain deontic statuses – let's call those *incompatibility commitments* – to which all the considerations regarding inferential commitments *mutatis mutandis* apply. Players should acknowledge all the incompatibility commitments they have, yet they usually acknowledge only some of these in fact (while also acknowledging some they don't have). Furthermore, scorekeepers track in practice both the incompatibility commitments they take a player to have and the ones they take him to acknowledge, by utilizing the whiteboard in some suitable way.

Interpersonal inheritance of entitlement

The three normative relations between types of vocalizations discussed – committive consequence, permissive consequence, and incompatibility – determine *intrapersonal* inheritances of commitments and entitlements to types. They determine, for any constellation of commitments and entitlements to types a player may acknowledge at a given stage, further commitments and entitlements to types *that player* should acknowledge consequentially and still further incompatible commitments and entitlements *that player* must not acknowledge. Yet norms regulating the *interpersonal* inheritance of commitments and entitlements to types from one player to another also characterize our games. The single most important norm of all these is that if a player avows a type Vx, all other participants *ipso facto* become *prima facie entitled* to Vx – both in the particular exchange going on and in other exchanges with different players – in the sense that, unless they have or acknowledge overriding commitments to other, incompatible types, they inherit entitlement to Vx automatically (MIE 170, 174). In our games, avowals of any types are thus highly contagious. They *prima facie* entitle every participant to re-avow that type anytime anywhere.

This feature distinguishes the basic moves in our game from the auxiliary moves we have introduced. Thus, issuing a query does not *ipso facto* entitle the addressee to re-issue the query, but has a different interpersonal deontic consequence: committing the addressee to respond by, as the case may be, avowing or disavowing the type queried. Similarly, disavowing a type does not entitle the other participants to disavow it as well, not even *prima facie*.

Indeed, it does not commit or entitle them to any type, but merely obliges them to change the score on the player who disavowed the type. Again, every player is presumably entitled at all times to withdraw any acknowledged commitment to any type (and, if so, responsible to adjust her collateral acknowledged commitments and entitlements accordingly). But it is not the case that someone's *making* a withdrawal *ipso facto* entitles everybody else to the same withdrawal. For example, it does not so entitle anybody who doesn't acknowledge commitment to the corresponding type in the first place. Everybody is only entitled to withdraw commitments he or she actually acknowledges. (Of course, these observations hold only for games that mimic structural features of assertional practices. There is nothing wrong with concocting deontic practices in which the interpersonal inheritances of commitments and entitlements to types differ. It's just that such games will not mimic – let alone *be* – assertional practices.)

A player's interpersonal inheritance of entitlement to Vx in response to someone's avowal of Vx is only *prima facie* and by default. The player may already be committed to types incompatible with Vx, and if she is also entitled to those types her commitment to them will frequently block, or override, her inheritance of a *prima facie* entitlement to Vx. On the other hand, the inherited default entitlement to Vx may instead override these incompatible background commitments, by contributing to outweigh her overall entitlements to the latter. The player may already have had some entitlement to Vx independently, and the additional default entitlement to Vx may now tip the scale in favor of her overall entitlement to Vx, in which case she should – openly or "in her heart" – withdraw acknowledgment to the incompatible background commitments.

As these reflections indicate, entitlement to types thus comes in degrees of strength. The weakest degree of entitlement is *prima facie*. Stronger degrees of entitlement may, for example, derive from the degree of reliability of a player's responses to perceptual observation (chapter 5). And a player's total entitlement to a type may add up, if different circumstances provide mutually independent entitlement for it. That entitlement comes in degrees of strength dovetails with Brandom's assimilation of the entitlement-preserving consequence relation to inductive inference, mentioned earlier, and it foreshadows his treatment of epistemic justification as a species of entitlement. After all, both inductive inference and epistemic justification come in degrees of strength.

The default and challenge structure

This specification of the interpersonal deontic consequences of basic
moves is the beginning of an answer to the question how a player
may gain entitlement to a type in the first place, that is, without
inheriting it intrapersonally from entitlements to other types (for
which the question as to how she got *those* arises again). What stops
the regress of intrapersonal inheritance of entitlements to types?
The beginning of the answer is that the player may inherit entitlement to the type interpersonally from someone else's avowal of it.
Intrapersonally, such interpersonally inherited entitlement is basic.
The player has it independently of any other entitlements he may
have. Yet of course, this immediately begs the further question as to
what, if anything, stops the regress of *inter*personal inheritances of
entitlement to types (MIE 176–7)? If our games are to mimic games
of giving and asking for reasons and if epistemic justification is to
be a species of entitlement, the most basic source of entitlement to
a type in our games must not just be anyone's avowal of that type.
That would correspond to the absurd claim that the ultimate justification of any claim in the game of giving and asking for reasons
is that someone has made it. In games of giving and asking for
reasons, Brandom assumes, making a claim – performing an assertion – is proper only if the assertion has some degree of justification
or warrant. Accordingly, in our games avowing a type is proper in
every respect only if the player is entitled to it, as said already. And
thus the question is: what stops the regress of interpersonal inheritance of entitlement to a type? How can a player be entitled to a type
without inheriting it from someone else's avowing it?

Brandom's answer is that at every stage of the game, every player
is entitled *by default* to many types: that is, entitled to them without
inheriting these entitlements intrapersonally or interpersonally at
all. Such default entitlement is yet another way for a player to be
prima facie entitled to a type. The general idea here is this:

> The worry about a regress of entitlements is recognizably founda-
> tionalist. It can be responded to by appealing to the fundamental
> pragmatic commitment to seeing normative statuses (in this case
> entitlements) as implicit in the social practices that govern the giving
> and asking for reasons. Those practices need not be … such that the
> default entitlement status of a claim or assertional commitment is to
> be guilty until proven innocent. … [A] grounding problem arises in
> general only if entitlement is never attributed until and unless it has

been demonstrated. If many claims are treated as innocent until proven guilty ... the global threat of regress dissolves. ... Which commitments stand in need of vindication ... is itself a matter of social practice

(MIE 177)

In accordance with the slogan "innocent until proven guilty," withholding attribution of entitlement to a claim from a player is in our games itself something the scorekeeper needs to be entitled to. If a player avows Vx, then the player has default entitlement to Vx. *Unless* a scorekeeper is entitled to a *challenge* – unless she either acknowledges commitment to a type incompatible with Vx or regards the player as incoherent (attributes commitment to a type incompatible with Vx to the player himself) – she must treat the player as entitled to Vx (MIE 177). To illustrate, as we shall see more clearly in chapter 5, speakers will under all circumstances acknowledge entitlements to observation reports, or language entries – "Here is a hand," "There's a barn," etc. – spontaneously, though non-randomly, in response to perceiving features of their environment. And they are usually also by default entitled to these acknowledgments. Unless a scorekeeper has reason to regard the player as an unreliable observer or as internally incoherent, or acknowledges a commitment to an incompatible claim herself, she must attribute default entitlement to these observation reports to the player. This feature of our practices is recognizably anti-Cartesian and classical American Pragmatist. According to it, withholding the attribution of entitlement to a type from a player ("doubt") is itself something a scorekeeper needs to be entitled to, and the fact that the player has not shown any grounds ("proof") for the entitlement does not constitute entitlement to withholding such an attribution. Rather, in the absence of grounds *against* the player's entitlement to a type, the player really is entitled to the type – by default.

Brandom regards challenges as yet another type of auxiliary move. Participants in autonomous discursive practices need not be able to issue challenges.[4] On the other hand, he thinks that challenges need not be new *kinds* of moves. Paradigmatically, a player may issue a challenge simply by making a basic move that is incompatible with the entitlement to a type thereby challenged.

Default entitlements to types serve as regress stoppers in our games. They are neither intrapersonally inherited from other entitlements the player has, nor interpersonally inherited from other players' avowals of these types. Once an appropriate challenge is issued, the player ceases to have default entitlement to Vx and is thus responsible to *demonstrate* entitlement to Vx – or else to withdraw Vx. In general, a player may successfully demonstrate entitlement to a type Vx in two ways. He may either show that he is entitled, intrapersonally, to other types of which Vx is a permissive consequence. In that case, the further entitlements the player will invoke will again terminate in regress-stopping default entitlements to types, which, under the circumstances, are not subject to proper challenges. Or, if the player inherited entitlement to Vx interpersonally, he may *defer* to the player from which he inherited it (by, let's say, vocalizing Vx while pointing at that other player). This deferral shifts the responsibility to demonstrate entitlement to Vx to that other player. *She* must now demonstrate entitlement to Vx, in one of these two manners. Of course, the player who originally avowed Vx, in whom the chain of deferrals will terminate, will only be able to discharge the responsibility to demonstrate entitlement to Vx in the first manner, by offering supporting intrapersonal entitlements – or else withdraw Vx, in which case every other player in the chain of deferrals ceases to have entitlement to Vx as well.

Given this *default and challenge structure*, the inheritance of entitlement in our practices is in a sense like the structure of inheritance of justification according to epistemic foundationalism. Under any given circumstances, some entitlements (the default ones) are foundational, in the sense that they are not inherited from other entitlements. All other entitlements directly or indirectly rest, under these circumstances, on this foundation. However, to borrow terminology from Michael Williams, this structure is merely formally, not substantively, foundationalist (Williams 1996: 114–21). No default entitlement is foundational in virtue of its own intrinsic epistemic nature, but is so only in the context of the given score. With a shift of score, it may be rightfully challenged, which annihilates its status as foundational and calls for the demonstration of its status as entitlement by recourse to other deontic statuses that terminate again in entitlements that, in the context of this shifted, new score, are now (formally) foundational.

Assertional practice

According to Brandom, our practices exhibit essential structural features of autonomous discursive practices. Moreover, I did my best to describe them exclusively in Brandom's favored normative pragmatic vocabulary, without using any central semantic, epistemic, cognitive, and logical locutions Brandom wishes to explain – except for occasional illustrations, which were intended to indicate the purpose and direction of our undertaking, but were meant to be inessential to the description of our practices themselves. To the extent that I succeeded, our practices, as described, may therefore in principle serve as a basis to explain the central semantic, epistemic, cognitive, and logical features of language and thought.

Indeed, Brandom thinks that our practices as described *are* instances of discursive practices. For any deontic practice to exhibit the described structure suffices for it to be an instance of autonomous assertional practice (MIE 221, 234). However, Brandom agrees in response to the objection that, for all that has been said, our games may merely mimic discursive practices without being real instances of them (McDowell 2008), that the identification of them with genuine discursive practices will have to be justified by greatly elaborating in normative pragmatic scorekeeping terms – or, anyway, in terms that do not presuppose any of the features of language and thought he is concerned to explain – the characterization of them so far provided (2008b: 218). Chapters 4, 5, and 7 will introduce these elaborations, and only in light of some of them will we be able to assess whether, and in which sense, they justify the identification of our practices as described with genuine discursive practices.

In the meantime, working on the assumption that the described practices are genuinely discursive, Brandom goes ahead and identifies features of them with central semantic, pragmatic, and cognitive features of assertional practices. In light of the last two chapters, these identifications are quite straightforward. The basic performances in our games literally are assertions and the corresponding types of vocalizations, accordingly, declarative sentences (or, anyway, assertible types of vocalizations). The overall significance of any assertion that p – what makes a certain avowal of a type an assertion that p as opposed to, on the one hand, an assertion that q, r, etc. or, on the other hand, a question, command, request, query, withdrawal, etc. that p – consists in the pragmatic significance of the corresponding declarative sentence, that is, in the totality of ways in which any possible, legitimate avowal of it would interact with the given score. Specifically, the *inferential role* of the assertion consists in the norms determining the assertion's location in the web of intrapersonal committive and permissive circumstances and consequences, and the incompatibilities, relative to collateral intrapersonal commitments and entitlements. This inferential role is the assertion's (and the corresponding declarative sentence's) location in the space of reasons, and hence, given Brandom's commitments to inferential role semantics and to the Kantian idea that conceptual content is normative, the assertion's *propositional meaning* that p.

Note that, on this view, any two declarative sentences occupying different locations in the (intrapersonal) space of reasons differ in inferential role and hence in meaning (MIE 175). This is true not only of pairs of sentences like "Fluffy is hungry" and "Philadelphia is larger than Pittsburgh," which obviously have different inferential roles in English, but also of pairs like "Phosphorus is a planet" and "Hesperus is a planet," which say the same thing about the same object and thus report, in this extensional sense, the same fact. Thus, as we will see more clearly in the next chapter, although the two last sentences are both incompatible with "Phosphorus is a star," the incompatibility between "Phosphorus is a planet" and "Phosphorus is a star" is immediate, in the sense that it is determined by a single norm of reasoning. On the other hand, the incompatibility between "Hesperus is a planet" and "Phosphorus is a star" is mediated, in the sense that it is determined by two norms of reasoning: one determining the incompatibility between "Phosphorus is a planet" and "Phosphorus is a star" and another one validating the inference from "Hesperus is a planet" to "Phosphorus is a planet". Thus, since "Hesperus is a planet" and "Phosphorus is a planet" relate inferentially in different ways to "Phosphorus is a star" – mediate and immediate respectively – they occupy different locations in the (intrapersonal) space of reason, and thus differ in meaning.

We thus see that Brandom's conception of propositional content and linguistic meaning will be broadly Fregean. Frege argued that the possibility for an English speaker who is rational, but unaware of the identity of Hesperus with Phosphorus, to simultaneously endorse "Hesperus is a planet" and to reject "Phosphorus is a planet" indicates that the two sentences differ in meaning, and hence that their meaning consists in more than the reference of the names and predicate in the two sentences. The two names "Hesperus" and "Phosphorus" refer to the same object (the planet Venus) and the two occurrences of the predicate obviously refer to the same property (the property of being a planet), yet still the two sentences differ in meaning. Thus, meaning (what Frege calls *sense*) consists in more than reference (Frege 1960). Brandom's conception of meaning concurs with this Fregean outlook. "Hesperus is a planet" and "Phosphorus is a planet" differ in inferential role, as just seen, and hence in meaning, and thus meaning consists in more than reference, according to Brandom – assuming that we can make sense of reference at all in a Brandomian inferential role semantic setting (see chapter 7). Inferential roles, we may say, are broadly Fregean senses.

The characteristic illocutionary force of an assertion that p, distinguishing it from, say, a question, command, or request that p as well as from any auxiliary moves (other than challenges) that p, consists in the interpersonal aspects of the assertion's pragmatic significance, according to Brandom, and in particular in the norm giving any interlocutor and overhearer *prima facie* entitlement to reassert the corresponding declarative sentence.[5] The defining feature of assertions, according to Brandom, is not so much their de facto tendency to spread through communities – although assertions often enough do that too – but rather a norm that makes such spread *prima facie* appropriate:

> An assertion in force licenses others to re-assert the original claim (and to assert its immediate consequences) *deferring to the author of the original assertion the justificatory responsibility which would otherwise thereby be undertaken.* That A's assertion of p has the social significance of authorizing B's re-assertion of p consists in the social appropriateness of B's deferring to A the responsibility to respond to justificatory challenges regarding B's claim. B's justificatory responsibility is discharged by the invocation of A's authority, upon which B has exercised his right to rely. Further challenges are appropriately addressed to A rather than B. If A is challenged concerning his assertion and fails to provide an appropriate set of justifying assertions, the socially constitutive consequence is to deprive his assertion of the authorizing force which it otherwise would have had.
>
> (Brandom 1983: 642)[6]

Note that in such spread from mouth to mouth, the content that p of the assertion is always preserved (MIE 175). After all, the corresponding declarative sentence's location in the intrapersonal space of reasons is always the same, no matter who is committed or entitled to it. True, as I've indicated throughout, what follows from being committed or entitled to the declarative sentence also depends on one's collateral deontic statuses, and collateral deontic statuses differ from speaker to speaker – more about this in chapter

4. Accordingly, different speakers inherit, relative to their different collateral deontic statuses, different consequential commitments and entitlements from being committed or entitled to the same declarative sentence. This does not imply, however, that the content of that sentence differs from speaker to speaker.[7] After all, what the sentence means is determined by its pragmatic significance, which in turn is determined by how properly asserting the sentence would interact with *any* possible score, not just by how it interacts with some particular actually given score. And how it would interact with any possible score is the same for all speakers, despite their actual differences in collateral commitments and entitlements. Accordingly, a declarative sentence's meaning – its location in the intrapersonal space of reasons, or its inferential role – is not determined by its consequences and incompatibilities relative to one set of collateral commitments and entitlements, but relative to any set. Thus, although any two speakers have different collateral commitments and entitlements, the declarative sentences they exchange have the same meaning for both of them.

To believe <u>that p</u>, according to Brandom, is to acknowledge or undertake a commitment to the corresponding declarative sentence <u>that p</u>. In Brandom's favored terminology, it is to acknowledge or undertake an *assertional*, or *doxastic, commitment* <u>that p</u>. A speaker may thus believe <u>that p</u> in a more empirical psychological sense and a more normative sense. To believe <u>that p</u> in the empirical psychological sense is to *acknowledge* an assertional commitment <u>that p</u>. In this sense, believing <u>that p</u> includes being prepared to assert <u>that p</u>. In the more normative sense, to believe <u>that p</u> is to *undertake* an assertional commitment <u>that p</u>. In this sense, believing <u>that p</u> is being rationally obliged to acknowledge this commitment in light of one's acknowledged collateral commitments and entitlements – whether or not one does so in fact (MIE 196). A speaker's *linguistic understanding,* or *interpretation,* of an assertion <u>that p</u> at a given time consists in his acknowledged inferential and incompatibility commitments regarding the assertion at the time, that is, in the inferential role the speaker at the time takes the corresponding sentence to have. A speaker's linguistic understanding is more or less accurate at a time and evolving over time; that is, it usually deviates more or less from the real meaning the sentence has. Brandom's theory captures this fact by allowing for a discrepancy between the real norms of inference and incompatibility governing a sentence and what a speaker takes these norms to be at a time (his acknowledged inferential and incompatibility commitments at the time). *Reasoning* is the ongoing activity of moving around in the space of reasons, that is, of updating and revising on an ongoing basis one's acknowledged assertional, inferential, and incompatibility commitments and entitlements, in response to someone else's assertions, or to one's own observations, or to one's own reflective efforts.

A relationalist, normative, social functionalism

Clearly, Brandom's theory is a version of linguistic pragmatism, the view that only speakers of public natural languages are able to think conceptually. Brandom does not, however, exactly reverse the traditional order of explanation regarding thought and communication, pursued by the Received View and rehearsed in chapter 1, which starts with an independent conception of representational mental content and explains linguistic communication in terms of it. Rather than offering an independent characterization of *discursive* practice and explaining cognitive mental states (belief) in terms of it, Brandom starts with a conception of *deontic* practice with a specific structure, in the context of which assertion and belief are explained simultaneously and, indeed, defined in terms of each other. Assertions are characterized in terms of their systematic interactions with doxastic commitments (beliefs), and doxastic commitments are, among other things, essentially commitments to assertions under certain circumstances. In this sense, Brandom offers a *relationalist* approach to assertion and belief (MIE 151, 230). This is nonetheless a *linguistic* relationalism, in the sense that Brandom regards the role of belief in the production and consumption of speech as more fundamental than its role in rational agency, in abstraction from speech (MIE 152, 155–6, 230). Of course, beliefs play a role in practical reasoning too (for this see chapter 5). Brandom regards this role as (strictly speaking) secondary to the role of belief in assertional practice, however: genuine assertional practice (hence beliefs) without practical reasoning and intentional agency is at least in principle possible, he thinks (MIE 234; see chapter 5).

Moreover, Brandom's theory is a version of *functionalism*, in the sense that Brandom regards the defining feature of assertion and belief, as well as of propositional content in the abstract, as the functional role of these items in the game of giving and asking for reasons. And according to Brandom, this functional role does not derive from any more fundamental features of assertion, belief, and content as such (MIE 16, 147–8; 2010f: 22–3). Yet Brandom's theory differs from more familiar versions of functionalism in being normative and social. Rather than couching the functional role of belief and assertion, as well as of content in the abstract, in more familiar naturalistic, causal, or teleo-functional terms, Brandom couches it in terms of norms governing the scorekeeping practice. And rather than characterizing this role in entirely individualistic terms, as the role these items play in the cognitive life of an individual person, Brandom treats this role as essentially comprising a social dimension: norms governing interpersonal inheritances of commitments and entitlements are constitutive of the functional role of assertions and beliefs.

Summary

This chapter introduced Brandom's normative pragmatic theory of the simplest kinds of genuinely discursive practices – autonomous discursive practices, or "language games one could play though one played no other" (BSD 27) – which are a structurally distinct kind of norm-governed social practices (deontic practices). Deontic practices in general, characterized in normative pragmatic terms, are social interactions in which each participant has a constellation of commitments and entitlements (deontic statuses) – paradigmatically to certain performances – at each stage of the interaction. The totality of these constellations is the score of the exchange at that stage. Any legitimate new performance by some participant alters the score in certain ways, in accordance with the norms governing the practice. Every participant also keeps score in practice, by adopting various kinds of deontic attitudes at each stage and by altering these attitudes in response to each new performance, in accordance with what she takes to be the norms governing the practice. Specifically, at each stage, every scorekeeper *acknowledges* a constellation of commitments and entitlements, paradigmatically to performances – the performances she takes herself to be committed or entitled to at that stage – and she *attributes* to every fellow participant *two* such constellations: first, the constellation that she takes the fellow to acknowledge in fact at that stage and, second, the constellation that he *should* acknowledge (according to her) at that stage.

The central type of performance in autonomous discursive practices is assertion, according to Brandom, and assertion is normative pragmatically characterized as follows. First, performing an assertion commits the speaker to that performance, and to the corresponding declarative sentence respectively. Unless and until his collateral entitlements change in certain prohibiting ways, the speaker must be prepared to reassert that sentence. Second, an assertion by a speaker *prima facie* entitles every interlocutor to reassert it. Unless the interlocutor has incompatible overriding collateral commitments, she is authorized to repeat the performance. If this interpersonally inherited entitlement to reassert should be challenged, the interlocutor may defer to the speaker from whom she inherited the entitlement: *he* is ultimately responsible for demonstrating entitlement to the original assertion. (Of course, he may discharge this responsibility by deferring to someone else from whom he inherited entitlement to the assertion, if so.)

Assertions and the corresponding declarative sentences stand in normative relations of committive and permissive consequence, and of preclusion (incompatibility), to each other. A speaker's commitment/entitlement to an assertion may be in consequence of his being committed/entitled to certain other assertions and it yields consequential commitments/entitlements on his part to yet further assertions. Furthermore, his commitment/entitlement to the assertion precludes his entitlement/commitment to certain further assertions. The web of intrapersonal normative consequence and preclusion relations, relating assertions and declarative sentences to each other, constitute the space of reasons, according to Brandom. An assertion's or declarative sentence's location in that web is its inferential role, hence, given Brandom's commitment to inferential role semantics, its propositional meaning that p.

Autonomous discursive practitioners have thus essentially two sorts of deontic statuses so far: commitments and entitlements *to assertions* and inferential and incompatibility commitments concerning the inferential and incompatibility relations *between* assertions/declarative sentences. To acknowledge an assertional commitment that p, according to Brandom, is to believe that p, in the empirical psychological sense of "belief". To acknowledge in practice a set of inferential and incompatibility commitments regarding that belief is to grasp the content that p in a certain way.

4

Sentence Meaning, Term Meaning, Anaphora

The last chapter introduced the basic features of Brandom's deontic scorekeeping model of autonomous discursive practices – the simplest possible genuine discursive practices. The deontic scorekeeping model characterizes autonomous discursive practices in purely normative pragmatic terms as a kind of norm-governed social practice with a distinct structure. Specifically, assertion – the central type of linguistic performance in autonomous discursive practice – is characterized as a type of performance to which a participant can become committed or entitled (or both) under certain circumstances, and whose core interpersonal structural feature is that its performance by a speaker *prima facie* entitles every other participant to repeat the performance. Intrapersonally, a speaker's commitment and entitlement to an assertion is holistically related to (actual or potential) commitments and entitlements on her part to other assertions. Thus, a speaker's commitment to assert A may be a consequence of her commitment to assert B, C, and so on, and it may in turn commit her to assert D, E, etc. as well as preclude her from entitlement to assert F, G, etc. Similarly, a speaker's entitlement to A may be a consequence of her entitlement to assert C, H, etc., and it may entitle her to assert E, I, etc. as well as preclude her from asserting J, K, etc. The deontic scorekeeping model characterizes these commitments and entitlements to assertions as well as these intrapersonal relations of committive and permissive consequence and preclusion between such commitments and entitlements to assertions in normative pragmatic terms, as commitments and entitlements to performances and intrapersonal, norm-governed inheritances and preclusions of such commitments and entitlements from other such commitments and entitlements. At this point, Brandom's key *semantic* move is his identification of these intrapersonal consequence and preclusion relations, characterized in normative pragmatic terms as links between one assertional commitment or entitlement and other such commitments or entitlements, with inferential and incompatibility relations linking the corresponding assertions and sentences – hence, given his commitment to inferential role semantics, with the propositional meaning that p of these assertions and sentences.

Yet so far all this is only a nice, if exceedingly abstract, idea. How plausible it is as a theory of assertion and linguistic meaning will depend on how well Brandom can develop it further into a theory that accounts for the semantic and epistemic features of thought and talk with which the philosophical literature is centrally concerned. First, the performances Brandom dubs "assertions" have so far no recognizable subsentential semantic structure, but are internally simple, unstructured semantic "blobs." Accordingly, Brandom owes us a theory, couched in normative pragmatic terms, of subsentential expressions – names and predicates – and their meaning, and of how speakers may combine and recombine names and predicates in ever-new ways so as to produce and understand ever-new assertions and declarative sentences. Second, he owes us a theory of distinctly *empirical* content and knowledge: a semantics and epistemology of our reports and knowledge of the largely non-linguistic, observable world. This will mean offering, in normative pragmatic deontic scorekeeping terms, a theory of the language entries in perception and language exits in action, and of how those relate to the meaning-constitutive norms of inference and incompatibility. Third, he owes us a theory of *logical* concepts and vocabulary – negation, conditional, quantifiers, modalities, etc. Autonomous discursive practitioners know how to follow the norms governing their practice, and in particular the norms of inference and incompatibility, "implicitly" or "in practice," without the aid of any logical concepts. Yet of course non-autonomous thought and talk is shot through with logical vocabulary and logical concepts, and Brandom needs to explain, in normative pragmatic terms, how such use arises from, and relates to, autonomous discursive practices. Fourth, assertions and beliefs are standardly regarded as representing, in virtue of their propositional content that p, the largely non-linguistic world to be a certain way – paradigmatically, as referring to individuals and as attributing properties and relations to them. Brandom agrees with this picture. Yet since in his view inference and incompatibility are the only semantically fundamental notions, the performances he dubs "assertions" are thus far not recognizable as representational – as being *of* or *about* anything – at all. Brandom accordingly owes us an account, in normative pragmatic terms, of how they get to be representational.

The next four chapters will introduce Brandom's efforts to make good on these four obligations. In the end, the success of his enterprise and the plausibility of the abstract characterization of assertional practice provided so far can only be assessed retrospectively, once his replies to these four challenges are in. This chapter will elaborate on Brandom's notion of propositional contentfulness. First, we will look a bit more closely at the crucial semantic notion of inference. Second, we will outline Brandom's theory of subsentential expressions – singular terms and predicates – and his reply to the question of how speakers can produce and understand evernew sentences. Third, we will introduce Brandom's theory of token recurrence: his theory of the mechanisms by which term-tokens occurring in one assertion may inherit their meaning from termtokens occurring in other assertions and thus may count as recurrences of the same term.

Truth

The first thing to stress is that Brandom's theory of inference and incompatibility in autonomous discourse does not tacitly rely on an unexplained notion of truth. Rather than introducing inference and incompatibility in terms of truth, as done in logic textbooks – good inference as what preserves truth, and incompatibility as what cannot be jointly true – Brandom introduces them in terms of his normative pragmatic deontic scorekeeping vocabulary. An inference is good if it preserves assertional commitment or assertional entitlement, and two sentences are incompatible just in case commitment to one precludes entitlement to the other. In general, truth plays no explanatory role whatsoever in semantics, logic, and epistemology, according to Brandom – the normative pragmatic deontic scorekeeping vocabulary does all the explanatory work – and Brandom is, in this sense, a deflationist about truth. This does not mean that truth-*talk* cannot play an important role in discourse. It clearly can, and Brandom accordingly has to offer, in deontic scorekeeping terms, an account of truth-talk – both of its semantics and of its discourse-facilitating functions – which he does by developing a version of the prosentential theory of truth, originally developed by Grover, Camp, and Belnap.[1] However, since truth is deflationary, according to Brandom, his prosentential theory of truth, albeit interesting in its own right, is not as central to his overall project as are other themes. Accordingly, due to the limited space here, I set it aside in this book.

Material inference

Next, the inferences and incompatibilities in autonomous discursive practices are all *material*, in the sense that their obtainment is independent of any premises containing specifically logical (formal) vocabulary. For example, as part of an autonomous fragment of English, the inference

> Pittsburgh is west of Philadelphia
> So, Philadelphia is east of Pittsburgh

is valid as it stands. In particular, its validity does not depend on suppressed premises containing formal logical vocabulary, such as the conditional

> **If** Pittsburgh is west of Philadelphia, **then** Philadelphia is east of Pittsburgh

Similarly, the pair of sentences

> Fido is a dog
> Fido is a cat

is incompatible as it stands, independently of suppressed premises like

> Fido is **not both** a dog **and** a cat

containing negation and conjunction.

Brandom agrees that many valid inferences and many incompatibilities are formal, in the sense that their validity or incompatibility depends on the logical form of the sentences involved – on the way specifically logical vocabulary is arranged in them – and that the material inferences and incompatibilities above in particular may be turned into formal ones by adding sentences containing logical vocabulary. Thus, adding the conditional statement above as second premise to the material inference concerning Pittsburgh and Philadelphia turns that inference into an instance of modus ponens – a formally valid argument form. Similarly for the statement containing negation and conjunction and the material incompatibility concerning Fido. Indeed, a chief aim of his project is to explain how use of logical vocabulary, and with it formally valid inferences and formal incompatibilities, emerge from simpler forms of discourse (ultimately, autonomous discursive practices) and how such emergence dramatically improves the scorekeepers' capacities to reason and discourse with each other (see chapters 6 and 7). All discourse involving logical vocabulary is non-autonomous, however, according to Brandom, and is an offshoot of, ultimately, autonomous discursive practices. Autonomous discursive practices themselves comprise no logical vocabulary. Hence, all inferences and incompatibilities in autonomous discursive practices are material.

This choice of material inference and incompatibility as his fundamental semantic notion seems mandatory for Brandom. If the inferences and incompatibilities structuring autonomous discursive practices were formal, then the scorekeepers' recognition of these inferences and incompatibilities would presumably depend on the scorekeepers' unexplained possession of logical concepts, contra Brandom's goal to explain in scorekeeping terms the use of *all* concepts and vocabularies. However, this choice is also not ad hoc. Anyone who wishes to offer a general inferential role semantics – one that includes a semantics for non-logical vocabulary – must appeal to a notion of material inference. After all, formally valid inferences are valid, and formal incompatibilities hold, as a matter of the logical form of the sentences involved, *in abstraction* from the meaning of the non-logical vocabulary occurring in them. Accordingly, formally valid inferences cannot shed any light on the meaning of such non-logical vocabulary. For example, the inference

If Pittsburgh is west of Philadelphia, **then** Philadelphia is east of Pittsburgh
Pittsburgh is west of Philadelphia
So, Philadelphia is east of Pittsburgh

is formally valid because it is an instance of modus ponens, that is, of the schema

If p, **then** q
p
So, q

The meaning of "Pittsburgh is west of Philadelphia" and "Philadelphia is east of Pittsburgh" contributes nothing to the formal validity of the inference. Substituting uniformly any arbitrary two sentences for the variables p and q into the schema will yield a (formally valid) instance of modus ponens. In general, formally valid arguments and formally incompatible sets of sentences can shed no light on the overall meaning of the non-logical sentences and terms occurring in them, since the meaning of the logical vocabulary and the logical form of the sentences involved, in abstraction from the non-logical sentences and terms occurring in them, suffices for accounting for their formal validity or incompatibility. Accordingly, if the meaning of non-logical sentences and vocabularies too is to be determined by their inferential role, as the inferential role semanticist claims, it must be determined by their *material* inferential role, that is, their inferential role *in abstraction from the ways logical vocabulary may contribute* to the validity of arguments and the incompatibility of sets of sentences in which these non-logical sentences and vocabularies occur. Given a commitment to inferential role semantics, the choice of material inference and material incompatibility as fundamental semantic notions is thus not ad hoc.

Inductive inferences

Since autonomous discursive practices comprise no usage of logical vocabulary, all the inferential and incompatibility relations structuring them are material. A striking feature of Brandom's theory is that he includes *inductive* material inferences and incompatibilities among the meaning-constitutive inferences and incompatibilities. For example, according to Brandom, a norm of material inference licenses the inductive inference

This match is well struck
So, it will light

and partially constitute these two sentences' meanings. Similarly, a norm of material incompatibility certifies the inductive incompatibility of

Lightning one mile away now

and

Silence here for the next ten seconds

and partially constitutes the meaning of these two sentences.

From the perspective of orthodox, classical empiricist theories of meaning, this view is anathema. Inductive inferences and incompatibilities reflect empirical laws and statistical regularities of the world, or, in Hume's words, "relations of matters of fact" (Hume 1975: 25–6). There is a sense in which these laws and regularities are contingent. Intuitively, the world could have been such that well-struck dry matches in an oxygen-rich, windless environment never light (but, say, grow or shrink instead, or turn blue). And, of course, well-struck matches don't light in our world if background conditions are unfavorable (the match might be wet or oxygen might be absent). In general, we can only know a posteriori which inductive inferences and incompatibilities hold, and how strong they are. To know what will happen with this well-struck match, we (or, anyway, someone) must have experienced well-struck matches regularly lighting up. Moreover, to know whether the inductive inference from the match's being well struck to it lighting up is weaker than the one from lightning one mile away to thunder here within the next ten seconds – whether the former correlation is less likely to obtain than the latter, even though the latter too is less than 100 percent (we might be submerged under water, or inside a soundproof room) – again experience needs to be consulted in some complicated way. And classical empiricism concludes from these considerations (with which Brandom agrees) that *therefore* the information enshrined in our explicit knowledge of, or implicit sensitivity to, inductive inferential and incompatibility relations cannot be due to our explicit or implicit *semantic* knowledge concerning the terms involved in the statements expressing such knowledge or sensitivity. Relations reflecting semantic features of our terms or statements, on this orthodox view, are necessary in the strongest sense and knowable a priori. In Hume's words, they are "relations of ideas" (Hume 1975: 25). Accordingly, inductive inferences and incompatibilities do not, from this classical empiricist perspective, reflect semantic features of the terms we use or the concepts we have.

However, *pace* such empiricist orthodoxy, the treatment of inductive inferences and incompatibilities as semantic makes sense from the perspective of Brandom's own Hegel-inspired project, and it dovetails with some broader twentieth-century philosophical developments. The orthodox perspective presupposes the two-phase model of inquiry that, as we saw in chapter 2, Brandom attributes to Kant (and similarly to classical empiricists such as Hume and Carnap) and rejects in favor of a one-phase model he attributes to Hegel (TMD 213–14). According to the Kantian model, gaining empirical knowledge occurs in two phases. *First* the subject determines the content of the concepts she will use, by selecting without the aid of experience the norms of reasoning constituting these concepts from an antecedently given heaven of possible norms. *Then* the subject applies these concepts, so determined, to the circumstances presented by the senses, thus gaining empirical knowledge. Yet according to Brandom's Hegelian one-phase model (which Brandom also attributes to revisionary empiricists such as Quine), there is only one unified dynamic process of rational empirical inquiry, in which the subjects apply concepts to the observed circumstances they encounter and *thereby* somehow gradually determine the content of the concepts they use. The process of gaining empirical knowledge *is* the process through which the subjects determine the content of the concepts in use, according to this one-phase model.

We will only be able to appreciate fully in chapter 8 how this one-phase model works in detail. Still, keeping in mind that meaning, for Brandom, is inferential role – the role of statements and terms in reasoning – the inclusion of inductive inferences and incompatibilities among the meaning-determining factors of the statements and terms in use makes much sense from the perspective of this one-phase model. Empirical inquiry is the effort of describing, explaining, and predicting the world we encounter in ways that make sense to us. And in empirical inquiry the world appears to us not as altogether chaotic, but rather as shot through with all sorts of regularities. Thus the world, so to speak, invites us to acknowledge inferential and incompatibility commitments, regarding the statements we make and judgments we form in empirical inquiry, that reflect these regularities. Through these acknowledgments, and given inferential-role semantics, the *meaning itself* of the empirical terms and concepts in use enshrines for us these empirical, worldly regularities, thus allowing us to take them into account in our empirical reasoning about the world whenever we use these terms and concepts. True, many of these regularities correspond to inductive inferences and incompatibilities. Still, empirical inquiry would be much less fruitful, and the world would make much less sense to us, if we did not acknowledge inferences and incompatibilities reflecting these regularities. Thus, *pace* the orthodox approach to meaning, the inclusion of inductive inferential and incompatibility relations among the determinants of the space of reasons, hence among the constituents of meaning and content, is natural from the viewpoint of Brandom's Hegelian one-phase model.

This inclusion should also be more palatable in light of broader twentieth-century philosophical developments initiated by Quine. Orthodox classical empiricism assumes a sharp distinction between analytic and synthetic statements. "Analytic" statements, such as "If Pittsburgh is west of Philadelphia then Philadelphia is east of Pittsburgh," are true in virtue of their meaning alone, and we can know them to be true a priori in the first phase of inquiry, according to the two-phase model. "Synthetic" statements, such as "If that match is dry, it will light," are true in virtue of their meaning *and* the way the world happens to be, and we can know them to be true only a posteriori, in the second phase of inquiry. Yet Quine has famously argued against the analytic-synthetic distinction, and advocated a one-phase view, akin to Brandom in important respects, according to which the meaningfulness of each statement and the contentfulness of each belief consists in the statement's and belief's overall roles in a whole web of statements and beliefs, which the subject maintains and updates with much leeway prompted by sense experience (Quine 1980: 42–6). Although Quine's and Brandom's thinking about meaning and induction are starkly opposed in other central respects (EE 64–5, 132–3, BSD 98–100), Brandom's inclusion of (what classical empiricism would call) "synthetic" inductive inferences and incompatibilities among the determinants of meaning – that is, inferences and incompatibilities that we would make explicit via (what classical empiricism would consider) synthetic statements such as "If this match is well struck then it will light" – should not be anathema in a contemporary philosophical climate influenced by Quine's holism about semantic significance, his one-phase model of empirical inquiry, and his rejection of the analytic-synthetic distinction.

It must be stressed, however, that Brandom's main influence on the matter is not Quine but Wilfrid Sellars. To gloss this inclusion of inductive inferences and incompatibilities among the semantic determinants of our terms and concepts, Brandom frequently cites the title of Sellars's early paper "Concepts as Involving Laws and Inconceivable Without Them" (EE 45, 141, 150), where by "law" here Sellars emphatically means empirical laws and statistical regularities of nature. It is constitutive of the *semantics* of many concepts, Sellars announces in this title, that we can use them to articulate certain empirical laws and statistical regularities. Brandom accepts this claim and wishes to make sense of it in terms of his material inferential role semantics. Specifically, Brandom's efforts to provide the technical details for this inclusion of inductive inferences and incompatibilities among the semantic determinants of our terms and concepts are an attempt to make sense of the following Sellarsian idea:

> although describing and explaining ... are *distinguishable*, they are also ... *inseparable*. It is only because the expressions in terms of which we describe objects ... locate these objects in a space of implications, that they describe at all, rather than merely label. The descriptive and explanatory resources of language advance hand in hand.
>
> (Sellars 1957: §108; cited from EE 135)

This passage is striking not so much because Sellars regards the meaning of empirical, descriptive terms ("being a match", "being well struck," "lighting up," etc.) as a matter of their locations in the space of implications, that is, the space of reasons – any inferential role semanticist today will be sympathetic – but because of Sellars's explicit inclusion of the *empirical* explanatory role of these terms as among the coordinates of these locations. Without also playing roles in empirical explanations, reflecting empirical laws and statistical regularities of nature, these terms would not have any *descriptive* meaning at all. That is, without playing such empirical explanatory roles, we would not be able to use these terms to describe a thing as, say, a match, as being well struck, as lighting up, etc. at all, but could merely use them to "label" that thing. Thus in order for us to describe the way the world is, we must also know how to use the terms and concepts used in the description in empirical explanations and predictions of the way the world is. Brandom adopts and defends this Sellarsian idea, by developing a detailed and comprehensive view of language and cognition that enshrines it.[2]

Non-monotonicity and counterfactual robustness

The following chapters will gradually introduce details of this view. For now, let's only highlight two important consequences. First, according to Brandom, many of the inferences characterizing autonomous discursive practices are *non-monotonic*. In general, an inference is non-monotonic if it is good but can be turned into a bad one by adding premises, or bad but can be turned into a good one by adding further premises. The validity of non-monotonic inferences may usually be alternately defeated and reinstated by successively adding premises, without definite end. Thus, cast in Brandom's normative pragmatic vocabulary, under "normal" circumstances a commitment to, for example, "That's a well-struck match" commits consequentially to "It will light." Yet adding a collateral commitment to "It's in a very strong electromagnetic field" as an additional premise defeats this inferential commitment – unless we are *also* collaterally committed to "It's in a Faraday cage," which reinstates the inferential commitment, *unless* we are also collaterally committed to "It's in a room evacuated of oxygen," which yet again defeats it, and so on (AR 88–9). Formally valid inferences such as instances of modus ponens, or instances of valid mathematical reasoning, are monotonic, as may perhaps be the inductive inferences characterizing the fundamental sciences: they may not be defeasible by adding further premises. Yet the "messy" inductive inferences and incompatibilities characterizing the non-fundamental sciences as well as our ordinary informal reasoning are typically non-monotonic. Thus, since Brandom includes these "messy" inductive inferences and incompatibilities among the determinants of the space of reasons characterizing autonomous discursive practices, he must hold that much of the inferential reasoning characterizing such practices is non-monotonic.

Given that reasoning in autonomous discursive practices is largely non-monotonic, a participant's inferential and incompatibility commitments essentially depend on the participant's background of *collateral* assertional commitments and entitlements under given circumstances. Successive changes in this background may alternately defeat and reinstate any of the participant's non-monotonic inferential and incompatibility commitments. This leads to a second consequence for Brandom, intimately related to the first:

The fact that we cannot intelligibly describe someone as deploying a concept unless he makes some distinction between materially good and bad inferences involving it has the consequence that we also cannot understand the practitioner as deploying the concept unless he treats the material inferences he takes to be good as having a certain *range of counterfactual robustness*, that is, as remaining good under various merely hypothetical circumstances. … [A]utonomous discursive practices *essentially*, and not just *accidentally*, involve the association of ranges of counterfactual robustness with at least some material inferences.

(BSD 104–5)

Autonomous discursive practitioners not only need to know which consequences and incompatibilities to acknowledge given their actual assertional commitments, but also how having alternative collateral assertional commitments would affect these inferences and incompatibilities. Specifically, they need to be sensitive to the boundary between alternative collateral commitments that would leave these inferences and incompatibilities unscathed vs. those that would weaken or defeat them. Material inferences and incompatibilities are *counterfactually robust* within more or less wide ranges of alternative collateral commitments, and a practitioner must be implicitly sensitive to these ranges, as an essential aspect of acknowledging inferential and incompatibility commitments – hence of their linguistic understanding of the sentences and terms in use – and, more generally, of keeping score. After all, being competent to keep score means mastering in practice the pragmatic significance of the assertions exchanged, and that means knowing how the assertion interacts with *any possible* score, not just with the actual score (see chapter 3: 79–80). Accordingly, drawing the inference from, for example, "This match is well struck" to "It will light" requires implicitly treating one's collateral assertional commitments as indicating that the actual circumstances are within the normal range (match struck by a guy in red t-shirt over there, oxygen present, match dry, no wind, etc.). And this includes implicit sensitivity to how circumstances might have been different while continuing to be normal – different without weakening or defeating the goodness of the inference (match struck by girl in blue t-shirt over *here*, oxygen present, match dry, no wind) – vs. how they might have been different and abnormal, that is, different in a way that weakened or defeated the goodness of the inference (match wet, or strong wind present, or very strong electromagnetic field present, or oxygen absent). Of course, the practitioner might draw this boundary mistakenly in some ways. She may, for example, not appreciate how the presence of a very strong electromagnetic field would affect the inference. Yet if she drew no such boundary at all, that is, if she were prepared to draw the inference under *any* circumstances, we would probably doubt that she has any sense of the meaning of "match," "being well struck," "lighting up," and so on.

This dependency on ranges of counterfactual robustness of many inferences and incompatibilities characterizing autonomous discourse, and autonomous discursive practitioners' implicit sensitivity to these ranges, is an important aspect of Brandom's theory of autonomous discourse. Brandom will use this aspect as the basis for his theory of explicit modal thought and talk: explicit thought and talk about what's possible and necessary. We shall pick up this thread in chapter 6.

Subsentential semantics: the problem

The notions of inference and incompatibility pertaining to autonomous discursive practices are explained in normative pragmatic deontic scorekeeping terms in Brandom's overall theory. However, *semantically* these notions are fundamental, in that Brandom will attempt to explain all other semantic notions – term-meaning, representation, truth, logical concepts, and so on – in terms of inference and incompatibility.

We may think of autonomous discursive practices, as described so far, as exchanges of assertions drawn from a finite and relatively small pool of declarative sentences. The participants master in practice the pragmatic significance of all these sentences, hence their inferential role, and thus understand and know how to use these sentences. However, they lack thus far the abilities to produce and consume ever new sentences and, indeed, to appreciate any systematic syntactic and semantic connections even between the old sentences in the pool. Consider the following sentences:

(1) Fluffy is smaller than Fido
(2) Fido is smaller than Fluffy
(3) Bugs Bunny is smaller than Fluffy
(4) Bugs Bunny is older than Fluffy
(5) **It is not the case that** Bugs Bunny is smaller than Fluffy

(6) **If** Fluffy is smaller than Fido **then** Bugs Bunny is smaller than Fido

(7) **Someone** is older than Fluffy

All seven sentences are syntactically and semantically connected to each other. 1–4 all are different combinations of names and predicates, taken from a pool of three names and two predicates, and the more complex sentences 5–7 are generated from three of these combinations – 1, 3, and 4 – using logical vocabulary. Pre-theoretically speaking, the meaning of 1–4 is determined by the meaning of the names and predicates, and the order in which these terms occur in these sentences, and the meaning of 5–7 is determined by the meaning of 1, 3, and 4 and, in 6, the order in which 1 and 3 occur, plus the meaning of the boldly printed logical vocabulary. Yet autonomous speakers, as described so far, have no sense of any of these systematic connections, because they have so far no sense at all of the fact that 1–7 have terms (names and predicates) or sentences as meaningful components. After all, the assertions exchanged in autonomous discursive practices, as described so far, lack any internal syntactic and semantic structure. They were so far not introduced as syntactically and semantically complex: as made up of subsentential syntactic elements (words and phrases) with their own subsentential meaning, but as internally unstructured holophrastic expressions with an inferential role. Thus, they lack so far precisely the features (subsentential meaningful syntactic elements) through the combination and recombination of which speakers might produce and understand ever-new sentences with ever-new sentential, or propositional, meanings – new sentences and sentential meanings that, since they result from recombining the same subsentential elements, are syntactically and semantically systematically related to each other and to old sentences.

Since Brandom accepts in outline this way of accounting for the systematic and productive (or, as Brandom prefers to say, projective) features of language, his task is to extend his theory of autonomous discursive practices. Brandom's theory must display the assertions exchanged, drawn from the original small pool of declarative sentences, as syntactically well-formed complexes consisting in such meaningful subsentential elements, and to explain both their systematic syntactic and semantic connections to each other and the production of ever-new meaningful sentences outside the original pool in terms of these elements. As the list above indicates, this task splits into two sub-tasks, corresponding to the distinction between atomic sentences such as 1–4, whose only meaningful subsentential components are singular and general terms (names and predicates), and molecular sentences such as 5–7, which contain logical vocabulary among their meaningful components. Atomic sentences combine singular and general terms only: they combine meaningful components whose freestanding performances in linguistic practice could not per se be assertions. And molecular sentences combine whole sentences (whose freestanding performances would be assertions) with logical terms to create larger sentences. Since, as seen earlier, all linguistic practices involving the use of logical vocabulary are non-autonomous, autonomous linguistic practices include only usages of atomic sentences. Moreover, since Brandom wishes to explain the meaning of any sentences outside the original pool, whether atomic or molecular, ultimately in terms of the meaning and use of the sentences in that pool, his task is twofold. He has to show how hitherto autonomous discursive practitioners come to produce and understand, based on their ability to use and understand only the old atomic sentences in the original pool, first, *new atomic* sentences and, second, ever-larger *molecular* sentences. The first task is by and large independent from the second, according to Brandom.[3] Accordingly, I shall now focus entirely on his attempt to tackle the first task, leaving his attempt to tackle the second task for chapter 6.

Decomposition and recomposition

To accomplish the first task, to show how to get new atomic sentences outside the original pool from the old ones in the pool, Brandom pursues

> [a] two-stage compositional strategy for the explanation of projection [, which] would take it that what is settled by proprieties of use governing the smaller, sample set of sentences … is the correct use of the subsentential components into which they can be analyzed or decomposed. The correct use of the components is then to be understood as determining the correct use also of further combinations of them into novel sentences.
>
> (MIE 366; see also AR 127–8, Brandom 2007: 176)

The slogan of this strategy is "decomposition and recomposition" (Brandom 2007: 176). The goal in the first, decompositional stage is, on the syntactic side, to analyze the sentences in the original pool as complexes of singular and general terms and, on the semantic side, to somehow distill from the given inferential roles of the sentences within this original pool the meaning of these singular and general terms. In order not to thwart the overall pragmatist explanation of meaning, it will be pivotal that this distillation be strictly top-down, flowing from the given meaning of the sentences in the original pool (their inferential role) to the meaning of the terms making up these sentences. That is, Brandom must take pains to avoid in his retrieval of term meaning any tacit appeal to semantic ingredients for the meaning of terms other than the original inferential roles. The meaning of a term must be gathered by way of abstraction from the meaning of the original sentences, and must appear as nothing but the *contribution* the term makes to the inferential roles of all the sentences in the original pool in which it occurs (MIE 95; Brandom 2007: 175). The goal in the second stage, the recompositional one, is to show, on the syntactic side, how new combinations of the terms retrieved in the syntactic portion of the first step yield new sentences and, on the semantic side, how these new combinations of terms, in virtue of the meaning of these terms retrieved in the semantic portion of the first step, determine the inferential roles, hence meanings, of these new declarative sentences.

Singular and general terms: syntax

Brandom's key notion in accomplishing both the syntactic and semantic aspects of this two-stage strategy is *substitution*.[4] Let's focus on the syntactic aspects first. Brandom stipulates that our practitioners are able to treat the original declarative sentences as complexes of terms by granting them the syntactic ability to detect, in each of the original atomic sentences, certain parts that can be *substituted into* these sentences *for* other such parts so as to yield new sentences. These parts are *singular terms*. For example, we may substitute the occurrences of "Fluffy," "Fido," and "Bugs Bunny" in the atomic sentences 1–4 for each other in any possible way without thereby producing anything but further syntactically well-formed atomic sentences. Thus, substituting "Fido" for "Fluffy" into 1 yields

(8) Fido is smaller than Fido

which, though blatantly false, is a new syntactically well-formed sentence. And a further substitution of "Fluffy" for the second occurrence of "Fido" in 8 yields 2. Brandom calls pairs of sentences such as 1 and 8, 8 and 2, 2 and 3, or 2 and 8, which are syntactically reachable from each other in a single substitutional step by substituting a singular term for a single occurrence of a singular term, *substitutional variants* (MIE 368).

According to Brandom, singular terms and whole sentences are the syntactically fundamental categories of atomic sentences. *Predicates* are syntactically derivative (MIE 368–70; AR 131; Brandom 1987: 128). They are what remains always invariant under substitution of singular terms for singular terms into sentences. Accordingly, Brandom also calls predicates *sentence frames* (AR 131; see also MIE 368). For example, what remains invariant under any substitution of a singular term for a singular term into 3 and 4 are the frames "__ is smaller than __" and " __ is older than __." True, any n-place predicate may be *replaced* by another n-place predicate without turning a syntactically well-formed sentence into anything but another syntactically well-formed sentence. Thus, replacing "__ is smaller than __" in 3 with "__ is older than __" yields 4, and 3 and 4 are thus substitutional variants in an extended sense of the word. This possibility to replace n-place predicates for n-place predicates into sentences while preserving syntactic well-formedness will be pivotal for Brandom's account of the semantics of predicates. Still, Brandom insists that, syntactically speaking, n-place predicates are identifiable only via substitutions of singular terms for singular terms into sentences – they become apparent as frames only through this further substitutional procedure – and they are in this sense a syntactically derivative category (MIE 368). Still, unless indicated otherwise, I shall use in the following "substitution" and "substitutional variant" in this extended sense.

Singular and general terms: semantics

For any given constellation of assertional commitments and entitlements a speaker may have, each sentence in the original pool stands in various material inferential and incompatibility relations to certain other sentences in the pool, determining the sentences' locations in the space of reasons. Moreover, some pairs of sentences in the original pool are substitutional variants: each member of such a pair is reachable from the other member in a single step, by substituting a singular term for a singular term or an n-place predicate. Combining these two features, *some* ordered pairs of sentences <S1, S2> in the original pool are *both* substitutional variants *and*, in the context of the overall constellation of assertional commitments and entitlements that a speaker has, S2 is validly inferable from, or is incompatible with, S1. That is, substituting for some occurrence of a singular term in S1 some other singular term, or for some occurrence of an n-place predicate in S1 some other n-place predicate, not only yields S2 but also generates either a valid one-premise inference (with S1 as the premise and S2 as the conclusion) or an incompatible pair of sentences (with S1 being incompatible with S2). For example,

(9) **Benjamin Franklin** invented bifocals

and

(10) **The first postmaster general of the United States** invented bifocals

are such a pair, according to Brandom (MIE 370, AR 133),[5] as are

(11) Benjamin Franklin **walked**

and

(12) Benjamin Franklin **was mobile**

as well as

(13) Benjamin Franklin **was tall**

and

(14) Benjamin Franklin **was short**

In each case, not only do we get the second sentence from the first in one step by substituting a term for a term, but also is the second sentence a consequence of, or is incompatible with, the first. Brandom calls one-premise inferences like the ones from 9 to 10 and from 11 to 12 *substitution inferences*. The incompatibility between 13 and 14 might be called a *substitution incompatibility*. (We need to distinguish between commitment-preserving and entitlement-preserving substitution inferences. In the following, unless indicated otherwise, I shall use "substitution inference" inclusively, first, to cover both cases and, second, to include, for brevity's sake, both substitution inferences proper and substitution incompatibilities in such uses.)

Note that for the first and third pair, but not for the second, reversing the order of the substitutional procedure also yields a substitution inference (in the inclusive sense). Thus, substituting into 10 "Benjamin Franklin" for "The first postmaster general of the United States" yields 9, and 9 is also validly inferable from 10 – and similarly for 13 and 14. On the other hand, 11 is not validly inferable from 12: being mobile does not imply being able to walk. This observation highlights an important essential difference between singular terms and predicates, concerning substitution inferences in the exclusive technical sense. For any valid substitution inference from S1 to S2 (in the technical sense), if the substituted-for expressions are *singular terms*, then the inference from S2 to S1 is also a valid substitution inference: the substitution inference from S1 to S2 is *symmetric*. Yet if the substituted-for expressions are *predicates*, the substitution inference from S2 to S1 need not be valid (though it may be): the substitution inference from S1 to S2 may be (though it need not be) *asymmetric*. Indeed, Brandom offers a detailed proof that this must be so for every predicate and every singular term (MIE 376–84). For every predicate P, *some* substitution inferences (in the exclusive technical sense) generated by substituting other predicates for P, or by substituting P for other predicates, are asymmetric while *others* are symmetric. For example, the inference from "Fido is a dog" to "Fido is a mammal" is asymmetric, whereas the substitution inference from "Fido is a dog" to "Fido is a specimen of man's best friend" is symmetric. On the other hand, all substitution inferences generated by substituting singular terms for singular terms are symmetric.

Now, for any pair of terms <T1, T2>, whether singular terms or predicates, if an occurrence of T1 in some sentence of the original pool is such that substituting T2 for that occurrence yields a valid substitution inference, then there are also many other occurrences of T1 in the sentences of the original pool such that substituting T2 for T1 will yield a valid substitution inference. For example, substituting "The first Postmaster General of the United States" for the occurrence of "Benjamin Franklin" into 9, and also into

(15) **Benjamin Franklin** invented the lightning rod
(16) **Benjamin Franklin** had a dog
(17) Deborah Read was the common-law wife of **Benjamin Franklin**

yields a valid (symmetric) substitution inference. Similarly for predicates: substituting "__ was mobile" for the occurrence of "__ walked" into 11 and also into

(18) Barack's dog **walked**
(19) Michelle **walked**,
etc.,

yields a valid (asymmetric) substitution inference. And substituting "__ was informally married to __" for the occurrence of "__ was the common-law wife of __" into 17, and also into

(20) Virginia Woolf **was the common-law wife of** Leonard Woolf
(21) Iris Murdoch **was the common-law wife of** John Bayley and,
etc.,

yields a valid (asymmetric) substitution inference.

Brandom calls any occurrence of a term T1 in a sentence – whether atomic or molecular – such that substituting T2 for T1 into the sentence yields a valid (symmetric or asymmetric) substitution inference, a *primary substitution-semantic occurrence* of T1 (AR 137). Every occurrence of any term in the sentences 1–21 is primary substitution-semantic, including in the molecular sentences 5–7. Not every term occurrence is primary substitution-semantic, however. For example, most people think that the occurrence of "Benjamin Franklin" in

(22) Bertrand believes that **Benjamin Franklin** invented bifocals

is not. The inference from 22 to

(23) Bertrand believes that **the first postmaster general of the United States** invented bifocals

is invalid: 22 may be true, yet if Bertrand does not know that Benjamin Franklin was the first postmaster general, Bertrand will probably not hold the belief 23 ascribes to him.[6]

All the materials are now assembled to introduce Brandom's key move concerning the semantics of singular terms and general terms. Relative to any set of collateral assertional commitments and entitlements concerning the sentences in the old pool, each singular or general term in any sentence of the pool is related to *some* other terms of the same syntactic category by norms of a new kind: *simple material substitution inferential norms*. Specifically, an ordered pair of terms <T1, T2> (where T1 and T2 are either two singular terms or two predicates) is governed by a simple material substitution inferential norm (relative to a set of collateral assertional commitments and entitlements) if for any primary substitution-semantic occurrence of T1 in any sentence "…T1…" of the original pool, substituting T2 for that occurrence yields a valid substitution inference, that is, a sentence "…T2…" that is a substitution inferential consequence, or substitution incompatibility, of "…T1…" (MIE: 360–99; AR 137–41). Every term is governed by a multitude of such norms, each of which relates it as the first or second member of an ordered pair of terms to one other term of the same syntactic category and codifies patterns of substitution inferences (in the inclusive, non-technical sense) involving this pair of terms. For example, the following ordered pairs indicate some of the simple material substitution inferential norms governing the singular term "Benjamin Franklin":

<Benjamin Franklin, The first Postmaster General of the US>

<The first Postmaster General of the US, Benjamin Franklin>

<The inventor of bifocals, Benjamin Franklin>

<Benjamin Franklin, The inventor of bifocals>

<Benjamin Franklin, Richard Saunders>

<Richard Saunders, Benjamin Franklin>

Etc.

For "__ is married to__" we have the following ordered pairs, among others:

<__ is married to__, __ is wedded to __>

<__ is wedded to __, __ is married to __>

<__ is married to __, __ is spouse of __>

<__ is spouse of __, __ is married to __>

<__ is married to__, __ is partner of __>

<__ is common-law married to__, __ is married to__>

Etc.

If T1 and T2 are singular terms, then the ordered pair <T1, T2> is governed by a simple material substitution inferential norm just in case the ordered pair <T2, T1> is governed by such a norm as well: the family of substitution inferences corresponding to <T1, T2> must be symmetric. If T1 and T2 are predicates, then <T1, T2> may be governed by such a norm although <T2, T1> is not: the family of substitution inferences corresponding to <T1, T2> may be asymmetric.

Brandom identifies the *meaning* of a singular term or predicate T (relative to collateral assertional commitments and entitlements), that is, the concept expressed by proper usages of T, with the totality of simple material substitution inferential norms governing T and relating T as the first or second member of certain ordered pairs of terms to certain other terms.

Corresponding to the simple material substitution inferential norms governing a term relative to a certain system of assertional commitments and entitlements, participants in autonomous discursive practices take on commitments of a new sort: *simple material substitution inferential commitments,* or SMSICs. Specifically, a participant has a SMSIC regarding a pair of terms <T1, T2> if <T1, T2> is governed by a corresponding substitution inferential norm.[7] If T1 and T2 are singular terms, the participant's SMSIC regarding <T1, T2> is symmetric, that is, she also has a SMSIC regarding <T2, T1>; if T1 and T2 are predicates, the participant's SMSIC regarding <T1, T2> may be asymmetric, that is, she need not also have a SMSIC regarding <T2, T1>. An autonomous discursive practitioner's *linguistic understanding* of a singular term or predicate T (given her system of assertional commitments and entitlements) consists in the totality of SMSICs she acknowledges regarding T and relating T as the first or second member of certain ordered pairs of terms to certain other terms. The participant fully understands T (given her system of assertional commitments and entitlements) just in case the set of SMSICs she acknowledges regarding T corresponds to the set of simple material substitution inferential norms that really govern T.

New sentence meaning

This completes the first, decompositional stage of Brandom's two-stage "decomposition and recomposition" strategy, to explain the meaning of the terms making up the old sentences in terms of the meaning (inferential role) of the old sentences. Understanding the second, recompositional stage is straightforward. Given their syntactic properties, the singular terms and n-place predicates making up the old atomic sentences may be recombined in multifarious new ways such as to yield new atomic sentences. And for each such new sentence S, the simple material substitution inferential norms governing the terms in S, recovered in the first step, determine all the substitution inferences in which S figures as premise or conclusion, relating S substitution inferentially both to certain old sentences from the original, small pool and to certain other new sentences – given *their* substitution inferential roles, which are determined by the simple material substitution inferential norms governing the terms in *them*. Relatedly, speakers acknowledge a set of SMSICs regarding each term in S, recovered from the inferential commitments they acknowledge regarding the old sentences in which the term figures. And these acknowledged SMSICs determine the set of substitution inferences in which they *take* S to figure as premise or conclusion with respect to certain old, as well as new, sentences. And Brandom thinks that knowing in practice S's *substitution inferential* role or, anyway, treating S in practice as having such a role, suffices for knowing enough of S's *overall* inferential role or, anyway, for assigning enough of an overall inferential role to S so as to use the new sentence S successfully in communication.

This concludes the outline of Brandom's theory of term meaning and of how speakers understand new atomic sentences given their understanding of a small sample of old ones. This theory raises a host of difficult issues, both technical ones internal to Brandom's project (see e.g. Brandom 2007: 177; MIE 346–52) and broader ones connecting Brandom's theory with theories of syntax and semantics for natural languages prevalent in linguistics (see e.g. Peregrin 2005). Unfortunately, I cannot address any of these issues in this limited space.

Anaphora

So far Brandom's account of term meaning was introduced in terms of *types* of sentences and terms – abstract linguistic items that may be used over and over again by different speakers in different contexts. Yet discourse is the norm-governed exchange of linguistic performances – *tokenings* of sentences and terms on particular occasions. Each such tokening is a unique, unrepeatable, spatio-temporal linguistic event. Any attempt to repeat a sentence-tokening yields a new token, numerically different from the first one. These observations raise two related questions for Brandom. First, apropos types of linguistic expressions, what determines whether an occurrence of a term in one sentence-type counts as a *recurrence* of a term in another (or even the same) sentence-type? Answering this question is pivotal for Brandom because his theory of term-meaning implies that any term may recur over and over again in many different sentences that are premises or conclusions of substitution inferences. Second, apropos tokenings of linguistic expressions, what determines whether an occurrence of a term-token in one linguistic performance is a recurrence of a term-token in another (or even the same) linguistic performance? Answering this question is pivotal for Brandom because his pragmatism attempts to explain the meaning of types of sentences and terms in terms of token linguistic performances in linguistic practice. From a pragmatist perspective, tokenings of sentences and terms are prior in the order of explanation to types of sentences and terms. Thus, we had better know under which circumstances a term-token in one linguistic performance is a recurrence of another term-token in another (or even the same) linguistic performance.

A natural first shot at a theory of term recurrence (type or token) is that two term occurrences are recurrences of the same term just in case they are lexically co-typical, that is, just in case they have the same phonetic or morphological features – roughly, the same "shape" when written out on paper. Alas, lexical co-typicality is neither necessary nor sufficient for term recurrence. For example, the inference

This organism is a mammal,

therefore, this organism is a vertebrate

is valid only if the occurrence of "this organism" in the conclusion is a recurrence of the lexically co-typical occurrence of "this organism" in the premise. Yet the two occurrences may well be two different demonstratives – referring respectively to, say, a cat and a dog – in which case they count as semantically different singular terms, and the second occurrence is not a recurrence of the first, despite their lexical co-typicality. Thus, lexical co-typicality is insufficient for determining term recurrence (MIE 450). Furthermore, the inference

This organism is a mammal

therefore, it is a vertebrate

is, on the most natural reading, valid. On this reading, the pronoun "it" in the conclusion is a recurrence of the "this organism" in the premise, that is, the two expressions count semantically as different occurrences of the same singular term, although they are not lexically co-typical. Thus, lexical co-typicality is not necessary for determining term recurrence (MIE 450).

Brandom's attempt to offer a better theory of term recurrence is his theory of *anaphora*. In general, anaphora is a mechanism due to which a term may inherit its meaning from another expression in the linguistic context. A paradigm example of anaphora is the use of the pronoun "it" in the conclusion of the last argument (on the most natural reading). On this reading, the "it" does not refer demonstratively (deicticly) to some salient object in the non-linguistic context, unmediated by the linguistic context – though the "This organism" in the premise may well be such a deictic expression – but rather inherits, regulated by the mechanism of anaphora, its meaning from the "This organism" in the premise and thus means and refers to whatever that "This organism" means and refers to. On the other hand, whether the first argument above is valid as it stands is indeterminate because it is unclear whether the occurrence of "this organism" in the conclusion is deictic or anaphoric. If it is anaphoric, it inherits its meaning from the "This organism" in the premise, and the argument is valid. If it is deictic, it picks out some organism in the non-linguistic context directly and thus counts semantically as a different singular term than the "This organism" in the premise, and the argument is invalid.

Brandom proposes that the phenomenon of anaphora extends far beyond such paradigmatic cases. In his view, *every* term-tokening in discourse – whether pronoun, name, or predicate – is an actual or potential link in a chain of anaphorically related actual or potential further tokenings of terms. Which anaphoric chain of term-tokenings a particular term in use belongs to determines the semantic identity of the term in use. That is, the mechanism of anaphora determines, for every term-tokening in discourse, which other term-tokenings are recurrences of it and which term-tokenings it is a recurrence of. Indeed, Brandom thinks that, metaphysically, there are no term-types over and above anaphoric chains of term-tokenings at all. A type of term simply *is*, metaphysically, a chain of anaphorically related term-tokenings, crisscrossing discourse (MIE 471, 467).

The familiar causal theory of reference for names and natural-kind terms provides a good entry point to this picture (Kripke 1972; Putnam 1975). According to the causal theory, tokenings of proper names or natural-kind terms in discourse inherit their reference from earlier uses of the same term, to which they are causally linked. That is, a tokening of the name or natural-kind term refers to whoever or whatever these earlier, causally antecedent uses refer to. The reference of these earlier uses in turn is ultimately determined by an initial, introductory use of the term – an "initial baptism" – paradigmatically vis a vis a non-linguistic individual, or a sample or instance of a certain natural kind, which initiates the entire causal chain of tokenings of the term. By virtue of their membership in one or another sociohistorical, causal chain of term-uses, later uses of a term refer, mediated by intermediate uses to which they are causally linked, to the individual or kind baptized at the initiation of the chain. For example, on this view, those uses of the name "Caesar" today that refer to the long-deceased Roman emperor do so because they are links in a causal chain of uses of the name that was initiated more than 2,100 years ago, perhaps by Caesar's parents vis a vis their newly born boy who was to become the Roman emperor. From this initial baptism, a causal chain of uses of the name spread through the family and Roman community to a wider and wider circle of speakers of Latin and other languages, down the decades and centuries, and to us. Thus, a speaker today cannot fail to refer to the long-deceased Caesar by using the name, even if she knows little about the man, because her use of "Caesar" today is a link in this causal chain of earlier and earlier uses of the name, terminating in the initial naming of the baby boy. Similarly for natural-kind terms. Thus, usages of the term "gold" today refer to the natural kind gold, even if the speaker knows little about gold, because they are causally linked via earlier and earlier uses of the term to some initial usage, presumably vis a vis a sample of gold, which stands as a representative of the kind.

Brandom is primarily concerned with the inheritance of meaning *qua* substitution-inferential role from term-tokening to term-tokening, not reference. Still, the anaphoric mechanism of meaning-inheritance he envisions has the same sociohistoric structure as the causal mechanism of reference-inheritance according to the causal theory. Indeed, "causal-historical theories of proper names [and predicates] ... appear as dark ways of talking about the sorts of anaphoric chains that link tokenings of proper names [and predicates] into recurrence structures" (MIE 470).

On Brandom's view, present uses of the term "Caesar," concerning the Roman emperor, inherit their meaning *anaphorically* from earlier and earlier uses of the term, culminating in some initial use vis a vis the Roman baby boy – and similarly for natural-kind terms and, indeed, for *all* singular terms and all predicates, including color predicates ("is red") or quantitative predicates ("has mass of twelve grams") (MIE 471). The initial introduction of the term vis a vis an individual or a sample, or in some other way, is, on this view, the ultimate anaphoric antecedent on which subsequent uses of the term depend, mediated typically by a sequence of anaphorically intermediary uses. Since the term in use reduces on this view to the whole anaphoric chain of its tokenings, *that chain* is the metaphysical bearer of the substitution inferential norms governing the term. Any particular use of the term today has the substitution inferential significance it has because it is a link in that chain. Metaphysically, the substitution inferential norms linking the term to some other terms (e.g., the symmetric substitution inferential norm linking the terms "Caesar" and "the Roman statesman murdered on March 15, 44 BC") are norms linking *different* anaphoric chains of term-tokenings to each other (e.g., the anaphoric chains constituting the terms "Caesar" and "the Roman statesman murdered on March 15, 44 BC") (MIE 467).

Different uses of the lexical type "Caesar," concerning different individuals such as the Roman emperor, Cesar Chavez, Julio Cesar (the Brazilian soccer goalie), or lesser-known Caesars, differ in meaning. The anaphoric theory explains these semantic differences in terms of the fact that different uses of the lexical type "Caesar" may belong to different anaphoric chains with different substitution inferential significances, concerning the Roman emperor, Cesar Chavez, Julio Cesar, etc. Again, the membership of any tokening of the lexical type "Caesar" in one of these anaphoric chains, hence the meaning of the tokening, does not depend on the token's lexical type nor on its lexical co-typicality with any anaphoric antecedents in the chain, but on the way the tokening is linked anaphorically with other tokenings in the chain, independent of their lexical types.

Of course, no speaker today has memory of the use over 2,100 years ago that initiated the anaphoric chain to which uses of "Caesar" today concerning the Roman emperor belong. In this regard, uses of "Caesar" today and the use of the "it" in the second argument above differ: everyone who understands the argument is exposed to the deictically used "This organism" in the premise, which initiates the anaphoric chain of which the "it" is a part. However, there is no problem here. We can think of speakers who refer to the Roman emperor today, using his name, as resembling speakers who join an ongoing conversation that includes anaphoric uses of pronouns whose antecedents they were not exposed to, and start using those pronouns themselves. The pronouns in use, out of these speakers' mouths, thus inherit their meaning from the earlier pronoun uses in the conversation, and mean whatever these pronouns mean, despite the speakers' lack of access to the anaphoric initiators of the entire chains. The speakers may nonetheless gradually gain a better understanding of these terms by gradually picking up substitution inferential norms governing them as the conversation progresses.

The most important difference between the causal and the anaphoric theory is that anaphoric relations are *normative* (MIE 452, 460, 472). Anaphora is a system of norms determining which bits of discourse are anaphorically related to each other. Accordingly, scorekeepers adopt yet another type of deontic status, besides assertional commitments, assertional entitlements, inferential commitments, and (by extension) SMSICs, and syntactic commitments: *anaphoric commitments*, or *recurrence commitments* (MIE 456–7). For example, speakers who read the second argument above in the natural way are anaphorically committed to treat the "it" in the conclusion as anaphorically depending on the "This organism" in the premise. In general, a scorekeeper has an anaphoric commitment regarding two term-tokens in discourse just in case one token depends anaphorically on the other. Relatedly, a scorekeeper acknowledges an anaphoric commitment regarding two term-tokens just in case she treats one token as a recurrence of the other. Acknowledging anaphoric commitments is yet again something scorekeepers usually do only implicitly in practice, but sophisticated, nonautonomous speakers may once again make any anaphoric commitments or anaphoric norms explicit, by articulating them in propositionally contentful claims (MIE 460, 472).

Although anaphoric norms and substitution-inferential norms are intimately related, anaphora is not per se semantic. It is

> a relationship among tokenings that is presupposed by, and hence not analyzable in terms of, substitutional commitments. Taking one individual's tokening to be anaphorically dependent on another is not attributing a substitutional commitment; it is attributing a more primitive sort of commitment, one that determines which substitutional commitments regarding other tokenings are relevant in assessing the substitutional significance of the one treated as anaphorically dependent.
>
> (MIE 167)

Anaphoric norms determine which bits of discourse go into the same anaphoric chain and are thus governed by the same substitution inferential norms. By contrast, the substitution inferential norms governing the chain, which are the only *semantic* norms governing it, link that chain to *certain other* anaphoric chains. For a term-tokening to be meaningful, that is, for it to have substitution inferential significance, norms of both kinds must govern it: "no (semantically significant) *occurrence* without (the possibility of) *recurrence*" (MIE 465). The meaning of the term-tokening consists in its substitution inferential role, that is, its potential to recur in the premises or conclusions of indefinitely many substitution inferences, each of which may be tokened over and over again by different speakers. And since the term-tokening cannot *itself* recur over and over again in (the tokenings of) these premises or conclusions (no token as such may occur more than once in the entire history of discourse) its potential to recur must be secured by anaphoric norms, which determine a never-ending supply of further tokenings as the term-tokening's anaphoric dependents and, as it were, deputies – each of these dependents *recurring in its stead* in the premises or conclusions of indefinitely many substitution inferences, tokened by one or another speaker, and having *its* meaning. For a term-tokening to recur or to be a recurrence – hence for it to be as much as capable of substitution inferential significance – is for it to have anaphoric dependents recurring in its stead or anaphoric antecedents in whose stead it recurs (MIE 462–5).

A deictic expression like "This organism" or "That boy," used vis a vis a cat or a baby, does not inherit its meaning from any anaphoric antecedent. So how does it mean what it means? According to Brandom, its meaning, just like the meaning of any other token in the anaphoric chain it initiates, consists in the substitution inferential norms governing the entire chain, and it has no meaning apart from it (MIE 466). In this sense, "deixis presupposes anaphora" (MIE 462). Brandom does not deny that deictic expressions (and their anaphoric dependents) also refer to objects, and that their reference is intimately related to their meaning. However, as we shall see in chapter 7, Brandom maintains that their reference is a semantically epiphenomenal consequence of their meaning, not *part* of their meaning.[8] The meaning of a deictic expression is solely its substitution inferential role, which it may have only because it belongs (as its initiating link) to a certain anaphoric chain.

Two features of anaphora will loom large in chapters 7 and 8. First, an anaphorically dependent tokening may be linked to its antecedent intrapersonally or interpersonally. For example, in Fred's linguistic performance

/**This organism** is a mammal. After all, **it** is a vertebrate/

the boldly printed pronoun token inherits its meaning *intrapersonally* from the boldly printed deictic token, and both tokens are produced by Fred.[9] On the other hand, in the little dialogue

Fred: /**This organism** is a vertebrate/
Sue: /Oh! So **it** is a mammal!/

The boldly printed pronoun token out of Sue's mouth inherits its meaning *interpersonally* from the boldly printed deictic antecedent out of Fred's mouth. Second, while different speakers usually exhibit significant differences in acknowledged assertional and (substitution) inferential commitments, they generally agree in their acknowledged anaphoric commitments, cases of defective communication aside (MIE 452). In other words, different speakers usually hold vastly different beliefs and differ in their views about the inferential roles of even the beliefs that they share – and, accordingly, they understand the corresponding linguistic performances in different ways. Yet they generally agree in practice as to which bits of their discourse count as recurrences of the same term. For example, Fred and Sue's respective understandings of the terms "organism," "vertebrate" and "mammal," and their beliefs concerning organisms, vertebrates, and mammals, may differ dramatically, but they will agree in practice as a matter of course that Sue's /it/ anaphorically depends on Fred's /This organism/. As we shall see in chapters 7 and 8, the phenomenon of interpersonal anaphora and the fact that in all cases of non-defective communication all participants acknowledge the same anaphoric commitments will be pivotal for Brandom's accounts, first, of how speakers may communicate successfully despite their differences in linguistic understanding and, second, of how speakers, in the course of their discourse, may institute, negotiate, and administer the very substitution inferential norms governing their discourse.

Summary

Brandom's fundamental semantic notions are the notions of material inference and material incompatibility. Material inferential and incompatibility relations obtain between sentences independently of specifically logical (formal) vocabulary. Brandom does not deny that inferences may also be formally valid: valid due to the logical form of premises and conclusion – and similarly for incompatibilities. Autonomous discursive practices are free from uses of logical vocabulary, however, and, accordingly, all inferential and incompatibility relations in such practices are material. These relations constitute the meaning of the sentences in use in such practices. An important aspect of Brandom's semantic theory is that many of these material inferences and incompatibilities reflect laws and statistical regularities of nature. Thus, the material inference from "This match is well struck" to "It will light" reflects the causal regularity of nature that well-struck matches light *and also* partially constitutes the meaning of these two sentences. Accordingly, contrary to how the orthodox empiricist tradition established by David Hume would have it, that inference reflects both a "relation of matters of fact" (a regularity of nature) and a "relation of ideas" (a semantic relation between propositions). Chapters 5 to 7 will expand on this aspect of Brandom's material inferential role semantics.

Brandom extends his material inferential role semantics concerning sentence meaning to a theory of *term* meaning and to an explanation how speakers may understand indefinitely many new sentences on the basis of understanding a finite set of terms (a vocabulary), where the latter understanding is derived from understanding a small set of old sentences. He stipulates that speakers have the *syntactic* ability to recognize in practice the sentences they exchange as concatenations of singular and general terms – names and predicates. Moreover, they have the *semantic* ability to recognize in practice that *some* material inferences and incompatibilities concerning pairs of old sentences are such that one sentence can be reached from the other in a single step, by substituting a singular term for a singular term or a predicate for a predicate. The inference from "Hesperus is bright" to "Phosphorus is bright" and the incompatibility between "Fido is a dog" and "Fido is a cat" are examples of such *substitution inferences* and *substitution incompatibilities*. The heart of Brandom's theory of term meaning is the idea that the meaning of a singular or general term T consists in a set of *simple material substitution inferential/incompatibility norms*, relating T to some other terms x of the same syntactic category. These norms determine that a substitution of x for T in any old sentence "...T...", or of T for x in any old sentence "...x...", (where T or x occur in extensional contexts) yields a valid substitution inference or a substitution incompatibility. More or less in accordance with these norms, speakers acknowledge in practice *simple material substitution inferential/incompatibility commitments* (SMSICs). A speaker's acknowledged SMSICs regarding any term T constitutes her linguistic understanding of T. Given these syntactic and semantic abilities, speakers can now generate and understand new sentences by combining and recombining the terms they understand in new syntactically permissible ways.

Linguistic practices are exchanges of linguistic performances – *tokenings* of sentences. Brandom's theory of *anaphora* explains under which circumstances a term-tokening in one linguistic performance counts as a recurrence of another term-tokening in a different (or even the same) linguistic performance, hence as a recurrence of the same term. Brandom models such term recurrence structures in discourse on anaphoric usages of pronouns. Just as in the sentence "John is happy because he is getting married" the pronoun "he" inherits its meaning and reference anaphorically from the occurrence of the name "John" in the same sentence, so a (singular or general) term-token in the context of a linguistic performance inherits its meaning and reference anaphorically from other (singular or general) term-tokens in discourse. A system of norms of a distinct kind – anaphoric norms – regulates which term-tokens count as anaphoric recurrences of which other term-tokens, and thus as tokens of the same term. Metaphysically, a term-type reduces to a chain of anaphorically related term-tokens in discourse, according to Brandom, and simple material substitution inferential norms, constituting the meaning of a term, are thus norms linking the anaphoric chain of term-tokens constituting *that* term to other such chains constituting other terms.

5

Empirical Content and Empirical Knowledge

In chapter 3 we saw that one way in which Brandom envisions scorekeepers inheriting entitlement to assert that p noninferentially and by default, besides inheriting it testimonially, is to inherit it based on observation of features of the non-linguistic environment. Such perception-based entitlements to assertions are, to use Sellars's term, language-entry moves. We also saw that a scorekeeper's assertional commitment that p, or her entitlement to such a commitment, has commitments or entitlements to further assertions as inferential consequences, and also, more or less directly, noninferential consequences in non-linguistic rational actions. That is, assertional commitments and entitlements have, using Sellars's term, language-exit moves among their consequences. Brandom's answers as to whether such language entries and language exits are essential to autonomous discursive practices vary. Sometimes he claims that they are, strictly speaking, inessential – strictly speaking, autonomous discursive practices are possible where the only noninferential inheritance of entitlement to assert is testimonial (MIE 221, 234, SOT chap. 4: 23–4) – whereas at other times he claims that they are essential (BSD 106, EE 52). Yet whatever his actual view on the issue may be, he consistently claims that the presence of language entries and exits in discursive practices makes a *semantic* contribution to the assertions exchanged. Their characteristic noninferential relation to observation and observed circumstances renders assertions figuring as language-entry moves, as well as assertions inferentially related to them, empirically contentful, and their characteristic noninferential relation to language exits in non-linguistic intentional actions render some assertions "practically contentful." Moreover, only discursive practices where many of the propositional contents asserted are empirically and practically contentful have any resemblances to usages of natural languages (MIE 234). Thus, to the extent that Brandom's theory of discursive practices is a theory of communication in the medium of natural languages – not just any languages – he consistently holds that language entries and exits are an essential aspect of such practices.

Brandom also holds that language-entry moves and the noninferential mechanisms giving rise to entitlements to them make an essential *epistemic* contribution to discursive practices using natural language. Under normal circumstances, language entries are, due to these mechanisms, both themselves bits of empirical knowledge and also bases for further, inferentially inherited empirical knowledge about the largely non-linguistic world. This chapter introduces Brandom's theory of empirical content and empirical knowledge, as well as his theory of rational agency.

Practical and discursive intentionality

Like all non-discursive organisms (such as amoebas, parrots, or leopards) and many of their organs and organic systems (such as kidneys or the immune system), and like certain artifacts (such as heat-seeking missiles or thermostats), we are what Brandom calls *practically intentional* creatures, that is, creatures capable of engaging in more or less complex feedback-governed ways with our environments. Practical intentionality, according to Brandom, is the most fundamental way in which sentient creatures may be intentionally directed toward environing objects (BSD 178). According to Brandom, the behavior of a system is practically intentional

> insofar as it is … specifiable … as having an algorithmic TOTE [Test-Operate-Test-Exit] structure in which each cycle is mediated by its differential responses to the effects of its own performances. Specifying the behavior of a system in such terms is taking or treating it as practically *directed toward* the features of its environment that play a suitable dual role in the reliably covarying causal chains of events that serve as both inputs to and outputs from the system that engages in a process with this structure.
>
> (BSD 182–3)

For example, the behavior of a leopard approaching and chasing down an antelope is a highly complex, feedback-governed practically intentional process of this kind. Each new perceptual input (inattentive antelope a certain distance away) reliably gives rise to a certain complex behavior (leopard crouching a bit closer), altering the perceptual information (antelope a bit closer, still inattentive), giving rise to adjusted behavior (leopard ducking and sitting still) in open-ended, feedback-governed loops – TOTE-cycles – manifesting a highly complex system of reliable dispositions on the leopard's part to approach and chase down game. Other examples of non-discursive practically intentional behavior are a flower's slowly moving its leaves in response to changes in the position of the sun, a cooling system's self-regulated flow of cold air in response to information transmitted by a heat sensor, an amoeba's moving toward a food source, and so on. In general, a system's behavior is practically intentional if the system's ongoing and changing reception of information about a certain environing feature serves as continuous feedback for the system's ongoing, continuously adjusted behavior regarding that feature. Such feedback-governed behavior is *intentional*, according to Brandom, in the sense that a complete characterization of it must describe it as directed toward the environing feature. Moreover, this characterization must include a characterization of that environing feature itself (BSD 178). It follows that two intrinsically type-identical systems that go through intrinsically type-identical sequences of motions do not necessarily engage in the same kind of practically intentional behavior, because the environing features toward which their respective behavior is directed may be of different kinds. Since it is essentially described in terms of the environing features toward which it is directed, practically intentional behavior is thick, in the sense that, according to Brandom, it literally *incorporates* the environing features toward which it is directed. A total practically intentional system thus essentially includes the perceiving and behaving system per se, in abstraction from the environing features toward which its behavior is directed, *and* those environing features themselves (BSD 178–9).

According to Brandom, the simplest cases of TOTE-cycles are entirely naturalistic and explainable in non-normative causal, information-theoretic, or teleo-functional terms (PP 10). Brandom agrees with standard cognitive scientific characterizations of such cycles as involving genuinely *representational* states, but insists (again in line with much cognitive scientific practice) that these representations are sub-personal, in the sense that the system is not literally responsible for them – that it is not praise- or blameworthy for being in these states – hence that these representations are not normative and *a fortiori* not conceptual (PP 12). Brandom has so far only offered cryptic remarks on the nature of these non-conceptual representations, characterizing them as mapping relations or tracking processes, where tracking is a process of continuously updating maps (PP 216). But in any case, he thinks of the TOTE-cycles of non-normative systems as fully describable in terms of naturalistic, reliable differential responsive dispositions, where each new feedback-governed behavior in the cycle is a manifestation of a more or less complex set of dispositions by the system to behave in that manner in response to incoming perceptual information (BSD 216).

Brandom regards the discursive behavior of language-using creatures as a "development and a special case" of their basic practical intentionality, as just described (BSD 179). Such behavior – *discursively* intentional behavior – is still practically intentional: it is perennially adjusted, feedback-governed behavior. Yet it is a "special case" in that among the states constituting each new feedback-governed loop generating feedback-governed behavior are now distinctly discursive, normative states: acknowledged discursive commitments and entitlements. Think of someone walking up to the fridge, opening its door, and grabbing a bottle of beer. The behavior is still a feedback-governed complex response to ongoing perceptual input, but it is also mediated by, and a feedback-governed response to, the person's system of doxastic and practical commitments – beliefs and intentions – and the person's perpetual updating of that system as he approaches the fridge. *(Practical commitments* are normative, conceptually contentful states of discursive creatures that give rise to intentional action: paradigmatically, intentions to act. We shall focus on them in the last section of this chapter. For now, let's just note that, in Brandom's terminology, not every practically intentional creature has practical commitments; only *discursively* intentional creatures do.) Discursively intentional behavior is moreover a "development" of simple, non-discursive practically intentional behavior in that it gradually develops in ontogeny out of cycles that, originally in a prenatal or neonate human, are non-discursive, simple practically intentional cycles.

Despite all these specific differences between simple practical and discursive intentionality, both are species of the genus "practical intentionality," according to Brandom, in that the TOTE-cycles characterizing each of them are still describable in terms of reliable differential responses to previous feedback-providing states – though in the case of discursively intentional systems, some of these states and responses are irreducibly normative (BSD 183). For example, the *sui generis inferential* processes of acknowledging new discursive commitments and entitlements based on old ones, in which a discursive creature's updating of her system of beliefs and intentions partially consists, is still describable in terms of reliable differential dispositions, according to Brandom (AR 99, KSR 896). This time, however, the process involves implicit sensitivity on the system's part to the norms of inference governing the process.

Brandom's treatment of discursive intentionality as a species of practical intentionality implies that discursive practices involving use of *natural* languages (which essentially include language entries and language exits) are thick. Like the practical intentionality of non-discursive creatures, a speaker's discursive practical intentionality literally incorporates the features of the environment toward which it is directed. This is a very important aspect of Brandom's theory and the basis for his theories of empirical knowledge, empirical content, and discursive representation. We can make justified and true empirical claims *about* the non-linguistic, perceivable world because our empirical discursive practices always already incorporate those aspects of the non-linguistic world toward which the corresponding discursively intentional states and processes are directed. By contrast to the way the Cartesian tradition thinks about these matters, according to Brandom the subjective and objective aspects of empirical discourse – rational thinking and acting subjects and the thought-about and acted-upon worldly objects – cannot be understood independently of each other, and their relations cannot be explained in terms of such antecedent independent understanding. Rather, rational thinking subjects and thought-about, acted-upon objects are per se abstractions from these antecedently understood, thick, world-involving discursively intentional practices and processes, and when the subjective and objective poles of these processes are understood in this way, we can also understand how subjects can think, talk, and know about the objective world (BSD 180).

Observational knowledge

An observational belief is an assertional commitment acknowledged by the subject in immediate response to perception of an external situation, according to Brandom, and an observation report is an assertion expressing such a belief. Paradigmatically, observation reports involve demonstratives or indexicals referring to a perceived feature of the environment and a predicate describing this feature in a certain way. Examples of observation reports are assertions such as /Whales over there!/, exclaimed by a whale watchman looking at a moving group of large sea animals, /Those were Toltec/, asserted by an expert of classical Central American pottery based on having seen some shards of pottery on a table, or /These are mu mesons/, exclaimed by a physicist looking at a vapor trail in a bubble chamber (MIE 226–7; AR 97–9; MIE 222–3).[1]

Observational beliefs are formed in immediate response to perceptual input, or the memory of such input, in the sense that the physical and psychological process leading to the formation of the belief – a segment of a TOTE-cycle that incorporates the perceived environing feature and yields the belief as response – does not include any inferential processes. The process leading from the environing feature via perception to the formation of such a belief, Brandom insists, does per se not include any reasoning, inferring, or justifying. Neither the perceived external situation itself nor the intermediary perceptual state is a basis for the observational belief in the sense that the subject would somehow *infer* the observational belief (or its content) from the situation or the perception (AR 99–100; MIE 204–5; 1995b: 249–51). At the same time, Brandom wants to claim that, in the normal case, the observational belief, *insofar as it has been formed by such a noninferential process*, is *justified*, hence that the subject is entitled to the corresponding assertion, and thus that the belief's being so formed adds to its standing in the space of reasons. To begin with, the belief stands in the space of reasons already *qua* contentful state that p. *Qua* contentful state, the belief has an inferential role, that is, certain norms of reasoning relate it to various other beliefs and statements. Moreover, the subject must to some degree be sensitive to this role by acknowledging multifarious inferential commitments involving the belief, more or less in accordance with this role. Accordingly, *qua* contentful state, the belief *is* involved in multifarious inferential relations and processes on the subject's part, and since the belief is a candidate for propositional knowledge only if it is, and is taken by the subject to be, propositionally contentful, its being involved in multifarious inferential relations and processes is thus essential for it to be a candidate for empirical, propositional knowledge (TMD

249–53). Yet Brandom insists that in normal cases, an observational belief, although it is formed based on a noninferential process, is nonetheless justified by the fact that it has been so formed, and that its status as being so justified adds to its standing in the space of reasons, in the sense that, *qua* being so justified, it may serve as a reason for someone to form certain beliefs *beyond* its serving as such a reason in so far as it is a contentful state (MIE 204–6):

> we must be careful in characterizing perceptual judgments or reports of observation as "noninferential." They are noninferential in the sense that the particular acts or tokenings are noninferentially *elicited*. They are not the products of a process of inference, arising rather by the exercise of reliable capacities to noninferentially respond differentially to various sorts of perceptible states of affairs by applying concepts. But *no* beliefs, judgments, reports, or claims – in general, no application of concepts – are noninferential in the sense that their content can be understood apart from their role in reasoning as potential premises and conclusions of inferences.
>
> (TMD 352)

The key to understanding these claims is the phrase "reliable capacities to noninferentially respond differentially." According to Brandom, an observational belief is justified just in case it is formed *by an epistemically reliable process*, that is, by a process that manifests a disposition on the subject's part to reliably form mostly true observational beliefs involving the relevant concepts under relevantly similar circumstances. For example, the report of the whale watchman above is justified if the watchman has a tendency to form similar observational whale beliefs under similar observable circumstances and in almost all of those circumstances the observed large sea animals are indeed whales. His report is not justified if, in those circumstances, the observed sea animals are quite frequently walruses, dolphins, etc. (MIE 226). Such reliability varies from observer to observer and topic to topic. The whale watchman may under the given conditions reliably discriminate nearby whales from walruses and hence produce justified whale or walrus reports, while a tourist on the same boat, producing the same observation report, may not have this reliable discriminatory ability and hence would not be justified. Similarly, the watchman may be a reliable whale observer under the given circumstances but an unreliable observer of '52 Pontiacs in traffic, and may hence produce justified observation reports of the former but not of the latter kind (MIE 226).

For observational beliefs and observation reports, Brandom thus endorses a version of the reliability theory of justification, originally developed by Alvin Goldman (Goldman 1976), according to which epistemic justification is a matter of reliable belief formation. Brandom shares several controversial commitments with proponents of more mainstream versions of the reliability theory. First, he accepts a qualified version of *fallibilism* – the view that a belief may be justified and yet be false, that is, that a (non-Gettiered)[2] justified belief need not be knowledge. An observer's epistemic reliability may, for the topic at issue and under the given circumstances, be less than 100 percent and thus lead to the formation of *some* false beliefs. Still, since these false beliefs have been produced by a largely reliable mechanism, they are justified (1995a: 899). For example, the watchman's observational whale belief may be justified even if it is formed, on this occasion, in the presence of walruses, assuming that his overall reliability to form observational whale beliefs under similar observational circumstances in the presence of whales, but not in the presence of walruses, dolphins, etc., is high. Second, Brandom accepts *externalism* about justification. He agrees that an observational belief that p may be justified – reliably produced – even though the subject may not be in a position to ascertain based on introspective reflection on her current cognitive states (including perceptions and memories), attitudes, and skills alone that her belief is justified and, indeed, even though she may in fact doubt that it is justified. As long as the belief was in fact reliably produced, the belief is justified and, if true, knowledge – even if the subject doubts that it was reliably produced. For example, the archeologist may in fact be highly reliable in discriminating Toltec from Aztec and other potsherds, when given random samples, and compulsively form the corresponding, mostly true observational beliefs about the sherds. But she may in fact also be suspicious about her abilities to form mostly true beliefs of this sort and always use further sources – the testimony of colleagues, or visual images from authoritative databases – to confirm her beliefs. Still, despite such doubts, all her observational beliefs regarding the sherds are justified as soon as she forms them, prior to consulting other sources, since they are in fact all formed based on her ability to reliably perceptually discriminate Toltec and Aztec potsherds (AR 98) – justified, that is, without her being able to ascertain them *as* justified on introspective reflection alone.

The exposition just given explains the notion of epistemic reliability in terms of truth: an observational belief is reliably produced, if and only if the process yielding the belief is one that likely yields true beliefs. Indeed, since Brandom accepts the classical justified true belief analysis of knowledge (the JTB analysis) – Gettier-style counterexamples aside – any reliably produced true observational belief is knowledge, according to him (MIE 201, including n. 1). Yet this does not mean that Brandom relies on the notion of truth as an explanatory *epistemic* primitive, in awkward contrast to his meticulous efforts to avoid appeal to truth as a semantic explanatory notion, as seen in the last chapter. To begin, autonomous discursive practitioners cannot explicitly ascribe knowledge <u>that</u> <u>p</u> to each other, since doing so would require possession of the concept of knowledge and, relatedly, the concepts of belief, truth, and justification, and having any of these concepts is essentially a matter of being able to engage in certain non-autonomous discursive practices, according to Brandom – as we shall see in chapter 7. Still, Brandom thinks that any autonomous discursive practitioner can, as part of her essential, elementary abilities to keep score, treat another as knowing <u>that p</u> *implicitly in practice,* by doing three things, corresponding to the three conditions of knowledge: first, attribute in practice to the other as acknowledged an assertional commitment <u>that p</u> (attribute belief), second, attribute in practice to the other entitlement to that acknowledgment (attribute justification), third, acknowledge assertional commitment <u>that p</u> *herself* (treat the attributed belief as true). Thus, apropos attribution of truth, Brandom claims that acknowledging assertional commitment <u>that p</u> oneself amounts, in the context of attributing an assertional commitment <u>that p</u> as acknowledged to another, to treating in practice the attributed commitment as true (1995a: 903; AR 117–9; MIE 202). Treating the other's belief <u>that p</u> as true does thus not require having the concept of truth oneself, but only requires having the elementary scorekeeping abilities to acknowledge an assertional commitment <u>that p</u> oneself and attributing assertional commitment <u>that p</u> as acknowledged to another. More generally, Brandom thinks that the ability to attribute knowledge *qua* true justified belief to another can be explained entirely in terms of the normative pragmatic vocabulary in terms of which the ability to participate in autonomous discursive practices is explained – the vocabulary of acknowledgments and attributions of commitments and entitlement. The JTB analysis of knowledge is for him merely a guiding light to craft this normative pragmatic account of attributing knowledge. To attribute knowledge, scorekeepers do not need any semantic, epistemic, and psychological concepts, but merely pragmatic know-how that they have *qua* autonomous discursive practitioners.

Based on this normative pragmatic approach to knowledge attribution, Brandom suggests that knowledge *itself* is a hybrid social deontic scorekeeping status, characterizable entirely in terms of the official scorekeeping vocabulary rather than in terms of truth and justification (1995a: 904). For a scorekeeper to know that p, Brandom claims, is for her to acknowledge assertional commitment that p, to be entitled to this acknowledgment, and for that entitlement to have the distinction to authorize any suitably positioned peer to acknowledge assertional commitment that p himself (MIE 203–4). (This interpersonal authorization must be distinguished from the way assertions as such authorize their own acceptance by interlocutors. The latter authorization is *prima facie* and is the defining feature of the speech act of assertion, as seen in chapter 3. The former interpersonal authorization is stronger and due to the fact that the speaker is *entitled* to the assertion.) Thus, Brandom thinks that he can account both for the nature of propositional knowledge itself and for a scorekeeper's ability to attribute propositional knowledge to another entirely in terms of the normative pragmatic vocabulary, which already fully describes autonomous discursive practices in general. If so, his acceptance of the JTB analysis of knowledge does not commit him to using the concepts of truth and justification as explanatory notions in epistemology.

Epistemic reliability

Brandom's most distinct contribution to epistemology proper is his elaboration of the nature of the justification condition of observational and, more generally, empirical knowledge – reliability – and the distinct way reliability licenses others to form beliefs. Brandom's version of epistemic reliabilism looks very different from more mainstream versions, prevalent in the epistemological literature today. To begin, whereas mainstream versions of epistemic reliabilism regard epistemic reliability as a naturalistic feature of a belief-forming process, fully describable in non-normative statistical terms and at best contingently dependent on processes of mutual social recognition, Brandom argues that reliability is irreducibly normative and essentially tied to normative social practices of assessing each other's reliability. Not only the semantic aspects of observational beliefs (their content) but also their epistemic aspects in abstraction from their content (their status as reliably or unreliably formed), is essentially normative and tied to processes of mutual social recognition (AR 112–22; MIE 214–15). Due to this added normative dimension, the epistemic status of a reliably formed observational belief contributes in its own right and in a distinct way to the belief's standing in the space of reasons, hence to its content.

Brandom's argument for this normative and social account of epistemic reliability takes Alvin Goldman's famous barn-façade case as its point of departure (Goldman 1976). Suppose Jones sees a nearby barn in good light and forms on this basis the observational belief that that's a barn. Since Jones is a cognitively normal adult speaker and as good as anybody at discriminating barns from other kinds of structures, we might think that no matter how we elaborate this scenario, Jones's observational belief is justified and, since it is also true, knowledge. Yet suppose the following elaboration: unknown to himself, Jones is in the middle of Barn-Façade County, a place dotted with hundreds of cleverly contrived barn façades – structures that look like barns but aren't barns. In fact, Jones is looking at the *only* real barn in the county. Goldman's intuition, which Brandom shares, is that under these circumstances Jones's belief, albeit true, is not knowledge after all. After all, Jones was epistemically lucky under the circumstances, and knowledge is incompatible with merely chancing on the truth. Specifically, had Jones been vis a vis any of the many nearby barn façades, he would still have formed an observational barn belief (as opposed to barn-façade belief) about it. Thus, Jones's actual barn belief is not justified because the process leading to its formation is, in the environment Jones finds himself in, highly unreliable. Goldman concludes that, in general, a belief is justified only if the process leading to its formation is reliable. Moreover, he concludes that, as the case at hand illustrates, such reliability often depends on external, environmental factors, inaccessible to the subject through reflection and introspection alone. After all, reflection and introspection alone cannot lead Jones to realize that he is in an environment dotted with barn façades.

So far Brandom concurs. However, Goldman goes one step further by claiming that the reliability of a belief-forming process per se, given the content of the belief formed, is a purely naturalistic feature of subject and environment, describable in entirely non-normative causal and statistical terms. Brandom rejects this further step (AR 112; MIE 210–3). The problem is that whether a belief-forming process is reliable, given the content of the belief formed, depends in part on the reference class of objects with respect to which such reliability is assessed. The process will count as reliable relative to some reference classes but not others. For example, the process leading up to Jones's barn belief in Barn-Façade County is unreliable relative to the reference class of barn-like structures in Barn-Façade County, which is the class we have in mind when we deny that Jones's belief is knowledge. On the other hand, the same token-process is reliable relative to the class of barns and barnlike structures in the entire nation. That reference class contains predominantly barns and only a few barn facades; that is, relative to *that* reference class the token-process giving rise to Jones's barn belief vis a vis the only barn in Barn-Façade County would yield mostly true beliefs and is thus reliable – though imperfectly so. Indeed, the same token-process is reliable with respect to the reference class containing as its only member the barn in front of Jones (the sole barn in Barn-Façade County): relative to that singleton, Jones's belief-forming process is perfectly reliable. In fact, the first reference class is the right one, Brandom and Goldman agree, for assessing the reliability of the token-process leading up to the formation of Jones's belief. But why? Brandom contends that no naturalistic causal or statistical feature of Jones's physiology and psychology and of his narrower or wider environment determines that this is the relevant reference class. Rather,

> [w]hat in practice privileges some of the reference classes with respect to which reliability may be assessed over other such reference classes is the attitudes of those who attribute the commitment whose entitlement is in question. Each interpreter implicitly distinguishes between reference classes that are relevant and those that are irrelevant to the assessment of reliability and hence of entitlement to claims, by the circumstances under which that interpreter accords cognitive authority to those claims. The sort of authority in question here is ... that of having an inheritable entitlement: the sort that supports successful deferrals by others (potentially including the interpreter). It is the scorekeeping social practices that actually govern the use of an expression (in particular the acknowledgment of entitlement to the commitments undertaken by its assertional use) that supply what is missing from pure reliability theories.
>
> (MIE 212–3)

Implicitly in practice we track and assess each other's assertional commitments and entitlements. For observational beliefs in particular, assessing entitlement involves assessing the reliability of the process leading up to the belief, which in turn requires selecting in practice the relevant reference class in the given context. And which reference class that is is determined by norms governing the scorekeeping practice. Accordingly, since a reporter's epistemic reliability depends on norms governing the scorekeeping practice it is thus a normative affair and, indeed, a mutually recognitive social affair.

Indeed, it is an irreducibly normative affair (AR 117). Any attempt to naturalize the norms for determining reference classes faces a version of the gerrymandering problem akin to the one regularist theories of rule-following face, as discussed in chapter 1:

> In the case of regularity theories of the correctness of the application of a concept, it is the boundaries of the concepts that can be gerrymandered in such a way as to preclude assessments of irregularity, and hence of error. In the case of reliability theories of entitlement, it is rather the boundaries of the reference class with respect to which reliability is assessed that can be gerrymandered in such a way as to preclude assessments of unreliability, and hence of lack of entitlement.
>
> (MIE 211)

No finite sequence of events, described naturalistically, determines how to correctly continue a sequence of past concept applications, because any continuation counts as correct in light of the sequence according to some rules, but not according to others, and no naturalistic feature of the past sequence of concept uses, or of the linguistic community, determines what the right rule is. Similarly, no token-process, described naturalistically, leading from an environing object to an observational belief determines whether the belief is reliably formed, because its formation counts as reliable in light of some reference classes but not in light of others, and no naturalistic feature of the token-process, the epistemic subject, and the subject's nearer or farther environment determines what the relevant reference class is. Instead, just as the rule capturing the correct continuation of a sequence of past concept applications is determined by implicit norms governing the social practices of correctly continuing the application of the concept, so the right reference class with respect to which reliability of a token belief-forming process is to be assessed is determined by implicit norms governing the social practices of correctly assessing reliability, which scorekeepers follow when they acknowledge and attribute assertional commitments corresponding to observation reports.

In accordance with this irreducibly normative and practice-dependent nature of epistemic reliability (though perhaps not implied by it), epistemic reliability, albeit external to the individual epistemic subject, is internal to the social practice of assessing reliability, in the sense that whether an individual's observational beliefs are formed reliably can in principle be found out by suitably positioned and informed scorekeepers. In principle (though often not in practice), an individual's degree of reliability in forming a certain observational belief can be determined through vigorous, persistent, collective engagement in the game of giving and asking for reasons: it is in principle accessible to reason itself. In this respect too Brandom's reliability theory differs from more mainstream reliabilist approaches to epistemic justification. The epistemic externalism of the latter, Brandom thinks, is extreme in severing the connection between reasoning and justification (reliability) entirely, holding that we may in fact be largely reliable observers and hence possessors of justified observational beliefs and knowledge, and yet in principle be unable to *ascertain* our epistemic status as reliable, justified observers through careful individual and collective reflective inquiry (1995a: 896–7). For example, someone who deems himself a lookout on a whale-watching boat near whale-like creatures, can, according to these mainstream approaches, in principle never ascertain through careful reflective reasoning and empirical inquiry, on his own or assisted by others, *that* he really is such a lookout in such circumstances, rather than merely someone to whom it appears that he is such a lookout in such circumstances because he has a vivid, coherent, long-lasting hallucination of that sort – a scenario familiar to students of Descartes. According to these mainstream reliabilist approaches, if he is in fact such a lookout on the sea, most of his observational whale beliefs are in fact reliably formed and hence epistemically justified. No individual or collective efforts to rationally reflect and inquire allow him to ascertain that fact, however. In general, according to mainstream reliabilist positions, a subjects' efforts to conscientiously and rationally reflect and inquire make no contribution to whether or not his observational beliefs are justified, nor do these efforts allow the subject to ascertain for himself the epistemic status of his observational belief. Rather, that status is entirely a matter of the kind of environment in which the subject happens to find himself – on the sea and seeing whales vs. in bed and hallucinating being on the sea and seeing whales.

In accordance with his view of epistemic reliability as irreducibly normative and social practice-dependent, though again perhaps not implied by it, Brandom thinks that such a radical divorce of epistemic reliability and justification from social practices of reason-giving and reason-seeking is absurd (1995a: 900). According to him, the combination of someone's de facto reliability in certain kinds of observational beliefs and her perfect insensibility to this fact can in principle be at most a local, isolated phenomenon, limited to an individual believer and specific kinds of observational beliefs (AR 110; KSA 897). Though an individual pottery expert may combine de facto reliability in discriminating Aztec from Toltec sherds with profound doubt that she has such reliability, it is in principle (though perhaps not in practice) possible for us, Brandom thinks, to ascertain the archeologist's de facto reliability in this case through sustained collective rational inquiry. Relatedly, Brandom maintains that it is impossible that most or all of the archeologist's observational beliefs may in fact be reliably formed without her having any sense of her by-and-large de facto reliability. If she were insensible to her de facto reliability as an observer of anything at all, she would not be a discursive scorekeeper speaking a natural language at all (199a: 905–6; AR 120–1). In short, epistemic reliability, albeit external to the individual in the described, limited sense, is internal to the social practices of giving and asking for reasons and assessing reliability, in the sense that social practitioners can in principle (though not always in practice) find out, in each case at hand, through sufficiently vigorous and sustained engagement in the practice, whether someone is epistemically reliable (1995a: 905).

The status of an observational belief that p as reliably formed *adds* to the belief's standing in the space of reasons, according to Brandom, in the sense that the belief is essentially a reason for others to form the belief that p:

the notion of reliability itself is essentially an *inferential* notion: a matter precisely of what is a reason for what. What must be kept in mind if one is to talk … the traditional language of justification as *internal* entitling and reliability as *external* entitling is that what they are internal or external *to* is not the practice of giving and asking for reasons, and is not the space of reasons, but rather the individual whose standings in that space are being assessed. For reliability is

precisely a matter of a *socially* articulated inference. For me to take
you to be a reliable reporter of lighted candles in darkened rooms is
just for me to endorse a particular pattern of reasoning; in particular,
it is for me to endorse the inference that could be made explicit by
saying:

> *If* in a darkened room *S* noninferentially acquires the belief that there
> is a lighted candle, *then* (probably) there is a lighted candle there. ...

> Knowledge is intelligible as a standing in the space of reasons,
> because and insofar as it is intelligible as a status one can be taken
> to achieve in the game of giving and asking for reasons. But it is
> essentially a *social* status

                                                          (1995a: 903–4)

Brandom calls the "inference" from attributing an acknowledged
observational assertional commitment that p to someone else as
reliably formed to acknowledging an assertional commitment that
p oneself a "reliability inference" (AR 120). The norms licensing
such a reliability inference are *sui generis* epistemic, that is, they
neither contribute to the semantic content that p of the assertional
commitment in question nor reduce to testimonial norms authorizing the default interpersonal inheritance of the assertional commitment that p (MIE 218). Reliability inferences are not literally
inferences, because genuine inferences are intrapersonal moves
while reliability inferences are interpersonal moves from implicit
attributions to acknowledgments of assertional commitments that
p. Hence the norms governing reliability inferences are not semantic norms contributing to the constitution of the content that p.
Calling reliability inferences "inferences" in an extended sense is
nonetheless fitting, because corresponding to the interpersonal
move from implicitly attributing to someone else an acknowledged
assertional commitment that p as reliably formed to acknowledging commitment to assert that p oneself is a genuine valid inference
from the *statement explicitly ascribing* the belief that p as reliably
formed to that person to the statement that p itself. Moreover, the
norms governing reliability inferences are unlike testimonial norms
authorizing the default interpersonal inheritance of the assertional
commitment that p, constitutive of the speech act of assertion,
in that reliability inferences are appropriate only in light of positive evidence of the observer's reliability. Whereas the *prima facie*
testimonial entitlement to acknowledging an assertional commitment that p based on someone else's say-so is overrideable by *any*
reason to the contrary, no matter how weak, the entitlement to

acknowledge an assertional commitment that p oneself based on an attribution of an acknowledged assertional commitment that p as reliably formed to another is overrideable only by specific evidence that that person is not reliable after all or that, despite his reliability (which, recall, is fallible), p is in fact false.

Empirical content

While the mechanisms and norms determining a speaker's degree of reliability to correctly apply a concept in observation reports are *sui generis* epistemic, in the sense that the semantics of the concept can be characterized substitution-inferentially in abstraction from them, the semantics of the concept "derives (at least in large part) from the *reliable differential responsive dispositions* that those who have mastered the concept exhibit with respect to their application" (MIE 119). The semantic norms constituting the concept are shaped by the epistemic practices and mechanisms of assessing each other's reliability in applying the concept to features of the non-linguistic environment and, in a sense, by these features themselves. This semantic dependency on these epistemic practices and these features renders a concept empirically contentful. Due to it Brandom's semantic inferentialism is broad (MIE 632).

The semantic dependency of concepts on features of the non-linguistic environment itself is possible because discursive practices *qua* practically intentional activities incorporate these features and *qua* practices comprising mechanisms for recollecting and revisiting these features on an ongoing basis allow these features themselves to constrain the semantic norms governing the game. Specifically, discursive practices include mechanisms to, on the one hand, deictically refer to environing features in the context of observation reports and to recollect such reference anaphorically and, on the other hand, more or less reliably apply general terms to these features in the context of these observation reports and to recollect these applications yet again anaphorically. Accordingly, players of the game of giving and asking for reasons are in a position, individually and collectively, to perpetually assess and reassess in practice the substitution semantic connections that they acknowledge regarding the general terms in use. In that way, the non-linguistic environment itself gradually leaves, mediated by the ongoing discursive practice and because the participants grant it that role, its mark on the very substitution semantic norms constituting empirical, predicative concepts. *This* is the mechanism due to which empirical concepts and terms are governed by substitution semantic norms reflecting, among other, laws and statistical regularities of nature, as discussed in the last chapter.

How exactly this works is a large and delicate topic for Brandom, which he has explored extensively over the decades. For one thing, the semantic dependency of empirical concepts and terms on the non-linguistic environment must not imply that the *reference* of these concepts and terms to these features becomes a constitutive feature of their semantics. Because that would undermine Brandom's commitment to strong inferentialism – his view that the substitution inferential features of terms and concepts alone constitute their semantics. For another thing, this semantic dependency on these non-linguistic environing features must not imply that these features themselves are intrinsically normative and, as such, the ultimate source of empirical semantic norms. For that would undermine Brandom's broadly Kantian commitment to our semantic autonomy – his phenomenalism about norms, according to which *we* are, by virtue of the normative attitudes we take in our discursive practices toward each other and the performances exchanged, the ultimate sources of the semantic norms binding us.

We will gradually deepen our understanding of Brandom's theory of empirical contentfulness by revisiting different aspects of it in the remaining chapters. For now, let's just get the ball rolling by looking at Brandom's appropriation, in MIE, of Hilary Putnam's famous twin-earth scenario (Putnam 1975):

> [A] broadly inferential approach can incorporate into its conception of the contents of empirical concepts the nonlinguistic circumstances in which they are correctly noninferentially applied. Thus the concept *water* and its twin-earth analog *twater*, which are by hypothesis alike except that one is appropriately applied to H_2O and the other to XYZ, counts as involving different *inferential* contents. This is so even though they fund inferential moves involving the same sorts of *noises*, from saying "That's water" to "That's liquid," for instance. For they involve different circumstances of appropriate application, and hence different inferential transitions from those circumstances to their consequences. So even though it is the practices of those whose concepts they are that confer on them their contents, the earthlings and twin-earthlings need not be able to tell that they have different concepts, if water and twater are indistinguishable to them. They are not omniscient about the inferential commitments implicit in their own concepts. For the [modern]

interpreter [familiar with modern chemistry] who is making sense of their practices, and who *is* able (not perceptually, but conceptually) to distinguish H_2O and XYZ, can understand transported earthlings as *mis*taking the XYZ they look at for water as *in*appropriately applying the concept they express with their word "water" to that unearthly stuff. The circumstances of appropriate noninferential application of the concept expressed by the English word "water" require that it be applied in response to a sample of H_2O.
          (MIE 119–20; see also MIE 631–2; BSD 185–6; EE 210–13)

Since speakers of English reliably produce observation reports involving the term "water" in the presence of water, samples of *water itself* – as ice, liquid, and vapor – have been incorporated into their discursive practices from the earliest beginnings. And since water is and has always been H_2O, there is a sense, vivid to us modern speakers of English, in which a (symmetric) substitution inferential norm has *always* related the concept expressed by our term "water" to the concept expressed by the modern English term "H_2O" – long before speakers concerned with the chemistry of earthly matter found out, after myriads of trial-and-error TOTE-cycles, that water is H_2O. From the perspective of modern English speakers, the meaning of "water" is thus external to individual speakers of English and indeed external to English speakers' collective understanding of "water" up to the development of modern chemistry, in the sense that, to us modern interpreters, pre-modern English speakers used, individually and collectively, the very concept <u>water</u> that all along was governed by this substitution inferential norm, even though these earlier speakers did not acknowledge (and, indeed, were in no epistemic position to acknowledge) this norm. On the other hand, from the viewpoint of modern interpreters, that semantic norm has nonetheless been all along internal to the *practice* of speaking English itself, since samples of water were all along incorporated into that practice, ready to be identified as H_2O (MIE 119–20; see also BSD 185–6).

Thus, from our viewpoint, if a pre-modern English speaker had, unbeknownst to herself, been teleported to twin-earth (a planet that superficially looks exactly like earth and that would have appeared to the pre-modern speaker exactly like earth in every respect, but whose underlying chemistry radically differs from earthly chemistry), she would have misapplied her English term "water" to the ubiquitous water-like, thirst-quenching, transparent liquid filling up the puddles and lakes on twin-earth, even though she was in no position to know that. That liquid is and has always been XYZ, not H_2O. Accordingly, since a symmetric substitution inferential norm has, sanctioned by the incorporated samples of water and the absence of samples of XYZ in pre-modern English discursive practices, all along related the English term "water" to the concept $\underline{H_2O}$, and not to the concept $\underline{XYZ}$, the pre-modern English speaker would have misapplied her term "water" to the transparent liquid on twin earth. Similarly, from our viewpoint, the noun "water" in twin-English – the language spoken by twin-earthlings, which is phonetically and syntactically exactly like English and *seems* to pre-modern English and twin-English speakers exactly like English in semantic respects as well – would have all along differed in meaning from the English term "water." After all, speakers of twin-English correctly apply *their* noun "water" in observation reports to XYZ and their practice thus incorporates samples of XYZ. Accordingly, a symmetric substitution inferential norm has always related *their* noun "water" to the concept $\underline{XYZ}$, never to the concept $\underline{H_2O}$. Their noun "water" has thus never expressed the concept water, but rather the concept twater.

Two features of Brandom's appropriation of Putnam's thought experiment are noteworthy. First, the appropriation does not compromise Brandom's commitment to strong inferentialism, that is, his view that inference is the only fundamental semantic notion. This appropriation indicates the sense in which Brandom's inferentialism is broad, because it indicates how the scorekeepers' practices of assessing each others' observation reports vis a vis the incorporated non-linguistic environing features for their reliability, and these features themselves, constrain the meaning of the empirical terms they use. However, neither the corresponding epistemic word-world relation of reliably applying these empirical terms in observation reports vis a vis these features nor any word-world relation of these features being *represented* by these empirical terms constitute the meaning of these empirical terms – not even in part. Rather, the meaning of these terms consists in their substitution inferential role alone. For example, the semantic significance of the samples of water incorporated into English discourse consists in the fact that these samples authorize, from the viewpoint of modern speakers of English in the context of these referential and epistemic activities, a substitution inferential relation between the English terms "water" and "H_2O." *That substitution inferential relation,* together with other such relations, constitutes the meaning of the English terms "water" and "H_2O," not the fact that observation reports involving these terms are justified just in case they are reliably produced vis a vis these samples or the fact that these terms represent the kind exemplified by these samples. Thus, in the semantic order of explanation, inference remains the only fundamental explainer, and Brandom's broad inferentialism remains, accordingly, strong.

Second, the appropriation of Putnam's thought experiment indicates how Brandom wants to resist the metaphysical realist view that the authority to determine the substitution inferential norm relating the English terms "water" and "H_2O" is *intrinsic* to water itself – as he should, in light of his broadly Kantian views about autonomy. According to Brandom, the authority of water to license this semantic norm depends, on the one hand, on all English speakers' normative social practices of referring and reliably responding to samples of water in discourse and, on the other hand, English speakers' *granting* water itself such authority. "Water" in English and twin-English differ, and have always differed, in their substitution inferential roles *according to us* modern speakers of English (who know about modern chemistry) – even when used by premodern speakers of the two languages – because *for us*, according to our honed practices, the terms are justifiably usable in observation reports only vis a vis, respectively, water and twin-water with their fundamentally different chemical compositions. Thus Brandom wants to resist the view that water and twin-water authorize these different substitution inferential roles intrinsically, in abstraction from the ongoing scorekeeping practices and interpretive activities on earth and twin-earth. These practices and activities, rather than merely relaying the inference license from water and twater themselves, "confer" this license, as Brandom says in the quote above, and are thus the ultimate sources of the license. We shall further examine this idea in chapters 7 and 8.

Observational and theoretical concepts

The mechanisms for producing observation reports are the source of the empirical contentfulness not only of natural-kind terms such as "water" or "gold," whose conditions of correct use depend on the essential micro-properties of the corresponding environing features (e.g., their chemical properties), but also of predicates such as "liquid," "transparent," "blue," "smooth," etc., whose conditions of correct use arguably do not depend on the corresponding features' essential micro-properties. The latter English terms can all be correctly used in observation reports about twin-water filling a lake on twin-earth on a sunny day.

Empirical concepts, according to Brandom, are any concepts that can be correctly applied in observational judgments as well as any concepts directly or indirectly substitution inferentially related to them – including theoretical concepts such as H$_2$O, DNA, or electromagnetic wave. At the same time, Brandom denies the traditional foundationalist picture of two essentially distinct kinds of empirical concepts – one kind usable to generate observational knowledge and the other usable only to generate empirical knowledge that is inferentially founded upon observational knowledge. That is, Brandom denies that there is, on the one hand, an essential semantic or epistemic distinction between observational vs. theoretical empirical concepts and knowledge and, on the other hand, a correlative essential ontological distinction between observable vs. theoretical objects, properties, or states of affairs. Following Sellars's suggestion, Brandom regards the distinction between the observational and the theoretical as methodological, rather than ontological (Sellars 1997: 84; TMD 362–3; EE 57–8). In one context, a certain empirical concept may only be properly applicable in non-observational empirical judgments. The context may shift, however – new scientific instruments and methods may be developed and scorekeepers may develop new sensitivities to reliably report environing features – and the same concept may then figure in the content of observational knowledge. Thus, at one point astronomers used the name "Neptun" to refer to an unobserved planet whose existence was stipulated to explain observed, unpredicted perturbations of the orbit of Uranus. In that context, Neptun was used as a theoretical singular concept. Later, astronomers managed to observe the stipulated planet directly, aided by more powerful telescopes, and in that shifted context they used the same singular concept observationally (TMD 362–3).

Even terms that are often considered to be paradigmatically theoretical may be used observationally, according to Brandom. Thus, a trained physicist may be able to reliably report the presence of mu mesons just by looking at a hooked vapor trail in a bubble chamber – hence to thereby express observational knowledge of the presence of mu mesons (MIE 222–3). In particular, Brandom resists the view that just because the physicist can also directly observe, in that context, the presence of a hooked vapor trail, and moreover offer her latter observation as a reason why she thinks mu mesons are present, her report of present mu mesons must after all be non-observational and inferred from her observational judgment of the presence of a hooked vapor trail. We must distinguish between inferential processes and inferential relations. The judgment that mu mesons are present is inferentially related to the judgment that a hooked vapor trail is present, given suitable collateral commitments. It does not follow, however, that the process of forming the former judgment involves an inference from the latter judgment. The trained physicist may form both judgments via two reliable, noninferential processes, just by looking at the bubble chamber – and then, when challenged, justify the riskier judgment by appealing to its inferential relation to the safer one. (On the other hand, a physics student may only be able to report the presence of muons inferentially, by observing the presence of a hooked vapor trail and inferring from that observation that mu mesons must be present.) In general, even entities that are traditionally considered paradigmatically theoretical can be directly observed by skilled observers, according to Brandom, and they are, in this sense, not ontologically, but at best methodologically, theoretical. Note, however, that although the same observable circumstances may give rise to proper observational uses of the concepts mu meson and hooked vapor trail the concepts are still different – because they have different consequences, hence different inferential roles. Thus, the presence of mu mesons can be inferred from the presence of a certain kind of vapor trail, but not vice versa. Mu mesons may be present in other ways than by forming a hooked vapor trail (MIE 223–4; 1997: 163–6; SOT chap. 6: 87–8; also Sellars 1997: 84).

These considerations extend to other kinds of concepts that are often thought to be essentially non-observational, such as dispositional concepts (fragile, toxic, courageous) and normative concepts (ungrammatical, entitled to enter the concert hall). All these concepts may be properly applied observationally by speakers who have cultivated the relevant sensitivities. Thus, normal native speakers of English, having the ability to reliably discriminate grammatical from ungrammatical speech and overhearing someone's ungrammatical usage of English, may form observational knowledge about the perceived speech: that it is ungrammatical (Brandom 2002c: 103). Indeed, unless they are linguists, they may do so without being able to offer persuasive reasons for their judgment when pressed – like the pottery expert. Similarly, the ticket checker at the entrance to the concert hall forms observational knowledge about the *normative status* of anyone presenting a valid ticket, <u>that she is entitled to enter</u>. And he can offer the validity of the ticket as a reason when pressed – like the expert physicist.

Intentional agency

The discursive practices of speakers of natural languages are tied not only to observable non-linguistic circumstances but also to non-linguistic circumstances realizable or realized through intentional action. The fundamental deontic statuses in theoretical reasoning are assertional commitments and entitlements to such commitments, as well as the inferential commitments linking them to each other. The fundamental deontic statuses in practical reasoning, that is, reasoning geared toward intentional action, are *practical commitments* and entitlements to such commitments, and the inferential commitments linking them to each other and to assertional commitments (MIE 234–6). Acknowledgments of assertional and practical commitments and of inferential commitments linking them to each other, and the correlative attributions of these deontic statuses in the scorekeeping practice, are thus the fundamental deontic attitudes of natural language users as such. Acknowledged assertional commitments are beliefs, in the empirical psychological, causally relevant sense of "belief." Acknowledged practical commitments, according to Brandom, are intentions, in the empirical psychological, causally relevant sense of "intention" (MIE 233).

Practical commitments are propositionally contentful, and their content, just like the content of their assertional counterparts, is their inferential role. Since the inferential role of practical commitments includes linkages not only to other practical but also to assertional commitments – what an agent might or must reasonably do depends not only on what else she is practically committed to, but also on what she believes and what it is reasonable for her to believe – the content of any practical commitment thus partially consists in its inferential relations to assertional commitments, and these inferential linkages also partially constitute the content of these assertional commitments. Brandom thus denies that the content of the assertions and assertional commitments of speakers of natural languages are determined merely by their inferential relations to other declarative statements and assertional commitments (MIE 234). A complete characterization of the content of assertional commitments for speakers of natural languages in Brandom's scheme of things must take into account their role in theoretical and practical reasoning.

Just as observational judgments and their ties to observable circumstances render discourse empirically contentful, so practical commitments and their ties to circumstances realizable through action renders them, as Brandom calls it, *practically* contentful (MIE 234). Brandom thinks of the relation between practical commitments and the non-linguistic circumstances realizable through action (as much as he reasonably can) by analogy to the relation between observable non-linguistic circumstances, perception, and assertional commitments. Just as observational judgments are directly elicited via noninferential processes of observing a non-linguistic circumstance, and these observational judgments are reasons for other assertional commitments, so certain kinds of intentions directly elicit noninferential processes of realizing certain non-linguistic circumstances in action, and other practical and assertional commitments are reasons for these kinds of intentions. Just as a constellation of observational judgments is a constellation of more or less reliable discriminatory responses to an observed situation, so realizing a non-linguistic circumstance through action is a more or less reliable discriminatory response to a constellation of intentions (MIE 235, 261). That is, perception stands to observed circumstances and to the more or less reliably produced observational judgments it gives rise to as action stands to the circumstances it more or less reliably realizes in response to a constellation of intentions. Both a participant's dispositions to more or less reliably form certain observational judgments under certain observable circumstances and in certain contexts, and his dispositions to act more or less reliably in response to certain intentions and in certain contexts, are brought into the space of reasons via their essential connection to reliability inferences. In the former case, this is the inference from the observation report and the treatment in practice of the observer as reliable to the *truth* of the report – acknowledgment of commitment to the content of the report oneself. In the latter case, it is the inference from the attribution in practice of certain intentions and of the reliability of the agent to fulfill these intentions, to the *success* of the action, that is, to the obtainment or realization of the intended state of affairs (MIE 236). Just as commitments to observation reports and to assertional commitments inferentially related to them are empirically contentful because these inferential relations are mediated by the noninferential processes of reliably producing them and the essential tie between these processes and normative practices of assessing reliability, so intentions that directly give rise to action and the practical commitments inferentially related to these intentions are practically contentful because these inferential relations are mediated by the noninferential processes to reliably realize the corresponding states of affairs in action and the essential tie between these processes and normative practices of assessing such reliability.

Just as what a speaker is really assertionally committed to usually deviates to some extent from the assertional commitments he acknowledges, so what he is really practically committed to usually deviates to some extent from the practical commitments he acknowledges. Practical commitments, like assertional ones, come in committive and permissive flavors. Thus in instrumental reasoning, being committed to a certain goal that is achievable in just one way commits one consequentially to realizing that goal by taking that way. On the other hand, if the goal is realizable in multiple ways, a commitment to the goal entitles, but does not commit, to realizing that goal by taking any of those ways: "there may be more than one way to skin a cat" (MIE 237). Brandom thinks that many of the norms of practical reasoning mirror the norms of theoretical reasoning (MIE 237). Thus, just as an assertional commitment that the car will go faster than 80 miles per hour today commits consequentially to an assertional commitment that it will be driven today, and entitles consequentially to an assertional commitment that it will be driven today by someone with a driver's license, so, Brandom thinks, a practical commitment that the car shall go faster than 80 miles today practically commits to that it shall be driven today and practically entitles to that it shall be driven today by someone with a driver's license (MIE 237).

Practical commitments, just like assertional ones, are essentially tied to their linguistic expressions. The linguistic statements expressing practical commitments are, according to Brandom and following Sellars, *shall-statements* (e.g. Sellars 1992, chap. 7). For example,

I shall open my umbrella

I shall wear a necktie

I shall not repeat the gossip about Bill Clinton

express the speaker's intentions to open his umbrella, to wear a necktie, and to not repeat the gossip about Bill Clinton (MIE 257–9). Shall-statements are not a species of assertion, but speech acts of their own kind. The main difference between assertions and shall-statements is that shall-statements do not in general have the dimension of interpersonal intra-content authority characteristic for assertions. Any assertion that p authorizes by default anyone who understands it to acknowledge an assertional commitment that p. Pre-theoretically, this feature of testimonial interpersonal authority reflects the fact that asserting that p puts p forward as objectively true, hence as true for everybody and thus in particular as true for everybody understanding the assertion. Shall-statements do not in general have this kind of interpersonal authority. They express intentions, and agents can legitimately differ and, indeed, conflict in their goals, plans, and projects. If I express to you my intention to drive to the airport to pick up a friend, that does not per se commit or entitle *you* to intend to drive to the airport as well, but would do so only under very specific circumstances – such as, for example, a prior agreement between us, or a private commitment on your part to do whatever I do, or certain quite far-fetched background conditions that would *morally* require you to go there too given that I go. In the absence of those, you could not demonstrate entitlement to intend to go to the airport as well simply by appealing to my statement ("Well, *he* goes") (MIE 239–40).

We saw in chapter 3 that other types of speech acts too lack the interpersonal authority characterizing assertions: assumptions, requests, questions, etc. One task that anyone elaborating Brandom's theory of practical reasoning and practical discourse faces would be to articulate the differences, in scorekeeping terms, between shall-statements and these other types of speech acts. True to his overarching Kantian predilections, Brandom alludes that the shall-statements expressing specifically *moral* practical commitments *do* share the dimension of interpersonal authority characterizing assertions. The morally good, like the true, is objective, Brandom insinuates, and moral shall-statements accordingly are like assertions in committing interlocutors and overhearers by default to acknowledge commitment to them in response (MIE 240). Once again, the task would be to articulate, in scorekeeping terms, what distinguishes assertions from moral shall-statements (which, after all, are practical statements) and moral shall-statements from non-moral ones.

Summary

Empirical inquiry is an ongoing feedback-governed process of rational engagement with the largely non-linguistic world. The feedback-governed process comprises the following: the non-linguistic features of the environment inquired into themselves; their perception; the noninferential formation of observational beliefs about these features based on such perception; the inferential formation of further non-observational beliefs and intentions to act based on these observational beliefs; and – often – the noninferential intentional alteration, based on these beliefs and intentions, of these environing features through non-linguistic actions. As part of these feedback-governed involvements, the environing features inquired into themselves literally become incorporated into the process of inquiry, according to Brandom: that is, they literally become part of discursive practices.

Brandom advocates a distinct *epistemically reliabilist* theory of observational and (more generally) empirical knowledge. Observational beliefs are formed noninferentially, based on perceptual encounters with the environment. They are justified, according to Brandom, to the extent that they are reliably formed. Pre-theoretically, forming an observational belief that p reliably means that the process leading to its formation tends to yield the formation of true beliefs. From the perspective of Brandom's theory, it means that the process leading to the formation of the belief authorizes a *reliability inference* from the attribution of the belief that p to the observer to the formation of the belief that p oneself. Knowledge that p is a hybrid deontic status, according to Brandon: to know that p means to acknowledge an assertional commitment that p (to believe that p), to be entitled to that acknowledgment (to be justified in believing that p), and for that entitlement to authorize others to acknowledge the assertional commitment that p themselves (to hold true that p). An observer's epistemic reliability to form certain observational beliefs noninferentially in particular is itself a deontic status, according to Brandom. Such epistemic reliability, Brandom argues, can only arise within irreducibly normative social practices of assessing each other's reliability and is therefore not merely a naturalistic, statistical feature of the observer – contra more familiar orthodox versions of epistemic reliabilism.

Brandom's epistemic reliabilism forges a middle path between orthodox epistemic externalist and internalist positions. It sides with orthodox externalism (hence with orthodox epistemic reliabilism) in accepting that we may occasionally be justified in forming an observational belief that p while being unable to ascertain through reflection and introspection alone that the belief is reliably formed (and hence justified). But it sides with internalism (contra orthodox epistemic reliabilism) in maintaining that the fact that the belief that p is reliably formed, and hence justified, is in principle (though not always in practice) detectable by someone through sufficiently vigorous *collective* engagement in rational, empirical inquiry – the game of giving and asking for reasons – and in particular through sufficiently vigorous engagement in the game of assessing each other's reliability. In this sense, Brandom's middle path amounts, as it were, to a social internalist approach to justification (AR 120).

The social deontic mechanisms of forming observational beliefs reliably are not only the source of empirical knowledge and justification, according to Brandom, but also (together with the similar mechanisms for reliable intentional agency) the source of empirical and practical content. Although the norms governing these mechanisms are not themselves semantic – they are not themselves substitution semantic norms – empirical concepts are, due to these mechanisms, governed by (for example) substitution semantic norms that reflect laws and statistical regularities of nature (witness the inference from being a well-struck match to lighting up) or the essences of natural-kind terms (witness the inference from water to H_2O). In general, due to these mechanisms, observational beliefs and all the beliefs and intentions inferentially related to them, as well as all the assertions and practical statements expressing them, have empirical (and practical) content.

6

Logical Discourse

The last three chapters brought into full view Brandom's theory of empirically contentful autonomous discursive practices – the practices we need to be able to engage in if we are to say anything at all using a natural language. What makes this theory philosophical is that, in Brandom's view (as we saw at the beginning of chapter 1), philosophy is ultimately concerned with the nature of reason, and the ability to participate in autonomous discursive practices constitutes, and hence demarcates, rational beings. Yet while Brandom's theory of autonomous discursive practices is philosophical, autonomous discursive practitioners as such are perfectly non-philosophical creatures. They can think and talk about the observable world and about what to do, draw inferences implicitly, track in practice each other's thoughts and commitments, coordinate their actions and hash out their disagreements in primitive discursive ways, etc., but they lack any words and concepts to say or think anything *about* any aspect of their rational activity. Using Hegelian language, these creatures are conscious but not yet self-conscious. They are capable of reasoning and rational discourse, but as yet perfectly incapable to reason and discourse *about* their reasoning and discoursing.

Brandom thinks that the concepts and vocabularies we use when we engage in thought and talk about reasoning and discourse – thought and talk that *makes explicit* essential features of our otherwise implicit rational and discursive abilities – are special, compared to the concepts and vocabularies we may use in autonomous discursive practices. The concepts and vocabularies used in such self-conscious thought and talk are in principle non-autonomous. Discursive practices that comprise their use can always in principle be stripped off them without rendering the remaining practice non-discursive.

This chapter introduces Brandom's theory of philosophical self-conscious thought and talk – its semantics and the pragmatic abilities needed to be a self-conscious, non-autonomous discursive practitioner.

Universal LX-vocabulary

Autonomous discursive practices vary vastly with regard to natural languages used, subject matters talked about, and the cultural or individual idiosyncrasies involved in such use. Yet as seen, Brandom thinks that behind such diversity is an essential, universal core. All autonomous discursive practices are exchanges of assertions and shall-statements. The performances exchanged have distinct normative inferential roles and interpersonal pragmatic significances, they have distinct subsentential structures and their semantically significant parts are anaphorically related in distinct ways. All participants in such practices are able to follow in practice the norms corresponding to these syntactic, semantic, and pragmatic features, by reliably acknowledging and attributing to each other in practice, in systematic interaction with the performances exchanged, certain constellations of assertional and practical commitments and entitlements, as well as (substitution) inferential and anaphoric commitments linking the acknowledged and attributed assertional and practical commitments and entitlements intrapersonally and interpersonally to each other and to the performances exchanged. And all participants respond largely reliably to these normative attitudes at any stage of the conversation, by saying something fitting to this context or by acting intentionally in certain ways, thus moving the discursive interaction to the next stage.

Merely autonomous discursive practitioners become non-autonomous and at least minimally philosophical discursive practitioners once their discursive practice begins to include thought and talk *concerning this essential, universal, reason-constituting core*. Philosophical concepts in the broadest sense, according to Brandom, are concepts that allow us to think and talk explicitly about any of those kinds of norms, attitudes, and structural features exemplified by, or present in, our hitherto autonomous discourse that are present in every autonomous discourse and belong to this core. These are special, "categorical," "pure," and "formal" framework concepts, according to Brandom, in a distinctly Kantian sense:

> To say that they are "categorical" ... means that they make explicit aspects of the *form* of the conceptual as such. For Kant, concepts are ... to be understood in terms of their role in judging. Categorical concepts express structural features of empirical descriptive judgments. What they make explicit is implicit in the capacity to make any judgments at all. ... [R]ather than describing how the world is, the expressive job of these concepts is to make explicit necessary features of the framework of discursive practices within which it is possible to describe how the world is. ... To say that these concepts are "pure" is to say that they are available to concept-users (judgers = those who can understand, since for Kant the understanding is the faculty of judgment) *a priori*. Since what they express is implicit in any and every use of concepts to make empirical judgments, there is no *particular* such concept one must have or judgment one must make in order to be able to deploy the pure concepts of the understanding.
>
> (EE 38–9; cf. also EE 175)

Consider an autonomous discursive practice where the participants make simple geometrical claims about environing objects, such as

A: That boulder is spherical
B: No. It's cubical. It has corners.

Now consider an expansion of this discourse, where the participants make the following claims:

(1) **It follows from the fact that** the boulder is cubical **that** it has corners
(2) **If** it is cubical **then** it has corners
(3) **Necessarily, everything** cubical has corners
(4) **Either** it has corners **or** it is spherical, **not both**
(5) It is **not** spherical, **because** it is cubical
(6) **Possibly,** it is spherical
(7) It is **not** spherical
(8) A **believes** **that the boulder is spherical**

(9) **Since** A **believes that** it is spherical, A **must believe that** it has **no** corners

(10) A **is committed to acknowledge that** it is cubical

Brandom wants to say that, due to the presence of the boldly printed vocabulary, each of these claims makes explicit a hitherto implicit aspect of the formerly unexpanded autonomous discursive practice. 1–5 make explicit *(substitution) inferential* and *(substitution) incompatibility* relations between some of the geometrical vocabulary: the general terms "being cubical," "having corners," and "being spherical." Depending on context, 6 may make explicit the *compatibility*, according to the speaker, of "The boulder is spherical" with actual concomitant assertional commitments (epistemic possibility), or the potential of the boulder to be spherical under *counterfactual circumstances* (metaphysical possibility); 7 makes explicit the speaker's *disavowal* of "It is spherical," and 8–10 make explicit the speaker's *attributions of assertional commitments* to A as, respectively, *acknowledged* and as *to be acknowledged consequentially* (undertaken). Furthermore, the features of the hitherto autonomous discursive practice so made explicit are all of kinds that must be present in every discursive practice at all. Accordingly, if we abstract away from the atomic component sentences contained in 1–10 (printed not in bold), belonging to the hitherto autonomous geometrical discourse, the remaining boldly printed sentence frames could be used in the context of any other sentences, belonging to any other discourse, to make explicit *the same kinds of features* present in these other discourses: (substitution) inferential and incompatibility relations, compatibilities and incompatibilities, acknowledged, attributed, and undertaken assertional commitments, and so on. In this sense, the boldly printed vocabulary is "categorical" or "formal." Rather than describing new, hitherto undiscovered features of the world, it helps make explicit structural features that must be implicitly present in any possible discourse at all.

Brandom calls any such categorical vocabulary *universally elaborated and explicative vocabulary* (universal LX-vocabulary) (BSD 47). Species of such vocabulary are logical and meta-logical vocabulary ("It is not the case that," "and," "or," "if … then … ," "some," "all," "is identical with," "follows from," "is (in)compatible with," etc.), modal vocabulary ("necessarily," "possibly"), normative vocabulary ("committed to," "entitled to," "should," "might," "must not," etc.), intentional vocabulary ("believes that," "intends that," "acknowledges commitment/entitlement to," etc.), traditional semantic vocabulary ("is true," "refers to," "represents," etc.), and epistemic vocabulary ("knows that," "is justified," "is reliable," etc.). The central use of all such vocabulary is to make explicit semantic and pragmatic features of the discourse the speakers themselves engage in, which are kinds of features that must be present in any discourse at all.

Algorithmic elaboration

Let's set aside for a moment the question in which sense universal LX-vocabulary is "explicative" and focus first on the sense in which it is "elaborated." All practices comprising the use of some universal LX-vocabulary are, ultimately, elaborated from some autonomous discursive practices, and they contain these autonomous discursive practices within them, in the sense that every participant in the expanded practice is also able to participate in the autonomous practice from which the expanded practice is ultimately elaborated (though not vice versa). These elaborations are, however, hierarchically ordered. Some are further removed from the original autonomous practice than others, in the sense that, though ultimately elaborated from that original practice, they are more immediately elaborated from some intermediate non-autonomous practice that is elaborated from the original practice in some more straightforward way. For example, the non-autonomous practice that includes use of the conditional "If it is cubical then it has corners" (second in the list above) is elaborated from the original autonomous geometric discourse, and that non-autonomous practice in turn may serve as the basis for elaborating the more removed non-autonomous discursive practice that includes the use of general statements *about* the conditional, such as

(11) The central use of "if p then q" is to make explicit that "q" is a consequence of "p"

The practice that includes uses of 11 is thus at least two levels of elaboration removed from the original autonomous geometrical discourse, though it is still ultimately elaborated from it.

What appears in elaborated form at each higher level, according to Brandom, are the *pragmatic* features and abilities necessary and sufficient for engaging in the lower-level practices, from which the higher-level practice is reached. Consider an arbitrary lower-level practice and a practice one level above. The pragmatic features and abilities present in the lower-level practice suffice to make certain statements using exclusively lower-level vocabulary. In Brandom's terminology, these features and abilities are practice-vocabulary sufficient (PV-sufficient) for making statements involving exclusively lower-level vocabulary (BSD 9). Similarly, the more encompassing pragmatic features and abilities characterizing the higher-level practice are PV-sufficient for making statements containing both lower-level vocabulary and new, higher-level universal LX-vocabulary that makes explicit structural features of the old, lower-level practice that were merely implicitly present in it.

Apropos elaboration, according to Brandom, the pragmatic abilities PV-sufficient to make statements in the higher-level practice are *algorithmically elaborated* from the pragmatic abilities PV-sufficient to make statements in the lower-level practice (BSD 33, 52–3). In general, an ability is algorithmically elaborated from a set of more basic abilities just in case "exercising the target ability just is exercising the right basic abilities in the right order and under the right circumstances" (BSD 26). For example, the ability to do long division is an algorithmic elaboration of the more basic abilities to multiply, to subtract, and to manipulate numbers in a few other elementary ways. Someone may be able to multiply, subtract, and do these other elementary things without being able to long divide, but not vice versa. Still, to long divide one number from another is nothing but going through a sequence of steps of multiplying, subtracting, and doing some of these other elementary procedures, and it thus is a novel skill only in the minimal sense that it applies the old, basic skills *in the right order* (BSD 26).[1] According to Brandom, the pragmatic abilities PV-sufficient for making statements in the higher-level practice, involving some universal LX-vocabulary, are similarly algorithmically elaborated from the pragmatic abilities PV-sufficient for participating in the lower-level practice. Applying the former pragmatic abilities, Brandom thinks, is nothing but executing, in the right order, a sequence of the latter abilities. Since the higher-level practice thus comprises new pragmatic ingredients only in the minimal sense of comprising old pragmatic ingredients applied in the right order, the pragmatic abilities PV-sufficient to participate in the old, lower-level practice are in this sense *practice-practice sufficient* (PP-sufficient) for the new, more expressive, higher-level practice (BS 26–7).

Furthermore, among the pragmatic abilities PV-sufficient to participate in the lower-level practice are pragmatic abilities essential to, and universally present in, any discourse at all – such as the abilities to assert, to infer, to respond differentially, etc. These abilities are, in this sense, *universally practice-vocabulary necessary* (universally PV-necessary) for using the lower-level vocabulary (BSD 41). Brandom claims that the pragmatic abilities PV-sufficient for using the new, higher-level universal LX-vocabulary per se, in abstraction from other more idiosyncratic (and hence non-universally PV-necessary) features of the higher-level practice that are carried over from idiosyncratic features of the lower-level practice, are algorithmically elaborated *exclusively* from such universally PV-necessary abilities present in the lower-level practice. What is more, they are algorithmically elaborated from precisely those universally PV-necessary abilities present in the lower-level practice whose exercising yields the universal, structural feature of the lower-level practice that this piece of new universal LX-vocabulary *makes explicit* in the context of higher-level statements (BSD 44). In other words, these lower-level universally PV-necessary abilities are PP-sufficient for the use of the new, higher-level universal LX-vocabulary per se (BSD 44). This is why the quote above describes the concepts expressed by universal LX-vocabulary as "pure" and "a priori" in a broadly Kantian sense. They are "pure" and "a priori" in the sense that there are "no *particular* [ordinary empirical] concepts one must have … in order to be able to deploy the pure [universal LX-]concepts" (EE 39). Rather, the pragmatic abilities universally PV-necessary for employing *any arbitrary* ordinary empirical concepts – necessary pragmatic abilities for the possibility of participating in any arbitrary discourse at all, in abstraction from any additional idiosyncratic pragmatic abilities needed for employing *some particular* ordinary empirical concepts – are PP-sufficient for deploying the universal LX-vocabulary.

These claims are at the core of Brandom's program of meaning-use analysis, concerned with algorithmically elaborating simple pragmatic abilities into more complex ones that allow speakers to say new things. Brandom considers this program as the point where his overall project makes contact with Classical AI. Classical AI is concerned with programming digital computers (Turing Machines, basically) such that the behavior of these machines is indistinguishable from intelligent behavior. The most important feature of digital computers, according to Brandom, is precisely that all of their behavior is algorithmically elaborated from very simple basic abilities – ultimately, the ability to manipulate sequences of "0"s and "1"s by going through potentially very long, tedious sequences of a handful of very simple operations in accordance with an equally tedious set of instructions (the program). Brandom thinks of meaning-use analysis as a generalization and pragmatization of classical AI, in the sense that, while the simple abilities from which the behavior of Turing Machines is algorithmically elaborated are essentially syntactic, symbol-manipulating abilities, the computational devices stipulated by Brandom's meaning-use analyses algorithmically elaborate elementary pragmatic abilities: the pragmatic abilities PV-sufficient for participating in autonomous discursive practices (and in particular the universally PV-necessary ones among those), such as acknowledging and attributing assertional, (substitution) inferential, and anaphoric commitments, etc. Still, Brandom thinks that the abilities of non-autonomous discursive practitioners to algorithmically elaborate these pragmatic abilities are in principle implementable by computational devices very much like Turing Machines (BSD 74–7).

Brandom illustrates what such an algorithmic elaboration of pragmatic abilities might look like by sketching how the practice of using conditionals, such as example 2, is algorithmically elaborated from an autonomous discursive practice, such as our geometrical discourse (BSD 45). Among the universally PV-necessary core of any autonomous discursive practice are the abilities to make assertions/acknowledge assertional commitments, to acknowledge inferential commitments relating certain statements P and Q of the practice, and to reliably respond differentially to assertions or changes in one's deontic attitudes by altering the score. These three core abilities, claims Brandom, may be algorithmically elaborated into the more complex ability to assert conditional statements under the right scorekeeping circumstances, and to update the score properly in response to such statements. Since the participants in autonomous discursive practices already know how to make assertions, they can in principle be taught to assert "If P then Q" (where the variables are replaced by the statements of the original practice that the variables stand for). Moreover, since they already know how to acknowledge material inferential commitments regarding P and Q and to respond differentially to features of their own score, they can in principle be taught to respond differentially to their own acknowledged inferential commitments regarding P and Q by acknowledging an assertional commitment to "If P then Q." These are the pragmatic *circumstances* of proper uses of "If P then Q": if one acknowledges an inferential commitment from P to Q, then one should acknowledge an assertional commitment to "If P then Q." Furthermore, participants in autonomous discursive practices can in principle be taught to acknowledge, in response to acknowledging an assertional commitment to "If P then Q" (entitlement to which they may have inherited interpersonally from someone else's assertion of the conditional), an inferential commitment from P to Q. These are the pragmatic *consequences* of acknowledging an assertional commitment to "If P then Q": if one acknowledges an assertional commitment to "If P then Q," then one should acknowledge an inferential commitment from P to Q. In this sense, thinks Brandom, mastery of the pragmatic circumstances and consequences of conditional statements is algorithmically elaborated from the universal PV-necessary abilities to assert/acknowledge assertional commitments, to acknowledge inferential commitments, and to respond differentially to assertions or changes in one's own deontic attitudes by altering the score (BSD 45). The pragmatic circumstances and consequences of other types of universal LX-vocabulary are similarly algorithmically elaborated, Brandom claims, from universally PV-necessary features of discourse. For example, we can think of the ability to use negations such as example 7, or belief ascriptions such as example 8, as algorithmically elaborated from the universal PV-necessary abilities to disavow or to implicitly attribute assertional commitments to others.

Someone might object that, according to this illustration, an expansion of the autonomous geometric discourse into one that also involves color vocabulary should count as an algorithmic elaboration too. Therefore, then, color vocabulary should also count as universal LX-vocabulary. After all, the expanded practice (involving color vocabulary) only involves more of the same old universal PV-necessary abilities to respond differentially (this time to the color of objects), to assert (this time regarding the colors of objects), and to acknowledge inferential commitments (this time connecting sentences involving color vocabulary). Yet Brandom would surely reply that, although the abilities PV-sufficient to use color vocabulary certainly involve these old universal PV-necessary abilities (which must, after all, be present in any discourse at all), it also involves *new idiosyncratic* pragmatic abilities which were not present in the old geometric discourse per se, such as the abilities to respond differentially to perceived color (rather than shape), to acknowledge inferential commitments involving color vocabulary (rather than shape vocabulary), etc. The pragmatic abilities PV-sufficient to use color vocabulary are thus not algorithmically elaborated *exclusively* from the old abilities PV-sufficient for the old geometric discourse per se, let alone from the universal PV-necessary abilities among those, and the new color vocabulary does thus not count as universal LX. Algorithmically elaborated abilities, after all, are new, complex abilities whose execution consists in the application of exclusively old abilities, in the right order.

Things are less straightforward than this, however, as John MacFarlane has commented. First, the ability to algorithmically elaborate discursive pragmatic abilities is not *itself* deployed in autonomous discursive practices, though it is certainly deployed when speakers use universal LX-vocabulary.[2] Thus, that ability does not seem to be a universal PV-necessary ability, but rather one that must be brought to bear in usages of non-autonomous, universal LX-vocabulary *in addition* to all the algorithmically elaborated old abilities deployed in autonomous discursive practices (MacFarlane 2008: 59). Second, according to MacFarlane, the ability to deploy universal LX-vocabulary appears to involve other new abilities as well (MacFarlane 2008: 58). Examples might be the new syntactic ability to use operators (locutions that allow us to form a single molecular sentence out of one or two smaller sentences) in addition to singular terms and predicates; or the ability to acknowledge commitments to new species of inferences, such as substitution inferences generated by substituting into molecular compound sentences whole component *sentences* for other component sentences (rather than inferences generated by substituting terms for terms) (MIE 338–60) or inferences involving premises that vary from the conclusion in syntactic complexity – all in contrast to the substitution inferences we are familiar with from autonomous discursive practices (see chapter 4). Third, MacFarlane argues that we can think of abilities to algorithmically elaborate as varying both in kind and in degrees of strength. Speakers with the same autonomous discursive abilities may be able to algorithmically elaborate these abilities in various ways and to varying degrees, depending on their respective abilities to algorithmically elaborate themselves. Accordingly, for the two speakers, different sets of vocabularies would count as universally LX (MacFarlane 2008: 60).

MacFarlane's commentary raises important issues about Brandom's program. Which algorithmically elaborative abilities do human speakers have? Are they universal? Are they innate? Raising such questions is less a critique of Brandom's program of meaning-use analysis than it is an indicator that this program opens up an area of research in cognitive psychology and, in particular, research that expands the program of classical AI (BSD 74–7; Brandom 2008(c): 141). Needless to say, in the present limited space we cannot even take a crack at exploring how any of these issues may be resolved.

Explication

Let's now clarify the sense in which universal LX-vocabulary makes explicit otherwise implicit universal aspects of lower-level discursive practices. Brandom distinguishes between what is said by, or follows from, a given claim *semantically*, in virtue of the proposition expressed, and what is said by, or follows from, someone's *making* the claim *pragmatically*, that is, how making the claim interacts with the score. For example, apropos conditional statements he says that:

> The view is that what I am *doing* when I say that … if this piece of copper is heated to 1084 degrees C, it will melt, is endorsing a certain kind of inference. I am not *saying that* that inference is good.
>
> (BSD 101)[3]

By claiming "If P then Q" the speaker makes explicit his acknowledgment of an inferential commitment from P to Q (circumstances of application), and the audience's proper default response to the claim, normatively expected by the speaker, is to acknowledge an inferential commitment from P to Q (consequences of application). But semantically the claim simply says <u>that if P then Q</u>. The proposition expressed does not involve the concepts <u>consequence</u>, <u>speaker</u>, <u>acknowledged inferential commitment</u>, <u>obligation to acknowledge commitment</u>, and thus does not semantically describe the circumstances and consequences it pragmatically makes explicit. Similarly for negations "Not-P" or belief ascriptions "A believes that p." They make pragmatically explicit, respectively, that P is (to be) rejected and that an assertional commitment <u>that p</u> is (to be) attributed to A, but they do not say any of these things in virtue of their respective propositional meaning <u>that not-P</u> and <u>that A believes that p</u>.

Any universal LX-vocabulary V is thus a *pragmatic meta-vocabulary* (BSD 10), according to Brandom, in the sense that assertions in which V is the main operator – that is, where V does not occur merely in a subordinated clause, embedded in a larger clause (see below) – allow speakers to make explicit what is (to be) done by scorekeepers leading up to, and in response to, the assertion without in general saying so in virtue of the proposition expressed. Those who master the circumstances and consequences of assertions involving V as the main operator *ipso facto* know what they need to do *qua* scorekeepers leading up to, and in response to, these assertions, and while the assertions pragmatically express that this is what needs to be done, they do not in general semantically say so.

Despite their semantic limits, expanded practices that allow for unembedded uses of conditionals, negations, or belief ascriptions nonetheless equip speakers with improved abilities to discourse. Thus, apropos conditionals,

> [w]here before one could only in practice *take* or *treat* inferences *as* good or bad, after the algorithmic introduction of conditionals one can endorse or reject the inference by explicitly *saying* something, by asserting or denying the corresponding conditionals.
>
> (BSD 46)

Although autonomous discursive practitioners acknowledge in practice inferences and incompatibilities between the ordinary empirical atomic statements – the only statements they are able to make – they lack the expressive resources to convey to each other which inferences are (to be) acknowledged. Thus, individual autonomous practitioners have to glean for themselves from these exchanges which inferences to acknowledge, in a perennial, cumbersome implicit, trial-and-error effort to make best sense of the ways in which their exchanges of ordinary empirical statements tend to go – presumably with considerable latitude and discrepancies between speakers. On the other hand, speakers able to use the conditional may convey to each other which inferential commitments between ordinary empirical statements are (to be) acknowledged. Asserting a conditional pragmatically thematizes, though it does not semantically describe, for every participant what follows from what, and it thus has the discourse-enhancing effect of unifying a group of speakers with regard to the inferential commitments they pragmatically express as (to be) acknowledged or (if the conditional is dismissed) as (to be) rejected.

Semantics for logical vocabulary

So far, this is a simple "expressivist" account of the sense in which universal LX-vocabulary explicates. As such, it faces all the thorny questions any version of expressivism faces, and unless Brandom addresses these issues, no one should be particularly impressed with it. In general, expressivism seeks to explain the significance of certain vocabularies by treating them as expressing subjective attitudes on the speaker's part, rather than as describing features of the objective world. To illustrate, a simple expressivism about aesthetic vocabulary ("beautiful") or semantic vocabulary ("true") may treat the significance of such vocabularies in statements such as:

(12) Grünewald's Isenheim Altar is beautiful
(13) It's true that silver is heavier than gold

as consisting in their expressing the speaker's attitude of aesthetic appreciation taken toward the Isenheim Altar or her attitude of endorsement taken toward the proposition that silver is heavier than gold. "Is beautiful" and "is true," in these contexts, do not describe the Isenheim Altar as beautiful or the proposition that silver is heavier than gold as true, according to simple expressivism – they do not ascribe the properties of, respectively, beauty or truth to these items – but rather express the subjective attitudes (of aesthetic appreciation or endorsement) taken by the speaker toward these items.

Brandom's pragmatically expressive account of universal LX-vocabulary, as presented so far, is expressivist in this sense. For example, by asserting "If P then Q," the speaker does not describe P and Q as standing in the consequence relation to each other, on this account, but rather expresses his subjective normative attitudes of acknowledging an inferential commitment regarding P and Q and of attributing such a commitment (as to be acknowledged) to his interlocutors. Brandom's theory of universal LX-vocabulary as pragmatically explicative is in the tradition of expressivist theories of the significance of a vocabulary.

A formidable technical challenge to any simple expressivist theory, as well as to its more sophisticated descendants, is the Frege-Geach problem. The problem is how to account for the significance of the targeted vocabulary in *embedded* contexts, that is, in subordinated clauses that appear within the context of a larger statement. For example, in the context of

(14) If Grünewald's Isenheim Altar is beautiful, then so is Bacon's portrait of Innocent X
(15) If it's true that silver is heavier than gold, then hydrogen is also heavier than gold

"is beautiful" and "is true," occurring in the subordinated clauses "Grünewald's Isenheim Altar is beautiful" and "it's true that silver is heavier than gold" do not express the speaker's attitudes of aesthetically appreciating the Isenheim Altar or of endorsing the proposition <u>that silver is heavier than gold</u>. Rather, by asserting 14 or 15, the speaker insinuates that she takes precisely the opposite attitudes toward these items. Similarly, in the context of

(16) It is not the case that if P then Q

the "if … then … ", occurring in the subordinated clause "if P then Q" does not make explicit the speaker's normative attitudes of acknowledging and attributing an inferential commitment from P to Q. Rather, due to the "It is not the case that," which is the main operator in 16 as a whole, someone asserting 16 makes, in Brandom's sense, pragmatically explicit the opposite normative attitudes – that the inferential commitment from P to Q is (to be) rejected – while the subordinated clause "if P then Q" does not, in the context of 16, make anything pragmatically explicit at all. Still, the subordinated conditional clause "if P then Q" is obviously significant or meaningful, and it makes a crucial contribution to the pragmatic significance and expressive power of 16 as a whole. Without that embedded conditional clause, the speaker, asserting 16 could not make pragmatically explicit that the inferential commitment from P to Q is (to be) rejected.

These considerations do not so much show that Brandom's expressivist theory of the pragmatically expressive powers of universal LX-vocabulary is to be rejected, but rather that it is to be supplemented by a *semantic* theory of the *propositions expressed* by sentences involving (embedded or unembedded) uses of universal LX-vocabulary. We need to know, in Brandom's official inferential role semantic and normative pragmatic terms, what, for any embedded or unembedded occurrence of a piece of universal LX-vocabulary in a potentially long sentence containing several pieces of universal LX-vocabulary, the overall proposition expressed is and how the various embedded or unembedded occurrences of universal LX-vocabulary in the sentence systematically contribute to that overall proposition. Relatedly, we need to know how scorekeepers may, in principle, calculate the overall proposition expressed by this long sentence, using only the resources that the theory of scorekeeping affords them – ultimately, the pragmatic abilities they have *qua* autonomous discursive practitioners plus the ability to algorithmically elaborate these pragmatic abilities.

This is a formidable technical challenge. To his credit, Brandom has to date made a serious effort to at least begin tackling it by developing, with his collaborator Alp Aker, a detailed semantic theory for four pieces of universal LX-vocabulary – negation, conjunction, and the modalities (possibility and necessity) – and their semantic interactions in any statements containing any mix of them (BSD chap. 5, especially 141–75).[4] In this limited space, I cannot go into the technical details of this effort, but shall limit myself to presenting two general features of it. First, Brandom and Aker can obviously not give the semantics of the four pieces of logical vocabulary in terms of truth, truth-functions, truth at a world, etc., familiar to students in an introductory class in formal logic, but must rather give it in terms of Brandom's favored normative pragmatic vocabulary: preservation and preclusion of commitment and entitlement to performances. Accordingly, the basic semantic explainer in their semantics for negation, conjunction, necessity, and possibility is the notion of the *incompatibility* of commitments and entitlements to linguistic performances in, ultimately, autonomous discursive practices, which captures one dimension of the performances' propositional meaning *qua* inferential role (the other two being commitment-preserving and entitlement-preserving inferences). Although this *incompatibility semantics* for negation, conjunction, possibility, and necessity avoids appeal to truth, truth-functionality, etc. Brandom and Aker claim to have proven that, within their incompatibility semantic framework, these four pieces of logical vocabulary turn out to behave logically in exactly the same way as they behave when treated classically in terms of truth. For example, on their incompatibility semantic approach, any sentence S is equivalent to its double negation Not-Not-S; S entails another sentence T just in case Not-T entails Not-S; a conjunction of any sentence S with its negation Not-S entails every sentence at all, etc. (BSD 128, 156–7). Similarly, on the incompatibility semantic treatment, the modal operators behave logically just as they behave within the standard system for modalities S5, given in terms of truth at a possible world. For example, if Necessarily S, then Necessarily Necessarily S; if Possibly S, then Necessarily Possibly S, etc. (BSD 129). In short, although the incompatibility semantic framework differs starkly from the classical framework, accepting this framework does not require (Brandom and Aker claim to have proven) accepting or rejecting any logical theorems involving the four pieces of logical vocabulary other than the classical theorems involving them.

Second, an important criterion of adequacy that Brandom claims the incompatibility semantics of the four pieces of logical vocabulary meets is that any extension of an old discourse by introducing any of these pieces is *conservative*. In general, an addition of new vocabulary to an old discourse is conservative just in case the addition does not change any of the old (substitution) inferential relations holding just between the old vocabulary (MIE 125; BSD 147–8). The requirement that the introduction of specifically logical vocabulary into an old discourse be conservative in this sense seems pivotal. The role of logical vocabulary is to enable speakers to make explicit otherwise implicit aspects of their old discourse *without changing the meaning of the old vocabulary*. Yet since the meaning of, for example, the ordinary empirical vocabulary used in some autonomous discursive practice consists in its substitution inferential relations to other such vocabulary used in that discourse, if the introduction of logical vocabulary altered these inferential relations, the old vocabulary would, in the context of the new extended practice, take on new meaning, and logical claims in the extended practice would thus fail to make explicit aspects of the old inferential role of that vocabulary, and hence fail to make explicit structural features of the old practice. Brandom and Aker claim to prove that any introduction of negation, conjunction, or the modalities into an old discourse does indeed, according to their incompatibility semantic account, meet this requirement of conservativeness.

It is important that the requirement of conservativeness is restricted to the introduction of logical and, more generally, universal LX-vocabulary. The introduction of new (non-explicitating) ordinary empirical vocabulary into some discourse often alters some of the (substitution-)inferential relations in the old ordinary empirical vocabulary, and its doing so is frequently even desirable. Thus the introduction of the Newtonian concept of gravity into pre-Newtonian physical discourse altered the old substitution inferential role of the concept <u>heaviness</u> in ways pre-Newtonian speakers would not have dreamed of, by obliging them to acknowledge an inferential commitment from "___ is heavy" to "___ attracts other heavy objects." What made the alternation acceptable and fertile was that the addition of Newton's concept of gravity *harmonized* the old pre-Newtonian physical discourse, in the sense that it eased old internal tensions within the space of reasons delineating that discourse (such as the problem why the planets move in regular elliptical orbits around the sun without being held by anything). In general, for the introduction of new non-logical vocabulary into discourse only the weaker requirement holds that adding the new vocabulary preserve or increase the harmony among the (substitution-)inferential relations in the old vocabulary, that is, that it does not oblige the speakers to new, obviously untenable commitments. Brandom uses an example from Dummett to illustrate what a non-harmonious extension of a discourse looks like: the introduction of the term "Boche" during World War I into English, where anyone who is German is *ipso facto* a Boche and any Boche is *ipso facto* cruel. The introduction of "Boche" into English discourse obliges anyone using this term to acknowledge a SMSIC from "___ being German" to "___ being cruel", hence, once quantifiers and modal operators are non-conservatively introduced, commits him assertionally to "Necessarily, every German is cruel." Since the latter claim is obviously false, the introduction of "Boche" thus amounts to a blatantly non-harmonious extension of previous English discourse and must be rejected (MIE 126–7).

In summary, whereas the introduction of new non-universal LX-vocabulary into discourse is often non-conservative, and such non-conservativeness is welcome to the extent that the introduction increases the harmony of the discourse, the introduction of logical vocabulary must, Brandom requires, always be conservative. And he and Aker claim to have proven that, on their incompatibility semantic treatment, the introduction of negation, conjunction, and the modalities into an old discourse is indeed conservative.[5]

Modality

We saw in chapter 4 that the material (substitution) inferential and (substitution) incompatibility relations governing ordinary empirical vocabulary come with ranges of counterfactual robustness. Many of these inferences and incompatibilities are actually good, or obtain, and would remain so under a wide range of counterfactual circumstances, but the occurring of circumstances outside that range would undermine their goodness, or their obtainment. Thus, the inference from "That match is well struck" to "It will light" may actually be good, and would have remained so had circumstances been different in many ways (match struck by a girl instead of a boy, boy struck it over *there* rather than over *here*, boy wore a red T-shirt rather than the blue one, etc.). But circumstances outside that range would have thwarted the goodness of the inference (match damp, oxygen absent, etc.). Similarly, "Lightning one mile away now" and "Silence here for the next ten seconds" may actually be incompatible, and would have remained so had circumstances been different in many ways (it's foggy here rather than clear, six people are here rather than three, etc.), but circumstances outside that range would have made the two statements compatible (we are in a soundproof room, lightning ignited inside a big vacuum chamber, etc.). As we saw, an essential aspect of being a minimally competent speaker is to have some sense of these ranges of counterfactual robustness for the inferences and incompatibilities to which commitment is acknowledged. That is, a speaker must know in practice how adding to, or subtracting from, the collateral assertional commitments she actually acknowledges would strengthen, weaken, override, or leave unscathed the inferential and incompatibility commitments she actually acknowledges. Of course, the speaker may misconstrue in practice the range of counterfactual robustness for some of the inferential and incompatibility commitments she acknowledges. For example, she may fail to appreciate how the absence of oxygen would affect her inferential commitment from "That match is well struck" to "It will light." Still, she must draw some line. If she would be altogether insensitive to how altered factual collateral circumstances might affect the inference, we might begin to doubt that she has any sense of what "match," "being well struck," "lighting up," etc., mean.

A consequence of this picture, according to Brandom, is that all discursive practices, including autonomous ones, essentially comprise a *modal* dimension, concerning what is *possible* and *necessary*, to which the participants must be sensitive. Modality is built into even the simplest forms of ordinary empirical discourse, according to Brandom. What follows from, or is incompatible with, what depends on what *must, must not,* or *may also* be the case. Oxygen must be present for the match to light, whereas strong wind must be absent, though the match may have been struck by a girl. Of course, the participants' sensitivity to this modal dimension does yet again not require that they employ modal concepts or modal vocabulary, according to Brandom. Rather, speakers may exhibit such modal sensitivity merely implicitly in practice.

On the other hand, speakers who have modal vocabulary at their disposal may use it to make aspects of this otherwise implicit modal dimension of their discourse explicit. Specifically, Brandom's central thesis regarding modal vocabulary is his *modal Kant-Sellars thesis*, which states that modal vocabulary is yet another species of universal LX-vocabulary:

1. In using ordinary empirical vocabulary, one already knows how to do everything one needs to know how to do in order to introduce and deploy *modal* vocabulary.
2. The expressive role characteristic of alethic modal vocabulary is to *make explicit* semantic, conceptual connections and commitments that are already *implicit* in the use of ordinary empirical vocabulary.

(BSD 102; see also EE 179)

First, the ability to use modal vocabulary is yet again algorithmically elaborated from abilities PV-sufficient to use the ordinary empirical vocabulary involved in the corresponding modal claims – and in particular from the universal PV-necessary abilities among those. Second, modal claims (where the modal operator is not embedded) make yet again explicit (in the pragmatic sense) otherwise implicit aspects of the inferential role of the ordinary empirical terms used in these claims, hence of the semantics of this vocabulary. Brandom calls this second part of the modal Kant-Sellars thesis *modal expressivism* (EE 205). Thus consider

(17) Necessarily bachelors are unmarried
(18) Possibly, some walls are red
(19) Necessarily, water is H$_2$O
(20) Necessarily, Cicero is Tullius
(21) Necessarily, this well-struck match will light
(22) Impossibly, this lightning strike will be followed by silence

According to Brandom's modal expressivism, 17 and 21 make pragmatically explicit that an (asymmetric) SMSIC regarding, respectively, "bachelor" and "being unmarried" and "being a well-struck match" and "will light" is (to be) acknowledged; 19 and 20 make pragmatically explicit that a (symmetric) SMSIC regarding, respectively, "water" and "H$_2$O" and "Cicero" and "Tullius" is (to be) acknowledged;[6] 18 makes pragmatically explicit that "being a wall" is compatible with "being red"; and 22 makes pragmatically explicit – roughly – that an incompatibility between "That's a lightning strike" and "It will be silent" is (to be) acknowledged.[7]

Brandom's choice of name for his modal Kant-Sellars thesis alludes to Kant's doctrine that having empirical concepts and empirical knowledge requires having "categorical," "pure" modal concepts of the understanding, of which Brandom's doctrine of modal vocabulary *qua* universal LX-vocabulary is a descendant, as discussed above. Moreover, it alludes to the fact that the modal expressivist part of the thesis is an elaboration of Wilfrid Sellars's thesis that "the language of modality is … a 'transposed' language of norms," that is, that through the use of modal concepts speakers may express aspects of the role in reasoning of ordinary empirical concepts (Sellars 2007: 21; see also BSD 100; EE 39–48). Using his distinction between what a claim says semantically vs. what a speaker making the claim expresses pragmatically, Brandom elaborates Sellars's thesis as saying *not* that modal vocabulary is normative vocabulary, used to describe norms of reasoning governing the use of the ordinary empirical vocabulary, but rather that, in making modal claims such as 17–22, scorekeepers implicitly *do* something that may be *described* using normative vocabulary (EE 204–6). Consider

(23) Necessarily, if this piece of copper is heated to 1084 degrees C it will melt
(24) Anyone asserting <u>that this piece of copper is heated to 1084 degrees C</u> should be prepared to assert consequentially <u>that it will melt</u>

Brandom wants to say that 23 is an *alethic* modal claim, describing in virtue of its semantic content the objective, nomologically modal, worldly fact that, necessarily, this piece of copper melts when heated to 1084 degrees C. That objective modal fact corresponds to a law of nature concerning copper, and it, and the corresponding law, would have obtained, Brandom wants to say, even if no scorekeepers had ever roamed the earth, hence even if the *concepts* <u>copper heated to 1084 degrees C</u>, and <u>melts</u>, and the substitution semantic norm relating them, had never existed. Copper's necessary melting at 1084 degrees C does not mandate a course of natural history leading up to creatures capable to make assertions about copper and drawing inferences from them. In general, Brandom wants to claim that alethic modal claims such as 17–23 describe, in virtue of their semantic content, worldly modal facts, and these modal facts are objective in the sense that they obtain metaphysically independently of any rational or discursive activity. This claim, that the world has this objective, mind- and discourse-independent modal structure, and that modal claims describe this structure in virtue of their semantic content, is Brandom's doctrine of *modal realism* (EE 194–9, 205–7). On the other hand, 24 is a normative (or *deontic* modal) claim, describing in virtue of its semantic content what scorekeepers should do when they are assertionally committed to the ordinary empirical claim that this piece of copper is heated to 1084 degrees C. In general, deontic modal claims describe, in virtue of their semantic content (and in particular the normative concepts in it), what rational *subjects* should do, while alethic modal claims describe, in virtue of their semantic content (and in particular the alethic modal concepts in it), what is the case, modally, in the *objective* world. Normative and alethic modal vocabulary is thus concerned with "the subjective and the objective poles of intentional relations" respectively (BSD 181).

The distinction, however, between what a claim semantically says vs. what a scorekeeper does (and makes pragmatically explicit in making the claim) allows Brandom to reconcile his modal realism with his modal expressivism, and to say that alethic modal vocabulary, despite its pragmatically expressive character, is not normative vocabulary. The relation between 23 and 24 is not that 23 semantically describes, or materially implies, what 24 semantically describes. Rather,

> what I am *doing* when I say that it is causally necessary that if this piece of copper is heated to 1083.4° C, it will melt, is endorsing a certain kind of inference. I am not *saying that* that inference is good; the facts about copper would be as they are even if there were no inferrers or inferrings. ... When Sellars says "the language of modality is ... a 'transposed' language of norms," he is saying in my terms that normative vocabulary codifying rules of inference is a *pragmatic metavocabulary* for modal vocabulary. His "transposition" is just this pragmatically mediated semantic relation between deontic normative and alethic modal vocabulary.
>
> (BSD 101; see also SOT chap. 2: 56–7)

The relation between 23 and 24 is pragmatic in the sense explained earlier. What a scorekeeper does, and normatively expects others to do, and pragmatically expresses when making the alethic modal claim 23, is what the deontic modal claim 24 semantically describes. Deontic modal (normative) vocabulary is, in this sense, a *pragmatic* metavocabulary for alethic modal vocabulary: it allows for semantically describing what scorekeepers do, and pragmatically express, when they make alethic modal claims. The relation between 23 and 24 is *semantic* only in the sense that 24 semantically describes the semantic relation that users of 23 pragmatically express: that that this piece of copper is heated to 1084 degrees C materially implies that it will melt. However, the relation between 23 and 24 is a *pragmatically mediated* semantic relation in the sense that 24 does *not* semantically describe what 23 pragmatically expresses because 23 would materially imply 24. If it did, 23 would be *reference dependent* on 24: the alethic modal fact represented by 23 could have obtained only if the deontic modal fact represented by 24 had obtained (SOT chap. 2: 56–9).[8] Yet Brandom's doctrine of modal realism is incompatible with the general reference dependence of alethic modal claims such as 23 on deontic modal claims such as 24, that is, incompatible with any metaphysical relativism according to which facts about the natural world – including alethic modal ones – metaphysically depend upon facts about norms of reasoning and normative statuses of scorekeepers. And his theory of how alethic modal claims such as 23 are in a "pragmatically mediated semantic relation" to corresponding deontic modal claims such as 24, provides, Brandom thinks, the space, first, for endorsing modal realism and rejecting such a metaphysical relativism; and second, for maintaining, with Sellars, that alethic modal claims about the objective world are "transposed" deontic modal claims about the normative structure of the space of reasons (SOT 56–9). (We shall discuss in the last chapter whether Brandom's twin thesis of modal realism and modal expressivism is compatible with his thesis that the norms of reason are instituted through mutual social recognition.)

Brandom attributes great significance to his modal Kant-Sellars thesis. If it is true, even autonomous discursive practitioners must have an implicit sense of what must, might, and cannot be the case in the world, as a necessary condition for having the specific ordinary empirical concepts used in their practices. Thus the thesis, if true, simultaneously contradicts longstanding empiricist worries about the justification, and indeed the meaningfulness, of alethic modal claims, and provides a philosophical foundation for the practice of using modal vocabulary freewheelingly in contemporary ("post-empiricist") analytic philosophy. According to empiricism, sense experience justifies ordinary empirical beliefs and determines the content of empirical concepts. Thus, since we don't seem to experience alethic modal features of the world – what might or must be – but only *actual* features, experience can, apparently, neither justify modal beliefs nor be the source of the content for modal concepts. Therefore, while on this view we can know and meaningfully talk about how things actually are, we apparently cannot know or meaningfully talk about how things might or must be. Yet if the modal Kant-Sellars thesis is correct, this empiricist line of thought is false: ordinary empirical concepts do not only describe how things actually are but also already comprise, as an essential aspect of their substitution semantic role, implicit information as to how things might or must be. Thus, thought and talk about how things actually are cannot be divorced from implicit considerations of how they must or might be, in contradiction to the gap assumed by Empiricists between thought about actualities and alethic modal thought (BSD 92–7). And this modal dimension, implicit in the semantics of ordinary empirical concepts, provides the semantic foundation for explicitly modal thought and talk, according to Brandom, thus justifying the free-wheeling use of modal locutions in contemporary philosophical analysis (BSD 92–7, 114–16; SOT chap. 5: 38–41).

A unified theory of alethic modality

As examples 17–23 indicate, Brandom intends his doctrine of modal expressivism to include what are traditionally considered to be three different kinds of alethic modal claims: "analytic" ones such as 17 and 18, which are classically thought to be verifiable a priori in virtue of the meaning of the empirical vocabulary in them alone (17, for instance, is classically thought to be verifiable through a priori analysis of the meaning of "bachelor"); metaphysical ones such as 19 and 20, which are synthetic and verifiable only based on experience (a posteriori), yet are thought to have peculiar modal strength in the sense that they concern essential features of the items talked about, and thus would have remained true under *any* counterfactual circumstances (for example, 19 describes water as essentially H_2O, and while the essence of water needed to be discovered through empirical inquiry, it is thought that water could not have been anything but H_2O, no matter what the world might have been like); and causal ones such as 21–23, which are synthetic and knowable only a posteriori too, but weaker than the metaphysical ones in the sense that, although they are true given the actual laws and statistical regularities of nature, they would be false in worlds where the laws and regularities of nature differed in relevant ways.

Brandom's modal expressivism offers a unified treatment of these three varieties of modality. According to it, modal claims of all three varieties make explicit semantic aspects of the ordinary empirical vocabulary involved in them (BSD 182, n. 4). His treatment of metaphysical modal claims such as 19 and 20 as expressing semantic aspects of the ordinary empirical vocabulary involved in them ("water"/"H_2O" and "Cicero"/"Tullius") accords with the contemporary semantic externalist orthodoxy arising from the classical works by Kripke (1972), Putnam (1975), and others. Heeding Putnam's slogan that "meanings are not in the head," most people today accept the claim that the meanings of many of our empirical terms are literally the very external individuals, properties, kinds, or conditions that these terms represent. Thus, the meaning of "Cicero" *is*, on this view, the real, long-deceased Roman orator, the meaning of "water" *is* the scatter of H_2O in the universe, etc. Accordingly, much about the meaning of our ordinary empirical terms and concepts cannot be found out a priori, on this view, but requires empirical inquiry. On this view, true metaphysical necessities, such as 19 and 20, thus carry simultaneously empirical information regarding the individuals and kinds they are about and semantic information about the empirical terms and concepts used. As seen already in chapter 5, Brandom agrees with much of this orthodox semantic externalist framework, except its semantic representationalism, and his expressivist take on metaphysical necessities can be seen as recasting this framework from a representationalist semantic setting into an inferential role semantic setting (BSD 99–100). On Brandom's view, 19 and 20 convey *semantic* information regarding the empirical terms in use not because they tell us which external individuals, or natural kinds, these terms represent – although they do tell us that also (see chapter 7) – but because they make explicit substitution inferential norms governing these terms that have been instituted in the community of English speakers in the context of empirical inquiry into Cicero and water respectively (see chapter 8).

Following Wilfrid Sellars's view, as captured by the telling title of his paper "Concepts as Involving Laws and Inconceivable Without Them" (Sellars 1980), and in accordance with Brandom's claim that some of the meaning-constitutive material inferential relations between empirical statements reflect laws and regularities of nature (as discussed in chapter 4), Brandom's most distinct contribution to these debates is his defense of the claim that causally modal claims such as 21–23 also convey semantic information about the empirical concepts in use: they simultaneously semantically describe (instantiations of) laws or regularities of nature and pragmatically express aspects of the meaning of the concepts in use.[9] For example, 21 simultaneously describes, due to its semantic content, the well-struck match as necessarily lighting up, in accordance with a regularity of nature, and pragmatically expresses a material inference from "This is a well-struck match" to "It will light." The key for Brandom's defense of this inclusion of causal modal claims as semantically informative is the fact that material inferences and incompatibilities reflecting laws and regularities of nature are good, or obtain, within ranges of counterfactual robustness. Accordingly,

> *modal* vocabulary specifying what is, at least, conditionally possible and necessary can then be introduced to make explicit those commitments to the, at least, limited counterfactual goodness of material inferences.
>
> (BSD 104–6)

This quote indicates that Brandom thinks of the modal operators figuring in causally modal claims such as 21–23 *as indexed to the corresponding ranges of counterfactual robustness for the material inferences or incompatibilities made explicit.* For example, 21 pragmatically expresses the material inference from "This is a well-struck match" to "It will light." The inference is valid, and would have remained valid had circumstances been different within the range of counterfactual robustness to which the modal operator in 21 is indexed (match struck by a girl rather than a boy, boy struck it over *there* rather than over *here*, etc.), but would have been undermined had circumstances outside this range obtained (match wet, oxygen absent, strong wind present). 21 pragmatically expresses the validity of the meaning-constitutive material inference from "This is a well-struck match" to "It will light" *within this range of counterfactual robustness.*

Given this idea of indexing the modal operators to corresponding ranges of counterfactual robustness, Brandom's theory can explain why, for example, 21 and

(25) Possibly, this well-struck match will not light

need not contradict each other and can both be true. The two sentences would contradict each other if the modal operators in them were indexed to the same range of counterfactual robustness. In that case, 21 would express that the substitution inference from "This is a well-struck match" to "It will light" is valid relative to the indexed range of counterfactual robustness, in the sense that the obtainment of no circumstance within the range would defeat that inference, while 25 would express that the same substitution inference is invalid relative to *that* range, in the sense that the obtainment of some circumstance within that range would defeat that same inference. On the most plausible interpretation of 21 and 25, however, the possibility operator in 25 is indexed to a wider range of counterfactual circumstances, which includes circumstances such as wetness of match, absence of oxygen, or presence of wind – circumstances that are excluded from the range to which the necessity operator in 21 is indexed. We have the presence of such circumstances in mind when we say that possibly the well-struck match will not light, yet we rule out the presence of such circumstances when we say that necessarily the well-struck match will light, that is, when we claim that 21 is true *ceteris paribus*. Since, on the most plausible interpretation, the modal operators in 21 and 25 are indexed to different ranges of counterfactual robustness, 21 and 25 do not, on this interpretation, contradict each other; they are both true. 21 makes explicit the substitution inferential relation between the empirical terms in use, corresponding to a regularity of nature, within a certain range of counterfactual robustness that excludes all the possible circumstances under which that regularity would not be manifest. And 25 makes explicit the defeasibility of that same substitution-inferential relation, by including (via the index of the "possibly") circumstances outside this range.

Summary

Participants in the simplest kinds of discursive practices (autonomous discursive practices) acknowledge and implicitly attribute assertional, (substitution) inferential, and anaphoric commitments and they treat each other in practice as more or less reliable observers and agents, in accordance with what they implicitly take to be the norms governing their practice. They are as yet unable, however, to make anything they do implicitly in practice explicit in the form of propositionally contentful claims. Autonomous discourse as such is perfectly irreflective, in that it comprises no expressive resources to explicitly think and talk *about* any aspect of discourse itself. This chapter introduced Brandom's theory of discourse through which scorekeepers make otherwise implicit features of their discourse explicit and thus become able to reflect in their reasoning and discourse about aspects of their discursive activity.

Logical vocabulary, normative vocabulary, and vocabulary to explicitly ascribe beliefs and intentions to someone are the most important expressive resources used in such reflective thought and talk, and Brandom offers a unified pragmatist theory of all such vocabulary, according to which all such vocabulary is *universally elaborated and explicative* (universal LX). Two central claims characterize this theory. First, the pragmatic ability to use any such vocabulary is algorithmically elaborated from pragmatic abilities that every speaker at all must have, hence abilities that must be employed in autonomous discourse. What this means is that the pragmatic ability to use any such vocabulary is nothing but the ability to execute in the right order a set of pragmatic abilities that any autonomous discursive practitioner as such must have, and thus is a new, non-autonomous pragmatic ability only in this minimal sense. Brandom thinks of a speaker's ability to algorithmically elaborate some of his autonomous discursive abilities into abilities to use some universal LX-vocabulary as, literally, a computational ability – albeit one that, by contrast to the tasks executed by a digital computer, does not map *symbolic* inputs into symbolic outputs but rather maps autonomous pragmatic abilities as inputs into non-autonomous pragmatic abilities as outputs.

Second, in the context of a statement, any piece of universal LX-vocabulary makes explicit some otherwise implicit *universal structural* feature of autonomous discursive practices: indeed, a feature that is centrally involved in the algorithmic elaboration that yields the ability to use that very piece of universal LX-vocabulary. For example, a conditional claim "If P then Q," in Brandom's view, makes explicit that Q is inferable from P and thus is concerned with a universal, structural feature of autonomous discursive practices: inferential relations. Moreover, the speaker's ability to draw inferences – an ability present in all discursive practices – is centrally involved in the algorithmic elaboration that yields the ability to make conditional claims. Brandom thinks that the two central claims of his theory of universal LX-vocabulary combined account for the formal and universal character of logical vocabulary: that is, for the facts that logical vocabulary is void of (empirical) content, and that it is applicable in the context of any discourse at all.

Brandom's theory of alethic modal claims is an effort to make sense of Wilfrid Sellars's claim that "the language of modality is … a 'transposed' language of norms" (Sellars 2007: 21), by trying to combine a doctrine of modal expressivism with a doctrine of modal realism. According to modal expressivism, alethic modal claims such as "Necessarily, this well-struck match will light" or "Necessarily, water is H_2O" express normative, (substitution) semantic relations between the empirical terms in use – "well-struck match"/"lighting" and "water"/"H_2O" respectively. According to modal realism, the two claims describe objective, mind-independent modal features of non-linguistic reality itself – the law-like necessity that the match will light and the metaphysical necessity that water is H_2O. The reconciliation between modal expressivism and modal realism is achieved, Brandom thinks, by drawing a distinction between what a modal claim pragmatically expresses vs. what it describes in virtue of its propositional content. A correct modal claim describes in virtue of its propositional content a certain objective modal feature of reality (modal realism), and scorekeepers appropriately *make* or *respond to* the claim by acknowledging in practice the corresponding (substitution) semantic relations among the empirical terms used in the claim (modal expressivism). One significant feature of Brandom's theory of alethic modal vocabulary is that it offers a unified treatment of "analytic," metaphysical, and nomological modalities – basically by treating modal claims as coming in degrees of strength, measured by their degree of counterfactual robustness. Another significant feature of this theory is that it provides a foundation and justification for the widespread use of modal vocabulary in contemporary philosophical analysis, because it treats alethic modal vocabulary as yet again universal LX and thus grounds such vocabulary semantically and pragmatically in features and abilities that must be manifested in any discursive practice at all.

7

Representation and Communication

The last four chapters developed Brandom's account of linguistic meaning and propositional content and, derivatively, his theory of concepts, in terms of his scorekeeping model of linguistic communication. So far, this approach to meaning, content, and concepts has nowhere appealed to any discursively representational notions. Rather than treating the semantics of contents and concepts as consisting at least in part in the fact that contents and concepts represent states of affairs, objects, properties, and relations, Brandom treats it as consisting entirely in the normative, inferential role contents and concepts play in reasoning, and he explains this role in turn entirely in normative pragmatic terms: in terms of the proper use of the corresponding sentences and terms in linguistic communication, without invoking any notions of representation at all (notions such as <u>reference to objects</u>, <u>representation of properties and relations</u>, <u>truth-conditions *qua* correspondences to states of affairs</u>). As we saw in chapter 5, Brandom sustains this thoroughly non-representational approach to the semantics of thought and talk even in his account of specifically empirical content, in terms of normative social practices of reliability responding to non-linguistic circumstances in one's observation reports (language entries) and reliably acting in response to constellations of assertional and practical commitments (language exits) and of assessing each other's reliability *qua* observer and agent. While engagement in practices of reliably interacting with the largely non-linguistic world explains empirical contentfulness as such, no discursively representational notions are invoked in Brandom's account of such reliability.

All this does not mean, however, that our thought and talk lacks a representational dimension. On the contrary, *all* thought and talk has a representational dimension, according to Brandom (MIE 306, 324), and, indeed, stands in representation *relations* to, often, non-discursive, worldly individuals, properties and relations, and states of affairs.[1] This *global* representationalism (PP 213) distinguishes Brandom's project sharply from other prominent, broadly pragmatist approaches to thought and talk in whose lineage he otherwise takes his project to be. For example, according to the later Wittgenstein, much empirically contentful speech is perfectly meaningful without being representational at all, and according to Brandom's teacher Richard Rorty, the very idea of thought and talk as representational is positively pernicious, as it is at the root of the (to Rorty) unacceptable predicament Cartesian epistemology has left modern Western philosophy stuck in. By contrast, Brandom's global representationalism makes his project look to a cursory view like nothing pragmatist at all, but rather like a standard representationalist approach to thought and talk in the tradition of the Received View discussed in chapter 1.

Yet what places Brandom's project into this broadly pragmatist tradition after all is that his account of specifically discursively representational *vocabulary* (such as "represents," "refers to," "is about," etc.) is *soft*. It is

> an account of the *expressive* role of representational vocabulary that shows [that] the same expressive function that makes it ubiquitously available to express a crucial dimension of conceptual contentfulness also *disqualifies* it from playing a fundamental *explanatory* role in an account of the semantics of at least some discursive practices. For the expressive role characteristic of representational vocabulary (like that of the logical, modal, and normative vocabulary) can itself be fully specified in a social, normative, inferential pragmatic metavocabulary that does *not* itself employ representational vocabulary.
>
> (PP 214)

Brandom envisions discursive practices and abilities involving the use of such representational vocabulary as yet again algorithmically elaborated from, ultimately, autonomous discursive practices (chapter 6). Yet since the envisioned algorithmic elaboration of our ability to use representational vocabulary draws only on the normative pragmatic resources constitutive of autonomous discursive practices, and since these resources are altogether free from discursively representational items, the envisioned algorithmic elaboration will not involve any discursively representational abilities. Accordingly, Brandom thinks, discursively representational vocabulary, so accounted for, cannot be used to explain the semantic dimension of thought or talk or even to explain its discursively representational dimension. That representational dimension is real and global and is, accordingly, properly characterized by using discursively representational vocabulary. Its reality, however, stems from independent and more substantial sources than its characterizability by using discursively representational vocabulary. In short, Brandom's account of discursively representational vocabulary is thoroughly deflationary: such vocabulary does not explain the semantic dimension of thought and talk, nor does it even explain its representational dimension.

It is worth highlighting in passing, however, that there is an important sense in which Brandom, in some recent work, seems to be open to being a *hard local* representationalist (as the "at least some" in the quote above indicates):

> I have talked so far only about *discursive* representational vocabulary. But this is not the only candidate for a representational semantic metavocabulary. In addition there are at least three others: those that express *mapping* relations (static), those that express *tracking* processes (dynamic), and those that express the *practical* intentional directedness of goal-seeking systems. ... Here, too, the possibility of an adequate nonrepresentational pragmatic metavocabulary for these varieties of representational vocabulary would not seem to rule out their playing fundamental roles in a semantic metavocabulary for some other vocabulary – quite possibly, empirical descriptive vocabulary.
>
> (PP 216–17)

We are practically intentional creatures, engaging in feedback-governed ways with aspects of the non-linguistic world (see chapter 5). Our discursively rational activity, including our activity of more or less reliably forming observational beliefs and performing intentional actions, is a segment of such cycles of feedback-governed interactions, and because it is such a segment our discursive activities and practices literally incorporate aspects of the non-linguistic world and become empirically contentful. Some segments of these feedback-governed cycles are thus rational, inferential, norm-governed processes; other segments are non-rational perceptual and behavioral processes, or non-psychological natural processes outside our skin. As indicated in chapter 5, Brandom thinks that the non-rational perceptual and behavioral portions of these processes involve various kinds of *non-discursive* – hence non-conceptual – representations, such as mappings, trackings, and goal pursuits. In some recent work, Brandom indicates openness to the idea that these non-discursive representations, and the vocabulary we use to describe them, *may partially explain* the semantic dimension of specifically empirical concepts and vocabularies (PP 216). Thus, although the *discursively* representational vocabulary in terms of which we describe rational thought and talk as conceptually representational ("refers to," "believes of," "claims about," etc.) remains both globally applicable and explanatorily idle, the *non-discursively* representational vocabulary in terms of which we describe the non-rational portions of TOTE-cycles ("maps," "tracks," "pursues") may be locally semantically explanatory, according to Brandom: it may in part explain specifically empirical contentfulness.

These thoughts raise the issue whether Brandom has to date begun to rethink his commitment to strong inferentialism – the view that inferential role alone constitutes meaning. However, since he has (as far as I know) to date not further developed these thoughts, I shall not further speculate about the matter here. The rest of this chapter will exclusively focus on three well-developed aspects of Brandom's theory of *discursive* representation: first, his theory of discursively representational purport; second, his theory of discursive representation as fall-out of the social dimension of the scorekeeping practice; third, his theory of this representational dimension as the key for successful communication despite the holistic nature of meaning. In the following, whenever I use the term "representation" I mean discursive representation, unless indicated otherwise.

Representational purport

Representational purport is the directedness of thought and talk toward features of the largely non-linguistic world. Brandom boldly claims that our rational, inferential activity itself is the source of representational purport. Representational purport is

> a matter of taking or treating one's commitments as subject to a distinctive kind of *authority*, as being *responsible* ... *to* things that in that normative sense count as represent*ed* by those represent*ing*

states. ... [R]ational ... integrative activity can be understood as instituting a specifically *representational* normative dimension of authority and responsibility. ... [W]hat becomes visible as a notion of conceptual content ... must exhibit also a representational dimension. Thinking *about* something is not a special kind of thinking. It is an aspect of *all* thinking.

[T]he relations of material incompatibility and inferential consequence among judgeable contents ... already implicitly involve commitments concerning the identity and individuation of *objects* they can accordingly be understood as representing or being about.

(RP 41–3; see also 2010b: 352; SOT chap. 2: 45–6; SOT chap. 10: 76–7.)

Representational purport is a semantic epiphenomenon, falling out from our ongoing efforts to rationally integrate our discursive commitments into a unified whole, by drawing out consequences, acknowledging compatibilities, weeding out incompatibilities, accommodating new observational and practical commitments, and so on. That is, representational purport flows from our ongoing efforts to get a better grip on the content (the inferential role) of the ever-changing swarm of acknowledged discursive commitments and entitlements that we aim to integrate at any moment of our waking life (RP 39–45). Metaphysically, the purportedly represented world is a world of states of affairs in a broadly Aristotelian sense (SOT chap. 5: 38), according to Brandom, that is, a world of individuals with certain properties and standing in certain relations to each other. Epistemically, that world exerts normative constraints on our rational activity, in the sense that we regard our ongoing integrative efforts as proper or improper in light of the states of affairs we purport to represent (RP 34–5). Brandom intends this to be a transcendental account of representational purport in the Kantian tradition. It is Brandom's effort to make sense of Kant's claim that "it is the unity of consciousness that alone constitutes the relation of representation to an object, and therefore their objective validity."[2]

Why such representational purport to an Aristotelian world in consequence of our reasoning? The quote above continues as follows:

The judgment that *A* is a dog is *not* incompatible with the judgment that *B* is a fox. The judgment that *A* is a dog *is* incompatible with the judgment that *A* is a fox. That means that taking a dog-judgment

to be materially incompatible with a fox-judgment *is* taking them to refer to or represent an object: the *same* object. And the same thing holds for relations of material inferential consequence. Taking it that *A* is a dog does *not* entail that *B* is a mammal. But taking it that *A* is a dog *does* entail that *A* is a mammal. So drawing the inference is taking it that the two judgments refer to one and the same object.
                    (RP 43–4; see also BSD 187–8; SOT chap. 2, 49–50.)

The subject treats "A is a dog" and "A is a fox" as both *about* the same single individual, A, and "B is a fox" as about a different individual, B, *because* she treats "A is a dog" as compatible with "B is a fox," as incompatible with "A is a fox," as implying "A is a mammal," and as not as implying "B is a mammal." In general, Brandom claims that because we treat various sentences with simple subject-predicate structure as standing in various inferential, compatibility, and incompatibility relations, we treat the singular terms in them as about individuals and, thanks to the monadic or polyadic predicates in these sentences, these individuals as having certain determinate properties and as standing in certain determinate relations to each other (see chapter 4). Metaphysically, the individuals so represented are "units of account for alethic modal incompatibilities," according to Brandom (RP 48), that is, they are nothing but items that take on counterfactually robust properties and relations – properties that they would continue to have and relations in which they would continue to stand within certain ranges of counterfactual circumstances, but that they would cease to have, or in which they would cease to stand, if circumstances outside these ranges obtained. These properties and relations in turn are Aristotelian universals, metaphysically speaking, that come both with converses and in hierarchies of species and genera, and hence include, preclude, or are compatible with each other – within ranges of counterfactual robustness – when exhibited by a single individual. For example, the converse of the property BEING A DOG is BEING NOT A DOG and its genus is BEING A MAMMAL. And BEING A DOG precludes BEING A FOX, BEING A LION, etc. (all of which are ways of being not a dog), includes BEING A MAMMAL, and is compatible with WEIGHING 85 POUNDS.[3] Individuals as such neither have converses nor come in hierarchies of species and genus. They have converses and come in such hierarchies only *qua* exemplifiers of properties and relations.

Why must we, given our efforts to integrate our discursive commitments and entitlements into a rational unity, treat these deontic statuses as representing an Aristotelian world of states of affairs, that is, a world of complexes consisting in individuals, properties, and relations in a broadly Aristotelian sense (EE 200–203, SOT 41–4)? As we saw in chapter 4, rational activity has a highly specific fine-structure, characterized by an elaborate interplay between a gamut of syntactic, modally robust substitution semantic and ana-phoric commitments and entitlements governing the singular and general terms in use, according to Brandom. And as we saw in chapter 5, this interplay in turn is part of an ongoing, larger, feed-back-governed process that, mediated by perception and action, incorporates aspects of the non-linguistic world. Brandom thinks that the purport to represent an Aristotelian world is a consequence of our efforts to rationally integrate discursive commitments and entitlements *with this fine-structure:*

> the representations of particulars [individuals], modeled on singular terms, are intelligible as such only in a context that includes repre-sentations of universals, in the sense of general properties, modeled on predicates and sortals. And … the representings that are them-selves particular, in the sense of being unrepeatable, modeled on the use of tokening-reflexive expressions, are intelligible as such only in a context that includes larger structures of [anaphoric] repeatability: ways of recollecting those unrepeatable events and taking them up as available in inferences made later.
>
> (SOT chap. 4: 14)[4]

The Aristotelian structure of the represented world – individuals as "units of account" for converse-repelling, species-and-genus-ordered universals – reflects the anaphoric, syntactic, and semantic fine-structure of our scorekeeping efforts, and in particular our efforts to integrate our own acknowledged commitments and enti-tlements into a rational unity. As seen in chapter 4, the notion of a singular or general term *token* as representing anything at all makes sense only in conjunction with the notion that the token is part of larger structures of repeatability ("recollection") via anaphori-cally dependent tokens of the same syntactic type, preserving such representation: "deixis presupposes anaphora" (MIE 462). And the reason singular term-tokens must represent individuals while general term-tokens must represent universals has to do with the systematically different syntactic and semantic principles govern-ing singular and general terms. On the one hand, as seen in chapter 4, singular term-tokens (and their anaphoric dependents) belong to anaphoric chains that constitute syntactically *substituted-for* expressions in the context of whole sentences – expressions that can be substituted for each other into sentences without turning a sentence into syntactic gibberish – while general term-tokens belong to anaphoric chains that constitute *sentence frames*, which stay invariant under substitution of singular term for singular term into a sentence. On the other hand, as also seen in chapter 4, any singular term must stand in exclusively *symmetric* substitution semantic relations to certain other singular terms – roughly, for any singular terms T1 and T2 and any sentences "…T1…" and "…T2…" reachable from each other in a single step by substituting T2 for T1 or vice versa, the material inference from "…T1…" to "…T2…" is valid if and only if the material inference from "…T2…" to "…T1…" is also valid – while every general term (sentence frame) must be such that some of the substitution semantic relations in which it stands to other general terms are asymmetric. Thus, due to the invariance of sentence frames under syntactically proper substitution of singular term for singular term, sentence frames purport to represent what is, in the language of traditional metaphysics, "one over many" (i.e., universals) while the singular terms themselves, varying (as they do) under substitution for each other into an (invariant) sentence frame, represent the "many" (i.e., individuals). And since sentence frames, by contrast to singular terms, include both asymmetric substitution inferential relations to some other such frames and substitutional semantic incompatibilities with yet other such frames, the "one" that each of them purports to represent both is essentially located, together with other "ones," in a structure of species and genera, and has other "ones" as contraries: that is, it exhibits the structural features of Aristotelian universals. In short, Brandom claims that assertions exhibiting subject-predicate structure represent Aristotelian individuals as instantiating Aristotelian universals because they are concatenations of token singular terms with token general terms, which in turn are parts of different anaphoric chains with their characteristically different syntactic and substitution semantic economies.

Thus, going back to Brandom's example above, a subject acknowledging in practice the inferential and incompatibility relations regarding the five sentences "A is a dog," "A is a fox," "A is a mammal," "B is a fox," "B is a mammal," *ipso facto* takes these sentences in practice to represent two numerically distinct individuals (A and B), represented by the instances of the singular terms "A" and "B," as exhibiting specific contrary properties – BEING A DOG vs. BEING A FOX – falling under the same genus

BEING MAMMALIAN. The very rational activity of (on the one hand) acknowledging commitment to /A is a dog/ and treating it as *incompatible* with an entitlement to /A is a fox/ but as *compatible* with a commitment to /B is a fox/, and as *consequentially* committing to /A is mammalian/ but as *not consequentially* committing to /B is mammalian/, and, on the other hand, of acknowledging a commitment to /B is a fox/ and treating it as *incompatible* with an entitlement to /B is a dog/ but as *consequentially* committing to /B is mammalian/ is the outcome of treating the "A" and "B" tokens in these assertions as singular term-tokens belonging to two different substitution inferentially *un*related anaphoric chains and, moreover, of treating the token general terms ("being a dog," "being a fox," "being mammalian") as belonging to three different anaphoric chains, two of which are treated as both substitution semantically incompatible ("being a dog" vs. "being a fox") and each asymmetrically substitution semantically linked with the third ("being mammalian"). These treatments all together bring it about, thinks Brandom, that the reasoning subject must also treat this system of assertions as purportedly representing two individuals, A and B, each of these individuals as exemplifying one of two mutually repelling species properties (BEING A DOG vs. BEING A FOX), and both of these individuals as exemplifying the same genus property (BEING MAMMALIAN).

Someone may object to this transcendental explanation of representational purport as follows. True, treating /A is a dog/ as incompatible with /A is a fox/ and as implying /A is mammalian/ requires recognizing the three occurrences of "A" in these assertions as recurrences of the same singular term. Regarding them as merely lexically co-typical occurrences of three different substitution semantically unrelated singular terms would require treating the three assertions as compatible and inferentially unrelated. Yet why shouldn't the subject's purely *intra-linguistic* recognition of the three occurrences of "A" as recurrences of the same term provide all the invariance between the three assertions needed for recognizing them as standing in these inferential and incompatibility relations to each other? That is, why can't a scorekeeper treat /A is a dog/ as incompatible with /A is a fox/ and as implying /A is mammalian/ simply by treating, in the context of her (equally purely intra-linguistic) substitution semantic treatment of the three predicates, the three occurrences of "A" *as recurrences of the same term – without* also treating them as purportedly representing an extra-linguistic individual A? Shouldn't treating the three occurrences of the symbol "A" as recurrences of the same term itself suffice as the "unit of account" required for acknowledging the incompatibility and the inference? In general, isn't it possible for someone to play the discursive scorekeeping game correctly without having any sense that the moves and states of the game purport to represent an extra-linguistic Aristotelian reality?

We will see in the next section that part of Brandom's answer to this challenge is given in terms of the essential social dimension of the scorekeeping practice: that is, in terms of the fact that the score-keeper's intrapersonal, integrative rational activity occurs in the context of her interpersonal activity of attributing commitments and entitlements to others (the matter of the next section). However, we should, I think, also interpret Brandom as giving another integral part of the answer in terms of the fact that such intrapersonal rational activity is part of wider, feedback-governed practically intentional processes that also include per se non-discursive perceptual and behavioral interactions with the environment, due to which portions of the environment themselves literally become incorporated into the discursive scorekeeping practice. Because the scorekeeper acknowledges the multifarious anaphoric, syntactic, and substitution semantic commitments concerning, say, the three assertions above as part of such wider, non-discursive processes, she treats the assertions as representing aspects of the incorporated non-linguistic environment: a single individual, A, AS A DOG, hence not AS A FOX, and AS MAMMALIAN (BSD 184–8). Brandom should concede, I think, that what's de facto doing all the work in providing the invariance between the three assertions needed for the subject to acknowledge their inferential and incompatibility relations is indeed the subject's purely intra-linguistic treatment of the three occurrences of "A" as anaphorically related to each other: as recurrences of the same term. After all, if the purported reference of these occurrences to a non-linguistic individual, A, generated by the fact that this intra-linguistic treatment is part of a wider environment-incorporating practically intentional process, did even part of this invariance-providing work, such referential purport would not be a semantically epiphenomenal consequence of the subject's intra-personal rational treatment of these three assertions – her anaphoric, syntactic, and substitution semantic treatment of them in which her understanding of these three assertions consists – in the context of this wider process, but rather a contributing factor to it. Representational purport would contribute to explaining meaning and understanding after all, and Brandom's strong semantic inferentialism would collapse into a hybrid version of the Received View. Still, although the referential purport of the three occurrences of "A" is de facto not a contributing factor to the subject's intrapersonal rational activity involving the three assertions, a necessary by-product of this activity is that the subject treats these three occurrences as representing an aspect of the environment incorporated into the discursive practice: a single Aristotelian individual A. We can put it this way: although from the viewpoint of theory the subject's intra-linguistic treatment of the three occurrences of "A" as recurrences of the same term is in fact the "unit of account" required for her ability to treat the three assertions as standing in their inferential and incompatibility relations to each other, from the subject's point of view, the three occurrences purportedly represent a single individual A as the "unit of account" for the three monadic properties invoked by these assertions.

The epistemic dimension of the purportedly represented states of affairs – the fact that, from the subject's point of view, they normatively constrain this rational, integrative activity – in turn is an aspect and consequence of their Aristotelian structure, thinks Brandom. Key here is the subject's experience of error. The scorekeeper frequently experiences her efforts to maintain a rational, unified doxastic and practical perspective as erroneous and as in need of revision *in light of what is purportedly represented*. In BSD (185–7), Brandom illustrates this point by considering an autonomous discursive practice in which the participants take, prior to time *t*, the predicate "___ is acidic" to be properly applied to all sour-tasting liquids – commitments to "That's sour-tasting" and "That's liquid" are taken to commit consequentially to "That's acidic" – and commitments to "That's acidic" in turn are taken to commit consequentially to "That turns phenolphthalein blue." In their collective experience up to *t*, any liquid the participants characterized as acidic always has turned phenolphthalein blue. Yet at *t* some participant observes a sour-tasting liquid that turns phenolphthalein red. Accordingly, that participant is now obliged to reshuffle her doxastic and substitution semantic attitudes in some way. She may, for example, alter and refine her substitution-semantic treatment of "___ is acidic," perhaps by acknowledging a SMSIC from "___ is a sour-tasting liquid" to "___ is acidic" only in the context of a collateral commitment to also apply "___ is transparent" to the environing liquid (BSD 185, also SOT chap. 3: 87). Or she may instead revise some of her doxastic attitudes, perhaps by disavowing that the powder applied at *t* is

phenolphthalein after all, or by discarding some of the old observations as, after all, unreliably produced. *How* the participant should
reshuffle her discursive attitudes is, Brandom thinks, underdetermined by the situation (see next chapter), though some potential
accommodations of the new evidence will appear to her more
"natural" than others. Here I only flag Brandom's insistence that,
for the subject, the purportedly represented sour-tasting red liquid
itself demands an adjustment of her intrapersonal scorekeeping
attitudes one way or another. That is, for the subject, that liquid
itself normatively constrains her rational activity: by discursively
representing a non-linguistic object one makes oneself "answer-
able (*for* the correctness of the endorsed judgeable contents ...)
to objects, which one in that normative sense thereby counts as
thinking about" (RP 40; cf. also RP 35, MIE 332, SOT chap. 2: 49–54,
SOT chap. 3: 87).

The social dimension of scorekeeping

Representational purport should not be conflated with the subject's
having an even implicit sense of her rational activity *as representational*. Using the Hegelian language of consciousness and self-consciousness again, representational purport is an aspect of the
subject's conscious, rational involvement with the largely non-linguistic world. Yet representation is a relation between representing
and represented items, and while *we* recognize the subject's efforts
to maintain, as part of her practically intentional involvement with
the world, a rational, unified system of doxastic and practical commitments as representational, the subject herself, insofar as she
makes these efforts, lacks any reflective self-consciousness of these
efforts as representational. These intrapersonal efforts, as such, do
not even implicitly appear to the subject as efforts to represent the
non-linguistic world.

The scorekeeper's efforts to maintain a unified doxastic and practical perspective, however, when involved with her non-linguistic
environment, occur in the context of her overall efforts to keep
score. In communication, not only do we acknowledge new discursive commitments and entitlements of various kinds and disavow
old ones ourselves – not only do we strive to maintain a unified
doxastic and practical perspective – but we also attribute to others
such commitments and entitlements, as acknowledged or as to
be acknowledged, in systematic interaction with the conversation.

We more or less accurately track each other's assertional and practical commitments (what the other does and should believe and intend) and, as part of these attributions, each other's correlative inferential and incompatibility commitments (how, correlatively, the other does and should reason) – and, as part of this twofold tracking effort, also each other's acknowledged syntactic and anaphoric commitments (which in cases of non-defective communication we always also acknowledge ourselves). Such tracking thus amounts to our implicit recognition of the other as a rational creature, that is, as a creature concerned with maintaining a rational unity of his doxastic and practical perspective. Such recognition is our first reflective (albeit still implicit) glimpse of rational activity as such. Brandom maintains that the combination in discourse of our interpersonal tracking efforts with our own intrapersonal rational activity adds up to an implicit recognition on our part of the doxastic and practical statuses and attitudes we attribute to others *as representational* and, indeed, as *of* or *about* the very individuals, properties, and relations we purport to represent due to our own intrapersonal rational activity.

Key here are the interpersonal anaphoric links between the term-tokens in the assertions and shall-statements through which the interlocutor does, or would, express *his* acknowledged assertional and practical commitments and the term-tokens in assertions and shall-statements through which the scorekeeper does, or would, express *her own* acknowledged assertional and practical commitments.

> Concern with what is talked about arises in the process of mapping the repertoire of commitments of an interpreted interlocutor onto the repertoire of commitments of an interpreting interlocutor. ... Use of an anaphoric proform implicitly *stipulates* coreference with the anaphoric antecedent upon which it is semantically dependent. ... To take one tokening to be anaphorically dependent on another is to take it that it should be understood as governed by whatever substitutional commitments govern its antecedent. Different scorekeepers may disagree about what these are, and they may disagree even with the ones producing the performances whose significance they are assessing. They may nonetheless all agree in attributing an anaphoric commitment, that is, in interpreting one tokening as being anaphorically dependent on ... the same antecedent tokening. A scorekeeper who takes it that the inventor of bifocals is the inventor of the lightning rod will take it that the first speaker claimed *of* the inventor of the lightning rod that he spoke French

well, and that the second speaker claimed *of* that same individual
that he did not speak French well.

(MIE 485–7)

Suppose C knows that Benjamim Franklin invented bifocals as well
as the lightning rod, but A and B know none of these things, and
that the score C keeps on A and B reflects this ignorance. C thus
acknowledges three symmetric SMSICs, concerning the three possible pairings of the singular terms "The inventor of bifocals," "The
inventor of the lightning rod," and "Benjamin Franklin," and thus
purports to represent a single individual when using any of these
terms, while neither A nor B acknowledge any of these SMSICs – as
C's score faithfully records – and thus A and B purport to represent
(from their points of view) three different individuals when using
these terms.[5] Consider a non-defective conversation between A and
B, overheard by C:

A: /**The inventor of bifocals** spoke French well/
B: /No, **he** didn't/

A, B, and C will all acknowledge an interpersonal anaphoric commitment regarding the boldly printed singular term-tokens, treating both tokens, coming out of different mouths, as belonging to
the same anaphoric chain. Moreover, A, B, and C will all agree in
practice as to which other actual or potential singular term-tokens
belong to that chain – cases of defective communication aside.
Thus, due to this agreement in anaphoric commitment, A, B, and
C treat all the assertional and practical commitments they *attribute*
to each other, involving singular term-tokens belonging to this
anaphoric chain, *because* they belong to this chain, as *of* or *about* the
individual each of them purports to represent via usages of tokens
belonging to the same chain in their own *acknowledged* doxastic and
practical perspective. For example, C acknowledges an assertional
commitment she would express via an assertion

C: /**The inventor of bifocals** is the inventor of the lightning rod/

and, moreover, attributes as acknowledged to A and B respectively
the assertional commitments each of them expressed in their little
dialogue above. Thus, since C treats the (boldly printed) singular term-tokens in the dialogue above, and in the corresponding
assertional commitments C attributes to A and B, as interpersonal

anaphoric recurrences of the (boldly printed) singular term token
in C's own potential assertion above, and in her corresponding
own acknowledged assertional commitment, she *ipso facto* treats
the assertional commitments she attributes as acknowledged to A
and B respectively, and in particular the (boldly printed) singular
term tokens expressing these commitments, as *of* or *about* the individual the boldly printed token in her own acknowledged commitment purports to represent: the inventor of bifocals. Moreover,
since C (though neither A nor B) acknowledges symmetric SMSICs
between this chain and two *other* anaphoric chains constituting the
singular terms "The inventor of the lightning rod" and "Benjamin
Franklin" respectively, C (though neither A nor B) identifies in
practice the inventor of bifocals with the inventor of the lightning
rod, aka Benjamin Franklin, and hence treats the (boldly printed)
singular term-tokens in A's and B's dialogue, and the two corresponding assertional commitments she attributes as acknowledged to A and B, as of or about the inventor of the lightning
rod, aka Benjamin Franklin – treatments that, of course, A and B
would reject.

In general, the scorekeeper treats the singular or general term-
tokens constitutively involved in her own system of acknowledged
and practical commitments as recurrences of certain singular or
general term-tokens constitutively involved in the systems she
attributes to each of her interlocutors. Accordingly, she treats in
practice the latter singular term-tokens, and the corresponding
commitments she attributes to the interlocutors, as discursively
representing the individuals, properties, and relations that the
term-tokens in her own system of acknowledged assertional and
practical commitments, and those commitments themselves,
purport to represent. Widening the perspective from the intrapersonal to the interpersonal aspects of the scorekeeping activity
reveals, Brandom thinks, that activity to the scorekeeper herself *as*
representational activity.

De re vs. *de dicto* belief ascriptions

As described so far, such reflective awareness of thought and talk
as representational in the context of the whole scorekeeping activity is still implicit. Even autonomous discursive practitioners have
this kind of awareness. So what needs to be added for scorekeepers
to make explicit in propositionally contentful thought and talk

which commitments and entitlements they acknowledge and attribute, and what these commitments and entitlements represent, so as to make these commitments and entitlements and their representational dimension themselves the topic of the conversation? Brandom thinks that the crucial addition is the ability to ascribe beliefs explicitly to each other, which is yet another algorithmic elaboration from, ultimately, autonomous discursive abilities. The contrast between ascribing beliefs *de dicto* vs. *de re* in particular is key here.

Consider C again. C may explicitly ascribe the assertional commitment A acknowledges above in two subtly different ways:

(1) A believes <u>that the inventor of bifocals spoke French well</u>
(2) A believes of the inventor of bifocals <u>that he or she spoke French well</u>

Sentence 1 is a *de dicto* ascription to A of the belief A expressed in the dialogue above. It specifies a complete, assertible propositional content (a *dictum*) – <u>that the inventor of bifocals spoke French well</u> – and states that A acknowledges an assertional commitment with that content. Sentence 2 is a *de re* ascription of, potentially, the same belief to A. It singles out an individual (a *res*) – the inventor of bifocals – and states of that individual that A believes <u>that he or she spoke French well</u>. Thus, by contrast to 1, 2 does not fully specify the content of the commitment A acknowledges, but makes instead partially explicit who or what A's belief represents. The "he or she" in the that-clause of 2 is an anaphoric expression that depends on the "the inventor of bifocals" in 2 and thus indicates that the belief ascribed to A *is about* the inventor of bifocals. But 2 does not indicate *how* – via which singular concept – A represents the inventor of bifocals. For all that 2 tells us, A may represent the inventor of bifocals through the belief ascribed not by using the singular concept <u>the inventor of bifocals</u> – which is what 1 would reveal – but instead <u>the first US Ambassador to France</u>, <u>the common-law husband of Deborah Read</u>, <u>Benjamin Franklin</u>, <u>Richard Saunders</u>, or any other singular concept that represents Benjamin Franklin uniquely. In fact, A represents him as the inventor of bifocals, given 1 and the little dialogue above, but 2 per se does not reveal this information.

In general, *de dicto* belief ascriptions have the form

S believes <u>that p</u>

They specify a complete, assertible content that p and display S as having a certain belief with that content. By contrast, *de re* ascriptions are paradigmatically of the form

S believes of x that ...it...

They pick out a certain individual, property, kind, or relation – x – and display S as having a certain belief *about* x – a belief whose content the ascription merely partially specifies but which it displays (via the anaphoric dependence of the pronoun "it" in the content-specifying that-clause on the expression "x" in the context of the "of") as about x. By contrast to *de dicto* ascriptions, which provide merely a that-clause context, *de re* ascriptions provide two contexts, the context of the "of" vs. the context of the "that". The terms in the context of the "of" purport to represent certain worldly items – paradigmatically individuals, properties, relations, or kinds – whereas the terms in the context of the "that" are of two kinds: they either are anaphoric expression depending on some terms in the context of the "of" and thus indicating that the belief ascribed represents the items the latter terms purport to represent, or they specify an aspect of the content of the belief ascribed (such as the "spoke French well" in 2) (MIE 539–47).

Occurrences of a term in a *de dicto* or *de re* ascription's that-clause behave substitutionally in ways different from occurrences of the same term in a *de re* ascription's of-clause. In the literature on belief ascriptions, the difference is usually couched in terms of co-extensionality and preservation of truth. Substituting for any term in a *de re* ascription's of-clause any co-extensional term – any term that designates the same individual, property, or relation as the term it is substituted for – never results in a *de re* ascription that differs in truth-value from the original one. By contrast, substituting a co-extensional term for a term in a *de dicto* or *de re* ascription's that-clause may yield an ascription that differs in truth value from the original one. Thus, substituting "Benjamin Franklin" for "the inventor of bifocals" into 1 and 2 gives us, respectively,

(3) A believes that Benjamin Franklin spoke French well
(4) A believes of Benjamin Franklin that he or she spoke French well

Since 2 is true, so is 4, given that Benjamin Franklin is identical with the inventor of bifocals. That is, in spite of A's ignorance about this identity, 4 has same truth-value as 2. Yet although 1 is true, 3 may very well be false, given A's ignorance about the identity of the inventor of bifocals with Benjamin Franklin. If 3 is true at all, it is so for independent considerations on A's part about the language skills of the person A purports to refer to by using the term "Benjamin Franklin" – which, unknown to A, is the inventor of bifocals – not because A would have formed the belief ascribed by 3 on the basis of the belief ascribed by 1.

Rather than accounting for this contrast between *de dicto* and *de re* ascription in terms of preservation of truth under substitution of term for term, Brandom offers a substitutional account of why everyone who ascribes beliefs explicitly to someone else *draws* this contrast in terms of his favored vocabulary of acknowledging vs. attributing commitment:

> The suggestion is that the expressive function of *de re* ascriptions of propositional attitude is to make explicit which aspects of what is said express substitutional commitments that are being *attributed* [by the ascriber to the ascribee as acknowledged] and which express substitutional commitments that are *undertaken* [i.e., acknowledged by the ascriber herself]. The part of the content specification that appears within the *de dicto* "that" clause is limited to what, according to the ascriber, the one to whom the commitment is ascribed would ... *acknowledge* as an expression of what that individual is committed to. The part of the content specification that appears within the scope of the *de re* "of" includes what, according to the *ascriber* of the commitment, but not necessarily according to the one to whom it is ascribed, is acknowledged as an expression of what the target of the ascription is committed to.
> (MIE 505–6. Compare also TMD 96–102; and 2007: 168–74).

Recall that, according to Brandom, scorekeepers track in practice not only each other's assertional and practical commitments – both the ones that the other acknowledges in fact and the ones that he should acknowledge, according to the scorekeeper – but also the acknowledged (substitution) *inferential* commitments in which the other's grasp of the content of the beliefs or intentions ascribed consists. Not only do scorekeepers track what every participant does and should believe and intend but also, as an integral part of such tracking, what inferential role every participant takes these beliefs and intentions to play. Brandom thinks that when a scorekeeper ascribes beliefs or intentions *de dicto* or *de re* to another, the difference, for her, in substitutional behavior of any term occurring in an of-clause vs. that-clause reflects, and is grounded in, this contrast between the substitutional commitments she herself acknowledges regarding that term at the time – which are usually also the ones she attributes to the ascribee as *to be* acknowledged regarding that term – vs. the ones she attributes as de facto acknowledged by the ascribee at the time.

For example, given the dialogue between A and B, C acknowledges not only an assertional commitment to the *de re* ascription 2 but also a substitution inferential commitment from 2 to 4, because C acknowledges a symmetric substitutional commitment concerning the singular terms "The inventor of bifocals" and "Benjamin Franklin." That is, C treats in practice the inventor of bifocals as identical with Benjamin Franklin, and hence will treat the inference from 2 to 4 as good – despite C's awareness of A's ignorance about the identity of the inventor of bifocals with Benjamin Franklin. By contrast, although C also acknowledges an assertional commitment to the *de dicto* ascription 1, C does not acknowledge a substitution inferential commitment from 1 to 3. After all, C attributes to A *as unacknowledged* a symmetric substitutional commitment regarding "The inventor of bifocals" and "Benjamin Franklin" (though C also attributes this commitment to A as *to be* acknowledged, given that C acknowledges it herself). From C's viewpoint, A does not regard Benjamin Franklin as the inventor of bifocals, and that viewpoint is reflected in C's not acknowledging a substitution inferential commitment from 1 to 3.

In general, substituting, for any term in a *de re* ascription's of-clause, another term that, according to the ascriber, purports to represent the same item always preserves, according to the ascriber, commitment to the resulting *de re* ascription, whereas substituting for any term in any *de re* or *de dicto* ascription's that-clause another term that purports to represent, according to the ascriber, the same item does not in general preserve commitment, according to the ascriber, to the resulting *de re* or *de dicto* ascription. It may do so, however, under different circumstances, according to Brandom. If A acknowledged in practice a symmetric SMSIC from "The inventor of bifocals" to "George Washington" – that is, if A misidentified the inventor of bifocals with George Washington – and C tracks A's acknowledgment without sharing it, C will, according to Brandom, acknowledge in practice an inferential commitment from 1 to

(5) A believes <u>that George Washington spoke French well</u>

but will not acknowledge one from 2 to

(6) A believes of George Washington <u>that he or she spoke French well</u>.[6]

This is Brandom's explanation of the difference in substitutional behavior from each ascriber's viewpoint between occurrences of a term in a *de re* ascription's of-clause and occurrences of the same term in a *de re* or *de dicto* ascription's that-clause.[7]

Brandom's theory of *de re* vs. *de dicto* belief ascriptions is a substantial, original contribution to the large literature on the topic. Here I can only highlight one interesting and, in light of this literature, controversial implication. According to Brandom, every belief is ascribable both *de dicto* and *de re*. More precisely, for every term-token in a correct *de dicto* ascription that is at all anaphorically linked to a term in the ascriber's repertoire that, from the ascriber's viewpoint, purports to represent an individual, property, or relation, there is, from the ascriber's viewpoint, a correct *de re* ascription, reached from the original *de dicto* ascription by creating an of-clause and exporting the term in question into its context – witness 5 and 6. This commitment is just a consequence of Brandom's view that *de re* vs. *de dicto* ascriptions mirror, from the ascriber's perspective, contrasts between the substitutional commitments she herself acknowledges regarding any particular term vs. the ones she attributes to the ascribee as acknowledged regarding that term.

Successful communication

Again, scorekeepers not only acknowledge, themselves, substitutional commitments regarding any term in their repertoire as an integral part of acknowledging a system of assertional and practical commitments in which the term figures, but also attribute to each interlocutor a usually deviating, though overlapping, set of substitutional commitments as acknowledged regarding the same term, as an integral part of attributing a system of assertional and practical commitments to the interlocutor in which the term figures. And given Brandom's inferential role semantics, the substitutional commitments a scorekeeper acknowledges regarding a term in the context of collateral commitments constitute the scorekeeper's linguistic understanding of the term. Thus an integral part of the overall scorekeeping activity is that each scorekeeper not only understands each term in use herself in a certain way but also tracks in practice how each interlocutor understands that term at the time. Accordingly, the difference in substitutional behavior of any term in the that-clause vs. the of-clause of a pair of *de dicto* and *de re* ascriptions concerning a certain belief or intention of an interlocutor reflects this difference between how the scorekeeper herself (the ascriber) understands the term vs. the way the scorekeeper takes the interlocutor to whom the belief or intention is ascribed to understand it, according to Brandom's theory of *de dicto* vs. *de re* ascriptions. The substitutional behavior, according to an ascriber, of occurrences of the term in an ascription's that-clause accords with the way the ascriber takes the ascribee to understand the term, whereas the substitutional behavior of occurrences of the same term in the context of the corresponding *de re* ascription's of-clause accords with the way the ascriber herself understands the term at the time.

This theory offers, Brandom thinks, a reply to a challenge, pressed prominently by Jerry Fodor and Ernest Lepore, for holistic theories of linguistic understanding such as Brandom's inferential role semantics. Couched in Brandomian terms, the problem is that different scorekeepers usually acknowledge different, though typically overlapping, inferential commitments regarding any sentence they exchange, reflecting their varying degrees of expertise and ignorance regarding the subject matter. Hence, since these acknowledgments constitute their linguistic understanding, given semantic holism, they usually understand any sentence exchanged in different ways. Yet if so, how can they be said to ever communicate successfully? Doesn't their variance in understanding imply that they constantly and systematically talk past each other? And if so, doesn't any joint assent or dissent regarding the sentences exchanged give the interlocutors merely the illusion of agreement or disagreement in discourse (Fodor and Lepore 1993: 19–20; Fodor and Lepore 1992)?

Brandom takes this challenge very seriously, and he thinks that his theory of scorekeeping includes precisely the resources to respond to it. He accepts that holism implies that different speakers usually understand any assertions exchanged in different ways. But he contends that the challenge is premised on the false assumption that successful communication requires *shared* understanding of what is said. Brandom calls the picture of successful communication this assumption presupposes the "transportation model" of linguistic communication, and identifies John Locke's theory of sharing ideas through speech as its historical origin (MIE 479). According to Brandom, communicative success does not require transporting an unchanging semantic item via speech from one mind to another, but rather requires from each participant an appreciation of every interlocutor's individual understanding of the linguistic performances exchanged. Communicating success-fully, thinks Brandom, is like engaging in a skillful dance together, where the varying moves made by each partner – the various lin-guistic understandings of what is said, distributed over the inter-locutors – amalgamate into one harmonious interaction (Brandom 2000b: 363).

> As long as there are differences in the collateral set of commitments with respect to which the content of the claim expressed by a sen-tence needs to be assessed, the sentence in one mouth means some-thing different from what that same sentence means in another mouth. So even in the smooth untroubled case of communication, if you want to understand what I say, you have to be able to associate with it a sentence that in your mouth expresses the claim that the sentence I uttered expresses in mine. For your understanding it (your knowing what I have committed myself to) involves your being able to trace out the inferences that claim is involved in ... in order to know what I am committing myself to. This means knowing ... what claims its endorsement would preclude you, as well as me, from being entitled to, and so on. Apart from that capac-ity, you cannot extract information from what I say and cannot be said to understand it.
>
> (Brandom 1994: 510, see as well 513, 586–601)

The theory of scorekeeping is, of course, Brandom's way to explain how each participant traces these similarities and differ-ences in linguistic understanding. The scorekeeper tracks in prac-tice, to the best of her abilities, the (substitution) inferential commitments each interlocutor acknowledges regarding any asser-tion exchanged, and thus captures how the interlocutor under-stands the assertion. Accordingly, the scorekeeper has a sense of the various ways in which her interlocutors understand the asser-tion and each of the term-tokens in it. Since each participant thus tracks every other participant's more or less idiosyncratic under-standing of any assertion exchanged, the participants, thinks Brandom, can be said to communicate successfully despite their variances, given semantic holism, in linguistic understanding. This, Brandom thinks, answers Fodor's and Lepore's challenge.

Yet a difficulty for this approach to successful communication is that while it may explain communicative success in cases where the scorekeepers already have a lot of information about each other's linguistic understandings of the terms involved, communicative success usually obtains in the absence of such information. Consider the following dialogue between two strangers:

D: Excuse me, where is the closest pharmacy?
E: At the downtown market.
D: How far is the walk? My arthritis is killing me.
E: The 47 gets you there. The bus stop is over there.

On any non-trumped-up understanding of "communicative success," this conversation is successful, steering, as it does, D via the bus stop to the pharmacy. Yet the exchange, even when taking into account the full non-linguistic context in which it occurs, dramatically underdetermines for D and E – and for us – how each understands the key terms "pharmacy," "downtown market," "arthritis," and "bus." D's and E's respective understanding of these terms may be quite idiosyncratic, and nuanced and sketchy in different respects. Thus, imagine D to be a physician from out of town and E the chair of the local chamber of commerce. Yet at no point of their short conversation will the scores D and E keep on each other capture any of these idiosyncrasies. Of course, should D and E get to know each other well and should they talk a lot about business, pharmacology, medicine, and public transportation, they may over time develop a better grip on each other's understanding of these terms. Yet such mutual enlightenment comes gradually and as a result of much successful communication, rather than as a condition for it. Therefore, it seems implausible that scorekeeping, on Brandom's account, can in general play the pivotal role Brandom envisions in yielding communicative success despite ubiquitous variances in linguistic understanding.

If that is right, is there a good way for Brandom to supplement or alter this theory such that it explains communicative successes between strangers such as D and E? It seems to me that he himself explicitly proposes an alternative in the passage quoted earlier. I requote:

Use of an [interpersonal] anaphoric proform implicitly *stipulates* coreference with the anaphoric antecedent upon which it is semantically dependent. Thus differences in the substitutional commitments that determine the propriety of inferences involving 'the inventor of bifocals' according to speaker and audience can be bracketed and a common topic of conversation secured by using a tokening that is anaphorically dependent on the speaker's tokening. To respond to the speaker by saying *"He* did not speak French well" is to disagree with the claim made, *whoever* the inventor of bifocals might turn out to be. ... Interpersonal anaphora achieves just the effect that matters for securing communication in the face of differences in collateral commitments.

(MIE 486)

This passage occurs in a context in which Brandom discusses and dismisses various alternative attempts from the literature to reconcile holism with communicative success.[8] Brandom regards what he says here as a preliminary introduction to his scorekeeping theory of successful communication, which he officially rolls out later in MIE and which I just challenged. We should, however, instead regard it as an alternative theory. Brandom here proposes that *bracketing* differences in linguistic understanding, rather than *tracking* them, is the key to communicative success, and that the anaphoric mechanism at the heart of his project allows for just that.

Here is one way to interpret this proposal. Given their agreement in practice as to which term-tokens belong to the same anaphoric chain, and their agreement in practice that all term-tokens belonging to the same anaphoric chain have the same meaning (and hence should be understood in the same way), all participants agree in practice, for any such chain and any token in it, that it is governed by a certain specific set of substitution semantic norms – the same set for everybody. That is, although the participants disagree in practice *which* set that is – they acknowledge different (though overlapping) substitution semantic commitments regarding the chain – they agree in practice that only one set of substitution semantic norms governs the chain, regardless of who produces the tokens in the chain. Accordingly, all participants recognize everybody, including themselves, as obliged to acknowledge the same substitutional commitments regarding any such anaphoric chain, that is, they treat in practice every token in such a chain as *to be* understood by all the participants – and indeed, by everybody at all – in the same way. This mutual normative expectation, regarding all the term-tokens in any assertion – that everybody should understand them in the same way – suffices for all the participants to treat the assertion as expressing a single claim. Of course, the participants usually vary in their de facto understandings of that claim. Still, on the present interpretation of the passage above, Brandom suggests that the combination of the participants' treatment of any assertion as *to be* understood in the same way by everybody and each participant's own more or less idiosyncratic de facto understanding of it suffices for successful communication. In particular, the de facto variances in understanding can be "bracketed" as long as they don't bubble to the surface, or matter for the purposes of the conversation. And when they do bubble to the surface, the discursive situation appears to the participants not as one in which they turn out to have talked past each other all along, and communication has failed all along, but rather as one that obliges them to align their understandings of the terms in question and, relatedly, their beliefs one way or another in the relevant respects, so as to honor the requirement that these performances are to be understood in the same way – "whatever it is" – by everybody.

For example, E may falsely believe that arthritis can strike both joints and thighs, hence acknowledge a substitutional commitment from "__ is arthritic" to "__ strikes joints and thighs", while D may know that arthritis may strike only the joints, hence acknowledge a substitutional commitment from "__ is arthritic" to "__ strikes only joints." Yet this difference in understanding of "arthritis" can be bracketed for the purposes of the dialogue above and, indeed, D and E may never notice it, without thwarting communicative success. What matters for communicative success is, first, that they both have at least the superficial, partial understanding of "arthritis" required for the purposes of their particular conversation – say, that they both acknowledge substitutional commitments from "__ is arthritic" to "__ is some kind of ailment" and, perhaps, to "__ is treatable with medication" – and, second, that they both treat in practice the arthritis-token out of D's mouth (and any token anaphorically related to it) as *to be* understood in the same way by everybody, that is, as a term governed by objective semantic norms (and expressing a single, determinate concept). Should, in a different context, their varying understandings of "arthritis" bubble to the surface, the new situation will appear to both D and E as a disagreement over arthritis that *ceteris paribus* needs to be resolved, not as a revelation that, since they have understood "arthritis" in different ways, they have miscommunicated all along. Suppose the little dialogue continues as follows:

E: I too have had arthritis for many years in my thighs now
D: Arthritis strikes the joints only

Now the hitherto hidden variance in D's and E's respective under-standings of "arthritis" has bubbled to the surface, and with it the obligation, dictated by their joint treatment of the various tokens of "arthritis" in their dialogue as governed by a single, determinate set of semantic norms, to align their acknowledged substitutional commitments regarding the term one way or another. If discourse proceeds as we would expect E will, once D has identified herself as a physician, adjust to D, that is, acknowledge a substitutional commitment from "__ is arthritic" to "__ strikes only joints" and disavow his last assertion. Still this variance, and the fact that it was hidden ("bracketed"), did not render the earlier parts of D's and E's conversation unsuccessful, according to this interpretation of Brandom's alternative proposal.

Summary

Although the semantics of speech and thought is not even partially a representational matter, but rather solely a matter of inferential role, all speech and thought has a representational dimension, according to Brandom. This chapter introduced Brandom's theory of the representational dimension of speech and thought, according to which this representational dimension results from the discur-sive scorekeeping activity.

According to Brandom, a scorekeeper's ongoing intrapersonal rational activity of integrating her beliefs and intentions into a coherent unity, by acknowledging inferential connections and weeding out incompatibilities, is responsible for the fact that these beliefs and intentions purport to represent a world of Aristotelian states of affairs – a world of individuals as having certain proper-ties and as standing in certain relations. This is so, first, because such rational activity is a segment of larger, feedback-governed cycles of the scorekeeper's more or less reliable engagement with the non-linguistic environment through which aspects of the environment themselves become incorporated into discursive practice, and, second, because such rational activity consists in a complicated interplay between assertional/practical, substitu-tion semantic, syntactic, and anaphoric commitments. Due to the combination of both dimensions, Brandom argues, the subject's rational activity appears to her as purportedly about the largely non-linguistic world, structured as a world of Aristotelian states of affairs.

While such representational purport is thoroughly irreflective, in the sense that such intrapersonal rational activity per se does not give the rational subject an even implicit sense of this activity *as representational*, the subject gains an implicit reflective sense of thought and talk as representational by placing her intrapersonal rational activity into the context of the interpersonal aspects of her scorekeeping activity, according to Brandom. Through attributing systems of assertional and practical commitments to peers in discourse in the context of her own intrapersonal rational activity, the attributed assertional and practical commitments implicitly appear to her – thanks to the interpersonal anaphoric connections between her own reasoning and the attributed systems – *as representing* the very individuals, properties, and relations that her own acknowledged assertional and practical commitments purport to represent.

Scorekeepers track in practice not only each other's beliefs and intentions but also, Brandom thinks, the more or less idiosyncratic ways in which each interlocutor understands the linguistic performances exchanged in discourse. That is, they track not only each other's acknowledged assertional and practical commitments but also each other's acknowledged (substitution) inferential commitments. Brandom thinks that scorekeepers may make explicit aspects of their otherwise implicit tracking of their own vs. another's linguistic understanding by explicitly ascribing beliefs to the other *de re* vs. *de dicto*. Moreover, he argues that such tracking of variances in linguistic understanding, built into the scorekeeping activity, resolves the challenge, famously raised by Jerry Fodor and Ernest Lepore, of how a holistic theory of meaning and linguistic understanding, such as Brandom's inferential role semantics, can explain the possibility of successful communication, given that such holistic theories imply ubiquitous variances in linguistic understanding among discoursing speakers. Communicative success, Brandom maintains, does not require shared linguistic understanding, as Fodor's and Lepore's challenge assumes, but rather an appreciation of how each participant understands the linguistic performances exchanged, as accounted for by the theory of scorekeeping.

8

Objectivity and Phenomenalism about Norms

Let us review the terrain we've marched through in the last seven chapters. Brandom's overarching ambition, to which all his philosophical efforts are subordinated, is to develop a nuanced, comprehensive, and attractive pragmatist account of the central semantic, epistemic, and cognitive features of thought and talk – meaning, propositional content, concepts, linguistic understanding, inference, representation, assertion, justification, knowledge, belief, intention, logic, truth, etc. – that is, an account of them in terms of the use of language in communication. To that end, he develops a normative pragmatic conception of communication, according to which communication (discursive practice) is a species of norm-governed social interaction (deontic practice). Deontic practices in general are norm-governed exchanges of performances between at least two participants. Described abstractly in normative pragmatic terms, at each stage of such an exchange, each participant has a constellation of commitments and entitlements, paradigmatically to certain performances. This constellation changes from one stage to the next, depending on the performance produced and on who produced it, in accordance with the norms governing the practice. Each participant tracks these commitments and entitlements as best as she can; that is, she keeps score by adopting at each stage a constellation of normative attitudes, and by altering this constellation from one stage to the next, depending on the performance produced and on who produced it, in accordance with what she takes to be the norms governing the practice. Specifically, at each stage each participant acknowledges an array of commitments and entitlements, paradigmatically to certain performances, and attributes in practice, among other things, two (overlapping) arrays of commitments and entitlements to certain performances to each participant: one array that she takes the participant to acknowledge in fact at that stage, and one that she takes the participant as required to acknowledge at that stage, in light of what she takes the norms to be.

Brandom insists that deontic practices and deontic practitioners, as described in these normative pragmatic terms, need not exhibit any of the semantic, epistemic, and cognitive features of interest. Neither need the performances exchanged be speech acts – propositionally contentful, inferentially related linguistic performances – nor need the participants be cognitive, rational, concept-using beings; that is, beings with beliefs and intentions and capable of propositional knowledge. Rather than being a cognitive affair in this sense, the participants' competence to participate in deontic practices, and their sensitivity to norms in particular, is ultimately entirely a matter of pragmatic and other know-how that does not require the ability to think and talk in the semantically, epistemically, and cognitive relevant senses.

Discursive practices are deontic practices with a distinct structure, according to Brandom. Brandom argues that due to this distinct structure, all the semantic, epistemic, and cognitive features of interest emerge as aspects of discursive practices so described. Thus, due to this structure, the performances exchanged, and the participants' commitments and entitlements to such performances, emerge as genuinely inferentially related to, or incompatible with, each other. That is, they have distinct inferential roles. Identifying these inferential roles with roles in reasoning and the space of inferential relations in which each actual or potential discursive performance is situated with the normative space of reasons, Brandom regards a scorekeeper's activity of acknowledging commitments and entitlements to performances in discourse as genuinely rational activity – reasoning – and his tracking of other participants' commitments and entitlements to performances as his tracking and assessing those other participants' reasoning. Discursive practitioners essentially are, and treat each other as, genuinely rational beings. Scorekeeping in discursive practices is the most fundamental form of rational activity, according to Brandom. Engaging in any other form of reasoning at all – thinking in private, making strategic decisions, and so on – requires being a minimally competent discursive practitioner, but not vice versa.

In light of Brandom's commitment to inferential role semantics, performances in discourse, and the participants' commitments and entitlements to them, emerge as propositionally contentful: their propositional content is their inferential role. Indeed, given the distinct structure of discursive practices, these performances emerge as genuine speech acts (assertions, practical statements, queries, disavowals, etc.) and acknowledged commitments and entitlements to performances emerge as genuine cognitive mental states (paradigmatically, beliefs and intentions). Furthermore, by placing the participants' scorekeeping activity into the broader context of their skillful engagement with their natural environment – their ability to form observational beliefs reliably in response to perceived inputs and to reliably act based on their constellation of assertional and practical commitments – and stipulating that the performances exchanged themselves have additional normative syntactic and anaphoric structure, Brandom offers accounts of singular and general terms and concepts, empirical content and knowledge, and conceptual representation of environing objects, properties, and relations.

Yet since discursive practice, even when placed in this larger context, is at bottom entirely described in normative pragmatic terms and other non-semantic, non-epistemic, non-cognitive vocabulary, recovering all these semantic, cognitive, and epistemic features of discourse and of discursive practitioners from this description amounts to a pragmatist explanation of them – or, at least, a philosophically illuminating elucidation (see Wanderer 2008, chap. 4, and the conclusion below) – in terms of the use of language in discourse.

As mentioned at the beginning of chapter 3, however, Brandom is actually invested in two pragmatist projects, one more fundamental than the other. The less fundamental one takes the norms governing deontic practices in general more or less for granted. It offers little philosophical explanation or elucidation of how these norms obtain and what their metaphysical status is, save for arguments that they cannot be naturalized and that their existence, and the participants' ability to follow them, nonetheless does not require that creatures governed by them must already exhibit the semantic, epistemic, and cognitive features and activities of interest (the arguments against regularism and regulism rehearsed in chapter 1). Rather, taking norms so understood for granted, this less fundamental pragmatist project limits itself to offering detailed normative pragmatic descriptions of discursive practices and correlatively detailed arguments that particular semantic, epistemic, and cognitive features reduce to, or otherwise metaphysically depend upon, particular aspects of these practices so described. Chapters 3 to 7 laid out Brandom's efforts along these lines.

The more fundamental pragmatist project aims to explain how norms in general, and the norms of reasoning governing discursive practice in particular, themselves come into existence. That is, it aims to explain how the specifically inferential norms constituting the propositional content of linguistic performances and, by extension, the substitution semantic norms constituting the meaning of the terms occurring in these performances, obtain. What determines them, and what is their metaphysical status? This is Brandom's project of "phenomenalism about norms," introduced in chapter 2, which is his attempt to revitalize and defend the enlightenment idea of the autonomy of reason. Brandom's point of departure here is Hegel's idea of the institution of norms through mutual social recognition. The key claim of this phenomenalist project is that the discursive scorekeeping activity is not only a process of following the inferential norms of reasoning governing discourse, but simultaneously also the process that creates, institutes, and determines these very norms of reasoning. In particular, according to Brandom, the social processes of scorekeepers' forming successive arrays of acknowledgments and attributions of commitments and entitlements in systematic interaction with the performances exchanged, distributed over the discoursing scorekeepers and seen as part of the larger sociohistorical process of discursive activity among the community of rational beings, gradually institutes and determines the very norms of reason governing these processes. The basic idea is that once each participant's intrapersonal reasoning activity – her synthesizing of her acknowledged assertional and practical commitments and entitlements into a unity of apperception, by acknowledging inferential commitments between them and by acknowledging incompatibility commitments repelling other actual or potential linguistic performances from this holistic web – is placed into the interpersonal context of each participant's mutual tracking and evaluating of other participants' intrapersonal reasoning activity, and once these mutually recognitive discursive micro-processes in turn are placed into the wider sociohistorical process of overall discursive practice among rational beings, the synchronic and diachronic interplay between such intrapersonal and interpersonal activity can be seen as instituting and determining the norms of reason governing this very activity. As seen in chapter 2, the contrast between what the norms of reason are and what a scorekeeper takes them to be under particular discursive circumstances – being right vs. taking right – is supposed to somehow fall out from the social contrast between what one scorekeeper acknowledges as her commitments and entitlements vs. what other scorekeepers attribute to her as commitments and entitlements she should acknowledge, distributed over the scorekeepers.

We have now in full view the fine-structure of Brandom's theory of discursively rational activity: the process of scorekeepers' adopting and changing normative attitudes of various kinds – of acknowledging and attributing assertional and practical commitments and entitlements, (substitution) inferential, syntactic, and anaphoric commitments, and of treating each other as more or less reliable observers and agents – through which scorekeepers both synthesize intrapersonally a unity of apperception and interpersonally mutually recognize each other in discursive practice as such synthesizing creatures. This chapter introduces how Brandom thinks this process institutes and determines the semantic norms of reasoning governing discourse.

I-thou vs. I-we sociality

In MIE, Brandom unambiguously asserts, with Kant, that norms of reason are objective in the sense that they may bind reason even though no one – past, present, and future – acknowledges their authority. By contrast to norms of taste, cultural norms, norms of certain ritualistic practices, or, arguably, aesthetic norms, any norm of reason is, Brandom thinks, such that it must be possible for the entire community of rational beings to go wrong with respect to it (MIE 53–4, 606–7). Yet phenomenalism about norms asserts a metaphysical dependence of the norms of reason on the normative attitudes scorekeepers adopt in discursive practices. And while Brandom's development of this idea in terms of Hegel's conception of mutual social recognition makes (in principle) room for accounting for the contrast between what the norms are and what someone takes them to be, in terms of the social contrast between what one vs. another scorekeeper takes them to be, this Hegelian move still suggests that the existence of a norm of reason depends on it being acknowledged as authoritative by someone or other. If so, the question is how such attitude dependence of norms of reason can be made compatible with the robust attitude independence that the objectivity of the norms of reason seems to assert.

In MIE, Brandom develops a line of argument designed to reconcile these two seemingly contradictory demands. He distinguishes between two ways in which a phenomenalist might think of the scorekeeping activity as instituting the norms of reason, only one of which is incompatible with the objectivity of norms of reason:

> [T]raditionally intersubjectivity has been understood in the *I-we* way, which focuses on the contrast between the commitments of *one* individual and the commitments of the *community* (collectively), or those shared by *all* individuals (distributively). ... [B]y contrast, intersubjectivity is understood in the perspectival *I-thou* fashion, which focuses on the relation between the commitments *undertaken* [acknowledged] by an [individual] ... interpreting others and the commitments *attributed* by that [individual] ... to those others.
>
> (MIE 599)

On the I-we approach, although the scorekeeping activity of each individual plays a role in instituting the norms of reason, it does so by contributing to the overall collective or distributive net-effect of such activity. This net-effect is a feature of the whole community of rational beings, and it sets the ultimate standard of what counts as right reasoning. In this sense, the community of rational beings, as such, has ultimate authority over what the norms of reason are. Brandom gives regularity theories of norms as examples to such I-we approaches (MIE 39). Each individual's use of, or her dispositions to use, language contributes to determining the overall regularity of (dispositions to) use, and this regularity – a feature of the community of rational beings – sets the standard of correct use for each individual. Yet any such I-we approach to norms of reason, Brandom thinks, is indeed incompatible with the objectivity of such norms. While the reasoning of individuals is right or wrong in light of the communal standard, the community as such can never be wrong. The perspective of the community, determined by the system of communal standards, is ultimate in that there is in principle no further perspective from which it can be rationally criticized, affirmed, or shown to be mistaken in certain ways (MIE 599–600; see also chapter 1).

By contrast, according to the I-thou approach favored by Brandom,

> Sorting out who should be counted as correct, whose claims and applications of concepts should be treated as authoritative, is a

messy retail business of assessing the comparative authority of competing evidential and inferential claims. ... There is only the actual
practice of sorting out who has the better reasons in particular cases.
The social metaphysics of claim-making settles what it means for a
claim to be true by settling what one is doing in *taking* it to be true.
It does not settle which claims *are* true – that is, are *correctly* taken
to be true. That issue is adjudicated differently from different points
of view, and although these are not all of equal worth, there is no
bird's-eye view above the fray of competing claims from which
those that deserve to prevail can be identified.

(MIE 601)

On the I-thou approach, the scorekeeping activity determines the
norms of reason in an always (in principle) open-ended, provisional, and further evaluable way. The authority of norms of reason
continues to depend on some – though not just any – scorekeepers'
acknowledging their authority under particular circumstances. Yet
such authority is in principle always subject to potential further
scrutiny, qualification, and reassessment in light of new evidence
or further considerations, provided by some scorekeeper under
different circumstances or by third parties brought into the conversation. Each scorekeeper has a perspective on many subject matters
at any time; that is, each scorekeeper acknowledges a certain system
of assertional/practical and (substitution) inferential commitments,
constituting her conceptual understanding of these subject matters
at that time. And by playing the game of giving and asking for
reasons, multiple scorekeepers determine among themselves who
has the better reasons "in particular cases": that is, which perspective on the subject matter at hand is comparatively best, what open
questions it raises, how it might be further refined, and who should
be considered as an expert comparatively most able to navigate the
relevant portions of the web of inferential relations (TMD 229–31).
What the comparatively and provisionally best perspective is
cannot be determined by an isolated individual alone, but depends
on the critical affirmation of others. Yet any results of such collective efforts are, and are recognized by all responsible participants
as, in principle subject to legitimate further scrutiny, reaffirmation,
or revision in light of new evidence and further considerations.

Thus, according to this I-thou approach, individual perspectives
"are not all of equal worth." Still, "there is no bird's-eye view above
the fray of competing claims from which those that deserve to
prevail can be identified" (MIE 601). That is, there never is an ultimate set of standards in light of which these provisional efforts can

be assessed as better or worse, but for which there is in principle no further, relatively independent perspective from which that set of standards could legitimately be critically appraised, reaffirmed, or reassessed. Instead, there are only the transient perspectives of individual scorekeepers, and for any one of these perspectives there are others that serve as a legitimate basis for evaluating and critiquing it. The I-thou approach thus contrasts with the I-we approach to norms of reason, which implies the existence of such an ultimate set of standards. However, it also contrasts with other prominent positions in Western philosophy that imply the existence of such a set – such as Platonistic approaches to the norms of reason, or approaches that stipulate a final set of standards in the mind of God, or in nature, or in some individual credited with ultimate epistemic and semantic authority.

A consequence of the I-thou approach is that propositional contents and concepts are essentially perspectival (MIE 197, 592–4), in the sense that there are *only takes* by individual scorekeepers at particular times on these contents and concepts, not also "real" contents and concepts over and above those takes and more or less completely apprehended or "grasped" by those takes. Cast in Brandom's normative pragmatic vocabulary, according to the I-thou approach, it is not the case that for any sentence or term there are, on the one hand, acknowledged (substitution) inferential commitments by particular scorekeepers at particular times constituting particular linguistic understandings of those sentences and terms at that time, that is, particular perspectives on their meaning, and, on the other hand, the "real" (substitution) inferential norms over and above any acknowledged (substitution) inferential commitments constituting the "real," non-perspectival meaning of these sentences on the term. Instead, there are only the various perspectives of linguistic understanding on any given sentence or term, and the scorekeeping activity of updating, coordinating, critically appraising, and improving these perspectives in piecemeal fashion on an ongoing basis. Brandom frequently expresses this point in terms of a prioritization of process over relation. Ultimately, the sentences and terms in use are not linked via any (substitution) inferential *relations* to each other. That is, they are ultimately not related to each other by any non-perspectival or supra-individual communally perspectival semantic norms. Instead, *processes* of particular scorekeepers' acknowledging (substitution) inferential commitments regarding these sentences and terms, and of updating these acknowledgments as part of the overall scorekeeping activity, are semantically ultimate (RP 88–90; SOT chap. 6: 92–3, chap. 9: 7–8, 60; BSD 178–80). Brandom regards such prioritizing of process over relation as the most characteristic feature of the pragmatist tradition (BSD 180).

Objectivity as a structural feature of discourse

How does the I-thou approach square with the objectivity of norms of reason? In MIE, Brandom proposes that due to the structure of the scorekeeping practice, all discursive practitioners have a *formal* sense of objectivity, which both suffices to account for the objectivity of norms of reason and is compatible with the I-thou approach.

> According to the *I-thou* construal of intersubjectivity, each perspective is at most *locally* privileged, in that it incorporates a structural distinction between objectively correct applications of concepts, and applications that are merely subjectively taken to be correct. But none of these perspectives is privileged in advance over any other. At first glance this egalitarian attitude may seem just to put off the question of what is really correct. … The alternative is to reconstrue objectivity as consisting in a kind of perspectival *form*, rather than in a nonperspectival or cross-perspectival *content*. What is shared by all discursive perspectives is *that* there is a difference between what is objectively correct in the way of concept application and what is merely taken to be so, not *what* it is – the structure, not the content.
>
> (MIE 600)

Each scorekeeper in practice treats the issue at hand as if there is one objectively correct way to reason about it; that is, one way in which the terms in use are *to be* understood by everybody – whatever that way is – regardless whether anybody does understand it that way. At the same time, each scorekeeper regards it as an in-principle open question whether the various ways in which he, or anyone else, reasons in fact about the issue, that is, in fact understands the terms in use, is the objectively correct way. This sense of objective correctness is merely formal, in that no non-perspectival content over and above anyone's de facto understanding of the terms in use, nor any fact regarding whether anyone or everyone understands these terms in a certain way, is constitutive of the objectively correct way to understand these terms. Neither is, for the scorekeeper, anyone's or everyone's reasoning objectively correct because anyone,

or everyone, de facto reasons this way – not even the expert is
objectively correct, according to the scorekeeper, *because* she (the
expert) reasons so – nor is anyone's or everyone's reasoning objectively correct because some non-perspectival content over and
above the individual scorekeeping perspectives ultimately authorized it. Although Brandom doesn't use these terms, we might say
that this formal sense of objective correctness is like a Kantian
regulative, as opposed to constitutive, idea. The scorekeeper's
treatment of any terms in use as to be understood by everybody
in the same way – whatever that way is – perpetually moves
him to critically examine and improve upon his and his peers' de
facto reasoning and understanding involving these terms, but this
objectively correct way of understanding is neither constitutively
determined by any non-perspectival content nor by anyone's de
facto understanding of these terms.

Why does every scorekeeper have this formal sense of objectivity? Brandom argues that every scorekeeper does so in consequence
of the contrast in scorekeeping perspectives he draws in practice
and made explicit by *de re* vs. *de dicto* ascriptions (as outlined in the
last chapter):

> From the vantage point of any particular scorekeeper, what one is
> *really* committed to by an acknowledgement . . , what *really* follows
> from the claim (and hence its objective content), is to be assessed by
> conjoining it with truths – that is, statements of fact. But what plays
> this role for a scorekeeper is the set of sentences by the assertion of
> which the scorekeeper is prepared to *acknowledge*, and so undertake,
> doxastic commitment. ... What appears to the scorekeeper as the
> distinction between what is objectively correct and what is merely
> taken to be or treated as correct appears to us [theorists] as the dis-
> tinction between what is acknowledged by the scorekeeper attribut-
> ing a commitment and what is acknowledged by the one to whom
> it is attributed. The difference between objective normative status
> and subjective normative attitude is construed as a social-perspecti-
> val distinction between normative attitudes.
>
> (MIE 596–7)

A structural feature of scorekeeping is that, at any stage of the
conversation, each participant acknowledges a system of assertional and inferential commitments and entitlements herself and
attributes in practice such a system as acknowledged to each interlocutor. And Brandom here proposes that, for the participant, the
former perspective enshrines what is right at that stage (right

reasoning, right understanding, true belief, etc.) whereas the latter enshrines what someone (the attributee) takes to be right. Thus, every scorekeeper draws in practice a contrast between what is right and what is taken to be right by someone, and Brandom proposes here that this is the sought contrast, for the scorekeeper, between what is objectively right and what is merely taken to be so by someone. This is still a formal sense of objectivity, first, in that it falls out from the structure of scorekeeping and, second, in that the theory of scorekeeping identifies neither any non-perspectival content nor the perspective of any particular scorekeeper as the ultimate standard that determines which scorekeeping perspective is really right.

While these considerations may show that each scorekeeper distinguishes between what is correct and what is merely taken to be so, however, Brandom's claim that this amounts to the scorekeeper's sense of *objective* correctness is problematic as it stands. After all, according to the argument, how the attributee should reason and understand, and what she should believe, is always determined, for the scorekeeper, by his (the scorekeeper's) own system of acknowledged commitments and entitlements. For each scorekeeper, his own system at the time is the standard of correctness at the time, according to the argument. Anyone's deviation from it is, from his point of view, *ipso facto* mistaken. Yet I think we should not identify such a sense of correctness with a sense of objective correctness. Having a sense of objective correctness implies having a sense that one might be wrong *oneself* – precisely what scorekeepers appear to lack, according to the argument. And even setting aside the issue of objectivity, the view the argument advocates seems implausible as it stands. We often appreciate the possibility that our own reasoning and understanding may be wrong in some ways. We do so vis a vis those who we regard as teachers or experts, and sometimes even when we are confident that our interpretations are by far the best – for example, when we have reached, after much study, a fruitful, harmonious, empirically adequate, predictively powerful cutting-edge position in a particular scientific field of study. We can, and in all non-trivial matters should, remain open to the in-principle possibility that we may be wrong after all. Cultivating such openness is epistemically virtuous – dogmatists and fundamentalists lack precisely this trait – and is required for one's ability to effectively and fruitfully learn from others. Yet as it stands, Brandom's argument makes it hard to see why we can, and often should, take others as better informed than we are ourselves, or why we should be open to counterarguments and different viewpoints. We shall return to this point below.

Common-law discourse as a model

Brandom's efforts in MIE to defend phenomenalism about norms along the lines just presented were widely considered unsuccessful. The key problem, I think, was that Brandom, despite advocating the idea of objectivity as a merely formal feature of discourse, also made it clear throughout MIE that he continued to aim to explain the institution of objective semantic *norms* in terms of the scorekeeping attitudes. Yet the continued pursuit of this aim in MIE was incompatible, I think, with the idea of objectivity as a formal feature of discourse. If objective semantic norms govern discourse, objectivity is not a formal but rather a substantial feature of discourse, consisting in the presence of these norms. Accordingly, the resulting phenomenalist explanation left most commentators dissatisfied.[1] In more recent writings, however, Brandom has significantly elaborated and refined his defense of the phenomenalism about norms.[2] Rather than defending the phenomenalist program entirely in abstract terms, he now frequently defends it by looking closely at specific examples of discourse. His favored example, which I shall introduce now, is legal discourse in a certain idealized common-law tradition (e.g. RP 84–8; TMD 13–15, 230–3). Following Wanderer (2008: 206), I interpret Brandom's use of the common-law case as not just an illustration or analogy but rather as a simplified model or paradigm for how *all* ordinary empirical concepts are instituted through a sociohistorical sequence of applications of concepts by scorekeepers.

In a common-law tradition, no written, statutory law constrains a judge's applications of legal concepts. Instead, judges apply or withhold a legal concept (such as being strictly liable or being contractually obliged) based on previous applications or withholdings of the concept in other cases by judges working in the same legal tradition and in light of the explicit rationales those judges provided for their previous decision. Each new case in which the question arises as to whether to apply the legal concept consists in a description, in non-legal language, of what are deemed to be the important facts. This non-legal description is in certain respects similar to those previous cases, and different in other respects. In making her decision, the judge first decides which of those previous decisions to regard as providing precedent: that is, as most similar in relevant non-legal respects to the case in her hands. Then she decides whether or not to apply the legal concept at issue based on the rationales provided by the judges in these precedents – that is, their justification of the application (or withholding) of the legal concept at issue in light of the non-legal facts of their cases and the rationales provided by still earlier decisions deemed to be precedents by them. To the present judge, these precedents and the rationales provided for them, which articulate as acknowledged (by those previous judges) overlapping systems of assertional and substitution inferential/incompatibility commitments linking the legal concept whose application is to be decided to other non-legal and legal concepts, *authorize* her present decision. That is, to the present judge, the tradition of previous, precedent-setting decisions, together with the accompanying rationales, gradually institutes and refines a system of normative statuses governing the application of the legal concept at issue and relating it to other legal and non-legal concepts. Moreover, by making her own decision and providing her rationale, the present judge contributes to instituting and refining this micro-system of normative statuses. Her decision and rationale, as part of the overall tradition, contributes to exert similar authority over future judges working on similar cases. In short, in such a common-law tradition, past decisions and their rationales, expressing past judges' systems of acknowledged assertional and substitution inferential/incompatibility commitments concerning the use of a particular legal concept, gradually institute without further ado a system of normative statuses for how to use this concept in future legal reasoning. In this sense, past judges and decisions exert authority over future ones (RP 86).

These moments of authority of past judges and decisions over future ones, however, are counterbalanced by moments of authority of future judges and decisions over past ones. Any future judge, in forming a decision and rationale for the case in her hands, *assesses* both which past cases are precedents for the current case, and which past rationales are most authoritative (persuasive) for it. That is, her efforts to be faithful to the legal tradition in her decision and her justification for her decision involve an implicit assessment of the claimed authority of past decisions and rationales, or of aspects of them: that is, an implicit treatment of these past claims to authority as responsible or irresponsible. Prior acknowledged assertional   and   substitution   semantic   commitments   that contravene what she regards as the cumulative normative weight of the prior tradition are deemed unpersuasive and dismissed (found as lacking standing as normative statuses), even if the non-legal facts of these dismissed prior decisions and rationales may greatly resemble the non-legal facts of the case at hand. Indeed, occasionally a judge may dismiss a whole tradition of using a certain legal concept in response to acknowledged commitments and entitlements from *outside* the legal tradition that, to her, are overridingly authoritative – such as widespread changes in popular opinions and attitudes or new persuasive scientific beliefs (think civil rights, right to gay marriage, and so on). In sum, in forming their decisions and rationales, past judges not only exert authority over future judges but also *petition* future judges to recognize (rather than reject) these decisions and rationales as authoritative. In this sense, future judges exert authority over past ones. Moments of authority and responsibility are symmetrically distributed over the historical succession of judges and judgments (RP 87–8).

Brandom's key claim, apropos phenomenalism about norms, is that the historic process consisting in the scorekeeping activities of successive judges in the tradition is, given this symmetric structure of authority and responsibility distributed over them, simultaneously a process of ongoing applications (or withholdings) of the relevant concepts and a process of instituting and gradually determining the substitution semantic norms constituting these concepts. The interplay between each judge's intrapersonal reasoning regarding her particular case in light of, on the one hand, her dual sense of being normatively constrained by, and of critically re-evaluating, past judges' applications (or withholdings) of these concepts and, on the other hand, her dual sense of further normatively constraining future judges in their use of these concepts and of petitioning them to treat her intrapersonal reasoning regarding the present case at hand – the synthetic unity of acknowledged commitments and entitlements expressed by her decision and rationale regarding that case – as authoritative, gradually institute and determine the norms of reasoning constituting the concepts in use.

Brandom elaborates on the sense in which this historical process determines the norms of reasoning constituting these concepts by holding that an essential aspect of the socially perspectival character of concepts – the fact that concepts are essentially interpreted by some scorekeeper or other – is a *temporally perspectival* dimension. Corresponding to a judge's twofold orientation on past and future applications of the concepts in use, she has a twofold sense in which she determines the substitution semantic norms constituting these concepts (RP 92–3). In light of her dual sense of being rationally constrained by, and of critically evaluating, past applications (and withholdings) of the concepts in use in her present synthesizing efforts vis a vis her present, historically novel case, she takes her efforts to determine the substitution semantic norms constituting the concept in the epistemic sense of a *discovery*. Her efforts to critically and selectively accommodate the myriad of normative pressures from past uses in her present case, if conscientious, appear to her as involving a retrospective rational reconstruction of the tradition as governed by a specific set of substitution semantic norms that always already have governed use of the corresponding terms and that past judges have only partially recognized and honored (RP 86). Looking back, the concepts in use appear to her to be determined in the sense of having sharp and complete boundaries: they appear to her to consist in fixed, eternal sets of non-perspectival substitution semantic norms that settle how each concept is to be used in reasoning under all possible circumstances, and the history of uses culminating in her present synthesis appears to her as a progressive process of gradually unearthing more and more of these norms (RP 92).

This epistemic sense of determining the concepts in use, involved in the judge's orientation on the past, is, however, counterbalanced by a constructive semantic sense of determining these concepts involved in her orientation toward the future. Looking toward the future, the fact that she applies (or withholds) the concepts at issue under historically novel circumstances – and her sense that her doing so involves a reconstructive recollection of past uses – make it appear to her that she *created* new substitution semantic norms governing those concepts to which future judges are responsible. And in light of this sense of creating new normative constraints for future judges, as well as in light of her sense of the tenuousness of these constraints – her sense that she petitions future judges to accept these constraints as authoritative, rather than to dismiss them, and that she is, in this sense, at their mercy – the concepts in use do *not* appear to her as determined (in the sense of consisting in fixed eternal sets of non-perspectival norms that settle the correctness of their use in reasoning under all possible circumstances). Rather, they appear to her as determined in the creative sense of being on an ongoing basis interpreted and re-interpreted – negotiated and administered – by conflicting, tenuous, potentially ever-shifting, contingent normative attitudes for which there is no non-perspectival standard of correctness. That is, looking into the future, the concepts in use appear to the judge as *in*determinate in the epistemic sense (RP 92–3; TMD 231; SOT chap. 9: 61–2, chap. 10: 80–3).

It is possible, I think, to motivate and refine this picture of concepts as temporally perspectival by looking at it again from the perspective of Brandom's theory of interpersonal anaphora. Judges usually differ to some extent in the way they understand the particular legal and non-legal terms in use. But they always agree in practice as to which term-tokens belong to which anaphoric chains: which are recurrences of the same term. Moreover, since the term-tokens in an anaphoric chain inherit their meaning from each other, all judges treat in practice all the term-tokens in an anaphoric chain – past, present, and future – as having the same meaning, hence as *to be* interpreted in the same way by everybody at all times. Accordingly, they treat every participant in their legal discourse as bound to converge on one set of acknowledged SMSICs regarding each such chain – the same set for everybody, whatever it is – linking that chain to some other anaphoric chains of legal or non-legal term-tokens.

Accordingly, each past judge's acknowledged SMSICs regarding the anaphoric chains constituting the legal and non-legal terms whose application is currently at issue appear to the present judge as an (overrideable) license or authorization to acknowledge the same SMSICs in her present case, so as to honor the requirement that each term-token belonging to the same chain is to be interpreted in the same way by everybody. Yet given the idiosyncrasies of her present case, and potential inconsistencies in the history of past acknowledged SMSICs regarding the terms whose use is at issue, the present judge is required to rationally reconstruct this history by disregarding some of these licenses and, also, by acknowledging some new SMSICs regarding the terms in use – required to acknowledge constellations of SMSICs regarding these terms that, depending on the degree of idiosyncrasy of her present case and the degree of inconsistency of the history of past acknowledgments, deviate more or less from past usages. In any case, looking into the past, the overall constellation of SMSICs she acknowledges regarding these terms appears to her as an improvement – after all, to her, her overall constellation captures her new case in addition to all the old ones, and (potentially) straightens out old inconsistencies – hence, given the way interpersonal anaphora works, as something that all past judges should have acknowledged all along too. Plausibly, all this adds up to a sense on the present judge's part of her synthesizing activity as determining the meaning of the terms in use in the epistemic sense of discovery. That is, her present synthesizing activity plausibly appears to her, looking into the past, as an unearthing, if not of the ultimate meaning of the terms in use, at least of something closer to how these terms should ultimately be understood by everybody.

Yet looking toward the future, the present judge's understanding of these terms appears to her in a different light. By acknowledging her overall constellation of SMSICs regarding these terms, she puts normative pressure on future judges to interpret them in the same way, given that future tokenings of these terms anaphorically depend on her present use of the terms and thus inherit their substitution semantic significance from it. She also, however, knows her overall constellation – enshrining, as it does, an extension of past acknowledged constellations to her new case and a critical appropriation and reconstruction of the history of past use – to be historically new and to be recognized as such by future judges. Moreover, depending on the degree of idiosyncrasy of her case and the degrees of richness and consistency of the history of past scorekeeping attitudes toward the terms in use, she will regard her present overall constellation of assertional and substitution semantic commitments as more or less underdetermined by that history – as being just *one* way, among a larger or smaller number of mutually exclusive other ways, to plausibly extend the tradition to her present case. (We will return to this point in a moment.) Furthermore, she knows that future judges will have to extend the tradition, including her present decision and rationale, to (to her) unforeseen new cases. Hence her decision, and the tradition, may call for further tweaking and revising. For all these reasons, she will regard her constellation as something future judges will critically examine and potentially reject in central respects in the context of their own synthesizing efforts. Plausibly, this sense that her constellation of assertional and substitution semantic commitments is historically new, that its propriety is underdetermined by the past, and that its authority depends on future affirmation under (to her) unknown, more or less idiosyncratic future circumstances, amounts to a sense on the part of the present judge, looking into the future, that her present synthesizing effort, and the normative pressure she thereby exerts on future judges, is created, rather than discovered. Her own and future judges' efforts plausibly appeared to her as part of an ongoing social effort to construct (institute, create) the meaning of the terms in use, rather than to unearth it.

Semantic underdetermination

As just mentioned, the present judge has a sense that the history of past scorekeeping attitudes regarding the terms in use underdetermines which constellation of assertional and substitution semantic commitments she should acknowledge in her present case. Brandom has been at pains to emphasize in his writings after *Making It Explicit* (though not so much in MIE itself) that this sense is accurate. Although the sum of past scorekeeping attitudes normatively constrains the present judge's synthesis, it does not metaphysically necessitate a single correct system of acknowledged assertional and substitution semantic commitments regarding the case at hand. In principle, and often also in practice, the past always gives judges some leeway. Brandom attributes this position to Hegel, but he clearly also endorses it himself:

> He [Hegel] is very much aware of the *openness* of the use of expressions that is the practice at once of applying concepts in judgment and determining the content of the concepts those locutions express. This is the sense in which prior use does *not* close off future possibilities of development by settling in advance a unique correct answer to the question of whether a particular concept applies in a new set of circumstances. The new circumstances will always resemble any prior, settled case in an infinite number of respects, and differ from it in an infinite number of respects. There is genuine room for choice on the part of the current judge or judger, depending on which prior commitments are taken as precedential and which respects of similarity and difference are emphasized.
>
> (RP 89; see also e.g. SOT chap. 10: 85–9.)

In principle, multiple mutually exclusive ways of selecting precedential decisions, of weighting aspects of the rationales accompanying them, and of extending them to the new case, are open to the present judge, and no further criterion is available for her or for future judges assessing her efforts to decide which of them is "really" correct. In practice, the degree of such leeway presumably varies with the degree of idiosyncrasy of the case at hand and the degree of sophistication, richness, and coherence of the tradition of past scorekeeping attitudes regarding the terms in use.

Still, in principle such leeway never shrinks to zero, according to Brandom.

What does this underdetermination thesis say about the metaphysics of meaning (norms of reason)? It would seem natural at this point for Brandom to place his project squarely into the "interpretationist" tradition in the philosophy of language developed by W. V. O. Quine and Donald Davidson.[3] Quine's and Davidson's central claim, pertinent to the underdetermination thesis, is that there is no linguistic meaning at all, metaphysically speaking, but only particular speakers' linguistic understanding at particular times: translation (Quine), or interpretation (Davidson). While a speaker's linguistic understanding of any linguistic performance is constrained in various ways – by naturalistic psychological mechanisms (Quine), and in addition by certain normative principles (Davidson) – the *real meaning* of the performance is no such constraint. Linguistic performances have no real meaning at all, according to Quine and Davidson, over and above the ways particular speakers may understand (translate/interpret) them. Moreover, the constraints on linguistic understanding leave *indeterminate* how a speaker should understand any particular linguistic performance, according to Quine and Davidson. Every linguistic performance is such that there are, in principle, many mutually exclusive and yet equally proper ways for a speaker to understand it. In light of his underdetermination thesis, it would seem natural at this point for Brandom to place his theory squarely into this Quinean and Davidsonian tradition. Brandom might say that since the totality of past scorekeeping attitudes constrains but underdetermines the propriety of reasoning and linguistic understanding, past attitudes and uses determine no norms of reasoning at all: that is, there are no such norms at all metaphysically speaking, and linguistic performances have no determinate meaning.

Yet while there are important affinities in spirit and detail between Brandom's project and Quine's and Davidson's theories, the conclusions Brandom draws from his underdetermination thesis seem subtly different from Quine's and Davidson's eliminativism about linguistic meaning. Brandom agrees, given the underdetermination of proprieties of present use by the totality of past scorekeeping attitudes, that no ordinary empirical term has determined meaning in the sense that the term would ever be governed by a set of semantic norms mandating, for all possible circumstances and scorekeepers (past, present, and future), a unique way of properly using the term in reasoning. Brandom now often calls a conception of determinate meaning in this sense the "Verstand conception" of meaning, in Hegel's pejorative

sense of *Verstand* (RP 89). Since determinate meaning in this "Verstand" sense would be non-perspectival, Brandom's rejection of it
thus reaffirms his I-thou conception of semantic norms: there are no
semantic norms over and above scorekeepers' acknowledging and
attributing commitments and entitlements in accordance with what
they take to be the semantic norms. Brandom claims, however, that
there remains a better, Hegelian "Vernunft" conception of semantic
determinateness, which takes into account both this socially perspectival character and the temporally perspectival character of concepts.
Brandom maintains that the scorekeeping practice determines, and is
governed by, semantic norms in this sense:

> are the contents of empirical concepts *determinate*, in the ... Verstand
> sense, as the retrospective epistemic perspective has it, or *in*deter-
> minate in that sense, as the prospective semantic perspective has
> it? ... [If] the only metaconceptual expressive tools one has available
> to describe the situation is the static, non-perspectival Verstand con-
> ception of determinateness, the answer would have to be "Both" –
> or, just as correctly, "Neither." That those two answers do not make
> any sense within the metaconceptual framework of Verstand just
> shows the expressive impoverishment and inadequacy of that
> framework. What we should say is that concepts have contents that
> are both determinate and further determinable, in the sense pro-
> vided by the dynamic, temporally perspectival framework of Ver-
> nunft. Do we *make* our concepts, or do we *find* them? Are we
> authoritative over them, or responsible to them? Hegel's model enti-
> tles him to answer "Both." For both aspects are equally essential to
> the functioning of concepts in the ever-evolving constellations of
> concepts and commitments. ... Authority and responsibility are
> coordinate and reciprocal, according to the mutual recognition
> model of normativity that is Hegel's successor to Kant's autonomy
> model. And when such a structure of reciprocal recognitive attitudes
> takes the special form of a historical-developmental process, the
> contents of those attitudes and the statuses they institute can be
> considered from both prospective and retrospective temporal recog-
> nitive perspectives. Those perspectives are two sides of one coin.
> (RP 93)

So, apparently contra Quine's and Davidson's meaning eliminativism, Brandom wants to preserve a sense in which linguistic
performances have determinate meaning – meaning in the *Vernunft*
sense – which combines the two senses in which a scorekeeper
takes herself to determine meaning, built into the temporally perspectival character of concepts: the retrospective epistemic sense

of discovering semantic norms that always already have governed the terms in use, and the prospective sense of creating semantic norms governing the terms in use. The two ways in which semantic norms seem to be determinate to the scorekeeper, who synthesizes a unity of apperception in light of past applications of concepts and in anticipation of future assessments of her present efforts, are not only subjective impressions, Brandom claims, but also revelations of the true metaphysical nature of meaning. Linguistic performances have determinate meaning, in Hegel's "Vernunft" sense, in seeming contrast with Quine's and Davidson's interpretationist, meaning-eliminativist program.

Yet perhaps the differences between Brandom's "Vernunft" theory of meaning and Quine's and Davidson's meaning-eliminativist approach may in the end be more terminological than substantial. After all, Quine and Davidson argue against the existence of meaning in the "Verstand" sense and never consider anything like Brandom's "Vernunft" conception of meaning, and they may thus agree that linguistic performances are meaningful in the "Vernunft" sense. Moreover, meaning in Brandom's "Vernunft" sense remains perspectival: no meaning (semantic normativity) exists over and above constellations of scorekeeping attitudes of acknowledging and attributing commitments and entitlements, distributed over past, present, and future speakers. This perspectival nature of meaning in the "Vernunft" sense thus seems to accord with Quine's and Davidson's insistence that there is no meaning over and above translation/interpretation. Finally, and perhaps most importantly, Brandom's claim that the totality of past scorekeeping attitudes underdetermines which SMSICs the present scorekeeper should acknowledge, arguably implies that the scorekeeper's retrospective impression that she discovers determinate meanings in the "Verstand" sense – specific substitution semantic norms that always already have governed the terms in use – far from being an insight into an aspect of the true nature of meaning, is an illusion. Multiple mutually exclusive ways of reasoning under the present circumstances are all equally proper in light of the totality of past scorekeeping attitudes, Brandom claims. If so, underlying the scorekeeper's retrospective *impression* of semantic determinacy in the "Verstand" sense is *real* retrospective semantic indeterminacy in the "Verstand" sense. And since there seems to be no further sense beyond this false impression in which meaning is determinate in the "Verstand" sense, according to Brandom's "Vernunft" conception of meaning, this conception arguably implies

that meaning, rather than in reality both indeterminate and determinate, is in reality only indeterminate, in accordance with Quine's
and Davidson's views.

Objectivity again: facts as true claims

Earlier we discussed Brandom's idea of objectivity as a formal,
structural feature of discourse. Yet Brandom also embraces the
seemingly different yet more familiar idea of objective correctness
as accordance with the facts: as correct representation of the largely
mind-independent, objective world:

> It is a feature of our assessments of the application of at least some
> concepts that we take it that besides correctness of discursive atti-
> tude in the sense of entitlement to the commitment undertaken ...
> there is also a kind of correctness that is determined by how things
> are with what is represented. Whether the application of a concept
> is correct or incorrect in this sense is independent of the attitudes of
> the one applying the concept. ... Making sense of this fundamental
> characteristic of our linguistic practice means funding a notion of
> discursive *success* ... that transcends our attitudes ... and answers
> instead to the *objects* of those attitudes.
>
> (MIE 280)

The world of facts not only contributes to determining causally
what we do believe and intend, but also normatively constrains
what we should believe and intend. Our beliefs and intentions in
this sense "answer" to the largely mind-independent world.

At first glance, this conception of objectivity seems to differ starkly
from the structural, formal one. The latter is the merely negative conception of objectivity as correctness for everybody independently of
what anybody or everybody takes to be correct. It does not imply
that some aspect of reality or discourse determines which lines of
reasoning are really correct. The formal conception of objectivity is
simply silent on the issue as to what, if anything, determines which
thoughts and lines of reasoning are correct. On the other hand,
the conception of objectivity as accordance with the facts gives an
answer to this question: those contents and lines of reasoning are
objectively correct that accord with the facts, because they accord
with the facts. It thus seems to be a substantial rather than a formal
conception of objectivity. Moreover, since Brandom elaborates this
conception of objectivity as one according to which the world of
facts normatively, and not merely causally, constrains our rational

activity, this conception of objectivity seems to imply that the largely mind-independent world is intrinsically normative. As mentioned in chapter 5, however, this implication would render Brandom's conception of objectivity as accordance with the facts incompatible with his pragmatist Enlightenment idea that norms of reasoning and concepts, rather than given by the mind-independent objective world, are instituted by scorekeeping processes of adopting and changing constellations of normative attitudes in discursive practice.

Yet Brandom works hard and, in more recent writings, with ever-increasing nuance to mitigate these impressions and to bring his conception of objectivity *qua* accordance with the facts in line with the overarching Enlightenment pragmatist bent of his project, using ingredients that we have already encountered along the way. To begin, Brandom defines facts, following Frege, as *true claims* – in the sense of true contents claim*ed* (contents asserted/believed), by contrast to true claim*ings* (true assertings/believings) (MIE 327–30, 622–5). A fact is an assertible content that is true, according to Brandom. Moreover, as Brandom makes clear in more recent writings, the notion of content he uses here is the alethically modal notion of an Aristotelian state of affairs representable by an assertion, not the deontically modal notion of a thought *qua* set of norms of inference and incompatibilities relating the assertion to other statements (RP 97–8). States of affairs are positions in the space of alethically modal relations of necessary co-occurrence (inclusion), possible co-occurrence, and impossible co-occurrence (preclusion), whereas propositional thoughts are positions in the deontically modal space of inferential entailment, compatibility, and incompatibility. The two spaces are isomorphic in the sense that the state of affairs p includes another one q, possible co-occurs with another one r, and precludes a third one s if and only if an assertional commitment to the thought that p consequentially commits to that q, does not preclude entitlement to that r, and precludes entitlement to that s. Since what constitutes the content of a thought is its location in the normative space of reasons, and since this deontic space is isomorphic with the space of alethically modal relations in which states of affairs are located, Brandom regards states of affairs as themselves conceptually contentful in a straightforward, extended sense. What constitutes the content of a state of affairs is its location in the space of alethically modal relations: its relations of inclusion, co-possibility, and preclusion relating it to other states of affairs (RP 97). In light of these elaborations, facts as true claimable contents, according to Brandom, are states of affairs that are actual (or obtaining, as opposed to merely possible).

Next, we saw in chapter 6 that the concept <u>state of affairs</u> and essentially related implicitly or explicitly *alethically* modal concepts regarding the objective world (the concepts <u>object</u>, <u>property</u>, <u>alethically modal relation</u>, etc.) are reference independent of the concept <u>thought</u> and essentially related implicitly or explicitly *deontically* modal concepts regarding rational subjects (the concepts <u>assertional commitment</u> and <u>(substitution) inferential commitment</u>, etc.), in the sense that, the existence and nature of Aristotelian states of affairs, objects, properties, etc., do not, in the relevant sense, depend on the existence of rational, discursive activity, assertional commitment, etc. (TMD 194–9, PP 125–7). That is, we saw that Brandom emphatically objects to any form of metaphysical relativism that claims that rational, discursive activity creates the world of facts, and that he agrees with the common-sense view that the world of facts existed long before rational, discursive creatures evolved and that it might have existed even if such creatures had never evolved. Brandom is, in this sense, a metaphysical realist – even a metaphysical modal realist (RP 98, EE 194–204).

Furthermore, we saw in the last chapter that, in the experience of error, scorekeepers may experience their empirical thinking as normatively constrained not only by other thoughts (reasons) but also by their non-linguistic environment. A scorekeeper may experience the non-linguistic environing objects, properties, and relations that are incorporated into her discursive practice, and represented by her thinking, as repelling her empirical thinking and hence her thinking as *ipso facto* erroneous. And this experience of worldly friction is experienced by her as a normative (not just causal) constraint on her thinking. Finally, we saw just now that, according to Brandom, reasoning and concepts are temporally perspectival and that the system of assertional, practical, and substitution semantic commitments a scorekeeper acknowledges at a given time appear to her retrospectively as a rational reconstruction of, and improvement over, her and her peers' past synthesizing efforts, and as a determination of norms of reason in the epistemic sense of discovery. To the scorekeeper looking back, Brandom wants to say, it seems as if she unearthed norms of reasoning that bind everyone at all times.

These are all essential, structural ingredients of the scorekeeping practice. Putting them together, Brandom argues that a scorekeeper must have a sense of representing, and of being normatively constrained by, an objective mind-independent world of facts:

The way the idea of <u>reference of *appearances* to an underlying *reality* that they represent</u> – the idea that they are appearances *of* some reality that was always already there, objectively (in the sense of being independent of the attitudes that are its appearances) – arises and is secured *for consciousness* itself [that is, for the scorekeeper] is through the experience of *error*. ... Prior error is acknowledged *internally* in each rational integration by engaging in the activity of repairing incompatible commitments. ... And using one's current commitments as the *external* standard for assessing which such prior developments and adjustments were *successful* is treating it as presenting the reality, how things are in themselves, that all the others were more or less adequate appearances of. A successful recollective reconstruction of the tradition shows how previously endorsed constellations of commitments were unmasked, by internal instabilities, *as* appearances, ... but also how each such discovery contributed to ... correcting the picture they present of how it really is with what they were all along representing.

(RP 100–1)

This is, I think, an elaboration of Brandom's earlier account in MIE of why, due to structural features of discourse, every scorekeeper must have a formal sense of objective correctness, in the sense that she draws in practice a distinction between a thought, or line of reasoning, being correct for everyone at all times vs. someone's or everyone's taking a thought or line of reasoning to be correct. As we saw earlier, in MIE, Brandom identifies the scorekeeping contrast between acknowledging and attributing commitments and entitlements as the relevant structural feature: for each scorekeeper, the commitments and entitlements she attributes as acknowledged to others, or to her earlier self, at a given time are correct or incorrect depending on whether or not they accord with the system of commitments and entitlements she acknowledges herself at that time. Our worry was that a scorekeeper's sense of correctness in this sense fails to leave room for her to have a sense that she might *herself* be wrong at the time, hence that this fails to be an account of having a sense of objective correctness.

Yet the present passage from RP appears to mitigate such worries by bringing all the additional structural ingredients just listed into consideration. To the scorekeeper, her present system of acknowledged commitments and entitlements is an improvement over her own and her peers' past synthesizing efforts, in the sense that she regards that system as both the result of many resolutions of past experiences of error and as a critical appropriation of, and improvement over, her peers' past applications of the concepts in use. Indeed, Brandom claims that in light of these recollective efforts, she takes her present system to accord with a system of norms of reason in the "Verstand" sense that always already has governed every rational being as such. If that is so, she also takes it as a system of representations of facts, that is, a system of representations of the way the world really is, as opposed to how it merely appeared to her and her peers in the past. Moreover, in light of the reference independence of facts from acknowledged commitments and entitlements, she also takes these facts to obtain independently of her present system and, indeed, independently of everyone's system of commitments and entitlements at all times. Finally, given her past experiences of error, she regards the objects, properties, and relations constituting these facts to normatively constrain her and her peers' reasoning.

Brandom claims, I take it, that all these considerations add up to an account of a scorekeeper's sense of correctness deserving to be identified with a sense of *objective* correctness. What about the worry that a scorekeeper may lack a sense that she might herself be currently wrong? Those who may feel that the present account still fails to fully address this worry may be steered toward the other half of Brandom's theory of the temporally perspectival nature of concepts. Looking into the past, the scorekeeper has a sense of having discovered a system of norms that has always already governed every rational being as such. Looking into the future, however, she has a sense that her present system of acknowledged commitments and entitlements might not be recognized as authoritative by future peers under their (currently unforeseen) circumstances. This sense of tenuousness, Brandom may say in reply to persistent worries, should suffice as the scorekeeper's sense of being potentially currently mistaken.

Assuming that, despite its many moving parts, this account of a *scorekeeper's sense* of objectivity can be successfully defended, what about objectivity itself? Are there objective norms of reasoning and objective, mind-independent facts, according to Brandom's mature theory of scorekeeping? The earlier MIE theory of objectivity as a formal feature of discourse would have it that nothing – and in particular nothing substantial – needs to be added to the account of a scorekeeper's formal sense of objectivity: this account is at the same time a complete account of objectivity itself. Unless it is in the end, however, a form of meaning eliminativism in the tradition of Quine and Davidson (as I suggested it might be), Brandom's mature theory of scorekeeping does say something substantial about the metaphysics of norms (and presumably facts) themselves, and it is, accordingly, incompatible with the theory of objectivity as a formal feature of discourse. According to the mature theory, norms (and presumably facts) exist, and they do not merely appear to scorekeepers as temporally perspectival but really are temporally perspectival. That is, they really are retrospectively determinate in the "Verstand" sense, and discovered, and prospectively indeterminate in the "Verstand" sense, yet determinable in the sense of being constructed. While this picture of the metaphysics of norms (and facts) may be obscure, it implies, I think, that metaphysically, norms (and facts) are retrospectively independent of scorekeeping attitudes and hence substantially objective, and prospectively dependent on the scorekeeping attitudes constructing them and hence substantially not objective (but rather relative to those constructing scorekeeping attitudes). If this is right, then while this view may be obscure, it clearly is incompatible with the merely formal approach to objectivity.

I indicated above, however, that the claim of the retrospective attitude-independence of norms (and presumably facts) is in tension with Brandom's thesis that the history of past applications underdetermines how concepts should currently be used: that this history allows for multiple mutually incompatible yet equally good ways to use them, and that therefore the scorekeeper's retrospective sense of norms as determinate in the "Verstand" sense (and as substantially objective) is illusory. In light of this underdetermination thesis, norms (and presumably facts), if they exist, are in fact *retrospectively* just as constructed and dependent on past and present scorekeeping attitudes as they are prospectively constructed and dependent on present and future scorekeeping attitudes. That is, the temporally perspectival realism about norms (and presumably facts), according to Brandom's mature theory of scorekeeping, when coupled with the underdetermination thesis, threatens to collapse into a form of full-blown relativism about norms (and facts).

Brandom has worked, and continues to work, extremely hard and stubbornly to reconcile his Hegelian pragmatism with a broadly Kantian commitment to objectivity, and such relativism is presumably the last thing he is prepared to accept. If so, perhaps one way for him to go forward, given his underdetermination thesis, is to firmly side with Quine's and Davidson's interpretationism: to advocate his mature scorekeeping theory while accepting it as a

form of meaning *eliminativism*. If so, Brandom would concede that
while there is much linguistic understanding (interpretation) by
particular scorekeepers at particular times, and while the mature
theory of scorekeeping shows exactly how that works, there are,
metaphysically speaking, no *semantic* norms (norms of reason) to
which such understanding answers. If Brandom were to take this
route, he could follow his broadly Kantian instincts about objectivity by reiterating his earlier view of objectivity as a formal feature
of discourse – which meaning eliminativism would allow.

Summary

An important part of Brandom's overall project is his advocacy of
phenomenalism about norms, which is the thesis that the scorekeeping attitudes speakers take in discursive practice create or
institute the objective norms of reasoning governing discourse, and
hence the objective meaning of the linguistic performances
exchanged. In one prominent strand of MIE, Brandom tries to
defend this thesis by combining an I-thou conception of semantic
norms with a conception of objectivity as a formal feature of discourse. According to the I-thou conception of semantic norms,
semantic norms are essentially socially perspectival in the sense
that there are no semantic norms over and above what particular
scorekeepers *take* those norms to be on particular occasions – over
and above the various ways scorekeepers understand the linguistic
performances exchanged. According to the conception of objectivity as a formal feature of discourse, it is built into the structure of
scorekeeping itself that each scorekeeper draws in practice a contrast between how a particular linguistic performance is in fact
understood by anyone (including herself) or everyone, and how
the performance should objectively be understood by everyone.
Since no substantial, non-perspectival objective semantic norms
govern discourse, according to the I-thou conception, the scorekeeper's sense of semantic objectivity, manifested in her drawing
of this contrast, is thus merely formal, rather than substantial.

Yet Brandom's overall case in MIE for phenomenalism about
norms has garnered mostly skeptical responses by commentators,
and Brandom has thus significantly elaborated and revised this
approach since then. In more recent works, Brandom reaffirms the
social perspectival character of semantic norms but also stipulates
an additional temporally perspectival dimension. To a scorekeeper

applying a certain term in light of the history of previous applications of the term (by her or by others), it appears as if she determined the norms governing the term in use in the epistemic sense of a discovery of those norms. Retrospectively, it appears to her as if she discovered the norms that always already governed the term. Yet in light of the fact that her present use will be critically evaluated and potentially dismissed by future users of the concept, her present use appears to her simultaneously as the determination of the norms governing the term in the semantic sense of a construction. Prospectively, it appears to her as if she brought the norms governing the term into existence. Brandom argues that this Janus-faced appearance of semantic norms to the scorekeeper do in fact reflect the true metaphysical nature of semantic norms themselves. The nature of semantic norms is that they are, on the one hand, essentially socially perspectival – acknowledged as authoritative by some scorekeeper or other – and both determinate in the epistemic sense and further determinable in the semantic constructive sense. I argued that one plausible way to interpret this otherwise potentially obscure proposal is to assimilate it to interpretationist approaches to linguistic meaning in the tradition of W. V. O. Quine and Donald Davidson.

Conclusion: Two Challenges

I would like to conclude by indicating two broader challenges to Brandom's project, one concerning the relation between this project and empirical work in the cognitive sciences and the other concerning the relation between the modeled scorekeepers and us.

Attributions "implicitly in practice"

Philosophy is often seen, and sometimes ridiculed, as an armchair discipline. The stereotypical philosopher proceeds in a priori fashion, is uncurious about work in the natural and social sciences, and dismissive about the possibility that such work could have any bearing on his or her projects. Although much philosophy today is thoroughly interdisciplinary and thus does not fit this description, one can see how Brandom might be accused of being such a stereotypical philosopher. In developing his massive theory of language and reasoning, he is much concerned with finding inspiration and support in ideas developed in what he sees as distinct "pragmatist" and "rationalist" currents in modern Western philosophy, and much less concerned with finding inspiration and support in contemporary debates in the cognitive sciences, in particular cognitive psychology and linguistics, that have a bearing on his project. This purely philosophical attitude is an advantage in the sense that it allows Brandom to lay out his unified and bold new vision of reasoning and linguistic communication without perpetually getting bogged down in specific, narrow empirical disputes. It can also be a liability in the sense that it provides the more antagonistic of his critics with opportunities to dismiss his project as empirically ill-founded. This is not so much a critique of Brandom himself – one man can only do so much – but a challenge for those sympathetic to his project to integrate it with, and further develop it in light of, the relevant empirical literatures.

For example, Brandom assumes that in the simplest kinds of discursive practices, in which all other instances of linguistic communication are grounded, the participants attribute to each other commitments and entitlements to assertions, both as acknowledged and as to be acknowledged, "implicitly or in practice." That is, he assumes that the participants in such practices attribute to each other both *de facto* beliefs that p and obligations and permissions to believe that q without conceptualizing in any way the attributed psychological states and normative statuses *as* beliefs or *as* obligations and permissions. The ability to explicitly ascribe to others beliefs that p, or obligations or permissions to believe that q – that is, the ability to form conceptualized meta-representations of these psychological states and normative statuses – is a later-coming ability of more sophisticated discursive practitioners, according to Brandom, which is grounded in their prior ability to attribute such states and statuses merely "implicitly in practice." This assumption is crucial for Brandom's pragmatist project. Without it, the normative pragmatic description of the simplest kinds of discursive scorekeeping practices, in terms of which Brandom wants to explain all reasoning and concept-use, would presuppose unexplained conceptual resources – the ability to conceptually represent others as believing that p and as obliged or permitted to believe that q – and thus his pragmatist project would falter.

Yet this assumption is also one of the Achilles heels of Brandom's project. While his regress-argument against regulism (chapter 1) motivates the view that in simple discursive practices all norms are followed merely implicitly in practice, Brandom offers no similar argument motivating the claim that in such practices all beliefs and normative statuses are similarly attributed merely implicitly in practice. And this absence is problematic in light of the large "theory of mind" literature in cognitive psychology, concerning our ability to recognize others as psychological beings, that is, as beings with beliefs, desires, intentions, emotions, perceptions, etc. Although a wide spectrum of theories of this ability are offered in this literature, and although no particular contender is currently widely accepted, most participants in these debates agree that recognizing others as being in certain psychological states in general, and as believing that p in particular, is essentially mediated by explicit meta-representations involving the relevant psychological concepts, such as the psychological concept of belief – contra Brandom's conception of simple discursive practices.[1] Thus, the more antagonistic of Brandom's critics, and certainly every supporter of the Received View, may use this conflict between an assumption at the heart of Brandom's project and an emerged consensus in the "theory of mind" literature, plus the fact that Brandom does not address the issue, as a reason for dismissing his project as based on a psychologically ill-founded *ad hoc* conception of scorekeeping in simple discursive practices.[2]

This example illustrates the importance for Brandom and like-minded contemporary "neo-pragmatists" to engage with relevant empirical literatures in the cognitive sciences. In this particular case, their task is to develop an argument, or at least a positive story, out of an engagement with the "theory of mind" literature: that, contra the wide consensus in this literature, Brandom's conception of attributions of beliefs and normative statuses "implicitly in practice" is plausible or at least acceptable. Indeed, in this particular case they might potentially find important support from the emerging literature on embodied cognition. In consonance with the overall drift of Brandom's project, proponents of the embodied cognition approach challenge the predominant cognitivist framework within which most of the "theory of mind" debate is conducted – roughly, the view that our cognitive abilities are to be fully explained in terms of mental representations in the brain – and argue for the constitutive dependency of conceptual thinking and other aspects of our cognitive life on non-cerebral embodied perceptual and practical skills and know-how. In particular, proponents of the embodied cognition approach concerned with our ability to recognize other minds are sympathetic to the view that much of such recognition is implicit and independent of applications of psychological concepts. For example, Shaun Gallagher holds that, regarding our ability to recognize each other's intentions,

> in most intersubjective situations we have a direct, pragmatic understanding of another person's intentions because their intentions are explicitly expressed in their embodied actions. For the most part this understanding does not require us to postulate a belief or desire that is hidden away in the other person's mind, since what we might

reflectively or abstractly call their belief or desire is directly expressed in their behavior. ... Prior to the possibility of knowing the other's mind in either a theoretical or simulation mode, one already requires (a) an understanding of what it means to be an experiencing subject; (b) an understanding of what it means that certain entities in the environment (but not others) are indeed such subjects; and (c) an understanding that in some way these entities are similar to and in other ways different from oneself. Furthermore, to form a theory about or to simulate what another person believes and desires, we already need to have specific pre-theoretical knowledge about how people behave in particular contexts.

(Gallagher 2001: 86)

Gallagher explicitly acknowledges that his approach to treating others as intending creatures is reminiscent of aspects of the existential phenomenology of Martin Heidegger – a framework that Brandom himself appropriates for his own purposes (TMD chap. 10, in particular 309–12). Supporters of Brandom's project should find this idea, that others' beliefs and desires are "directly expressed in their behavior" and directly detectable by others without the aid of the psychological concepts of belief and desire, congenial. It should be important, for the sake of this project, to develop an idea along these lines further and to explore whether it may provide suitable underpinnings for Brandom's discursive scorekeeping model, and in particular his conception of attributing beliefs and normative statuses to each other "implicitly in practice."

Scorekeepers and us

A second challenge concerns the issue of whether Brandom's theory has the resources to account for *our* reasoning and discoursing. Obviously, if it does not have these resources, Brandom's theory should be of little interest to us. Yet some commentators have challenged the prospects for Brandom's theory in this regard. For example, following McDowell (2008), Wanderer has argued in his book on Brandom that even if the practices Brandom calls "autonomous discursive," as described in chapter 3, are gradually algorithmically elaborated, as described in chapter 6, into more sophisticated practices called "non-autonomous discursive," encompassing all sorts of universal LX-vocabulary – in particular vocabulary dubbed "logical," "psychological," and "semantic" – we are left without a compelling reason to regard the resulting practices, or their "autonomous discursive" origin, as instances of genuine rational linguistic communication at all, as opposed to non-discursive social games with some structural similarities to genuine rational discourse. That they are instances of genuine rational discourse begs the question, according to this challenge, and Brandom lacks further resources to make this claim plausible – let alone to prove it – if pressed by someone skeptical about the matter, such as a proponent of the Received View (Wanderer 2008: chap. 4, especially 84–9).[3]

In order to respond to the challenge, Wanderer ingenuously recommends that Brandom should abandon his explanatory pragmatist ambitions – to reduce the semantic, epistemic, and cognitive features of our discourse and reasoning to normative pragmatic features of discourse – and reinterprets his pragmatism as a more modest explicatory doctrine. Brandom's pragmatism, understood as a reductively explanatory doctrine, faces the challenge just described, and the best way out for Brandom, Wanderer proposes, is to regard the normative pragmatic descriptions of discourse (encountered in chapters 3 and 6) as explications and elucidations of important aspects of *our* discoursing and reasoning. These normative pragmatic descriptions highlight essential ties that the semantic, epistemic, and cognitive aspects of our reasoning and discoursing have to pragmatic features and skills involved in *our* discursive practices – ties that *we* would otherwise have merely implicitly appreciated – but they should not be regarded as the bases for a reductive explanation of the semantic, epistemic, and cognitive features of our discoursing and reasoning. Since this reinterpretation of Brandom's pragmatism from an explanatory into an explicatory doctrine dissolves the skeptical challenge – after all, the reinterpreted doctrine takes our discursive reasoning for granted from the start and does not attempt to explain it in normative pragmatic terms – we should understand Brandom's pragmatism in this less ambitious reinterpreted way.

Since I have interpreted Brandom's pragmatism throughout as explanatory – in line with how Brandom himself understands the doctrine (as Wanderer agrees) – and since this is, if I'm right, the main difference between Wanderer's and my take on Brandom's work, it is appropriate for me to conclude by saying at least a few words in defense of Brandom's pragmatism as an explanatory doctrine. The key to assess Wanderer's (and McDowell's) challenge is to get clearer on what the essential features of autonomous discursive practices are. The challenge relies heavily on Brandom's claim in MIE that, strictly speaking, all social practices fitting the bare-bones normative pragmatic description given in chapter 3 of the present book (and, incidentally, also the third chapter of MIE) – hence any social practices algorithmically elaborated from these practices and comprising universal LX-vocabulary – are genuine rational discursive practice (MIE 221, 234). I agree that *this* claim opens Brandom up to the challenge that such practices may be merely social games, and that the best way to respond to the challenge may be to reinterpret his pragmatism as an explicatory and elucidatory doctrine, rather than a reductively explanatory one.

Throughout his entire oeuvre, however, Brandom frequently attributes essential features to discursive practices that go far beyond the bare-bones description in chapter 3. He claims, first, that any discursive practices resembling usages of *natural languages* – which, really, should be the only discursive practices of interest to us – essentially comprise language entries in perception and language exits in behavior (MIE 234; see also 2008b: 219; 2010f: 33; BSD 106; EE 52), and that the discursive and rational processes tied to language entries and exits are portions of larger feedback-governed TOTE-cycles that incorporate aspects of the non-linguistic environment (chapter 5). Second, Brandom claims that all discursive practices must involve anaphoric recurrence structures (SOT chap. 4: 23–4), and since he does not stipulate, for *autonomous* discursive practices, a mechanism by which *sentence*-tokens are anaphorically linked to each other,[4] this claim is most plausibly interpreted as saying that in autonomous discursive practices anaphora links *term*-tokens to each other – and, more specifically, tokens of singular and general terms. If that is right, then this second claim implies that all autonomous discursive practices must exhibit the whole gamut of anaphoric, syntactic, and substitution-inferential (SMSIC) structures encountered in chapter 4. Note that Brandom nowhere says that these anaphoric, syntactic, and substitution inferential features are generated through algorithmic elaboration. Thus, if the presence of universal LX-vocabulary, generated via algorithmic elaboration, is the mark of non-autonomous discursive practice, these features may well be part of autonomous discursive practices, according to Brandom's overall oeuvre – *pace* his claim in MIE that every social practice fitting the bare-bones normative pragmatic description of chapter 3 is genuinely discursive.

Brandom's first and second claim combined in turn imply, in light of the considerations in chapter 7, that all discursive practices resembling usages of natural languages purport to represent a largely non-linguistic Aristotelian world of states of affairs (dis-course-incorporated, non-linguistic, worldly objects having certain properties and standing in certain relations to each other). In other words, *pace* his claim in MIE that, strictly speaking, every social practice fitting the bare-bones normative pragmatic description of chapter 3 is genuinely discursive, Brandom also makes claims throughout his work that strongly suggest that, according to him, all discursive practices resembling usages of natural language exhibit precisely the anaphoric, syntactic, and representational fea-tures that linguistic communication exhibits according to the Received View. *These* are, I would argue on behalf of Brandom, the practices with respect to which McDowell's and Wanderer's chal-lenge should properly be raised. To my mind, Brandom should simply scrap the needlessly controversial claim in MIE that every social practice fitting the bare-bones normative pragmatic descrip-tion of chapter 3 is genuinely discursive, and hold – as he often suggests he does in more recent work – that the simplest kinds of genuinely discursive practices must comprise the anaphoric, syn-tactic, and substitution inferential structure laid out in chapter 4, language entries and exits (chapter 5), and the representational features discussed in chapter 7.

Brandom introduces all these structural features in the technical, normative pragmatic language of acknowledging and attributing assertional, practical, syntactic, anaphoric, (substitution) inferential commitment and entitlement in the context of overall feedback-governed, world-involving perceptual and behavioral activity. None of these features, if I'm right, presupposes any of the key semantic, epistemic, and cognitive features of our discourse and reasoning that Brandom wishes to explain. In particular, the (sub-stitution) inferential feature is officially introduced, in the context of this entire normative pragmatic machinery, without relying on the prior assumption that it is also the key semantic and rational feature of the practices described. Similarly, referential purport to an Aristotelian world of states of affairs falls out from the way these normative pragmatic components interact with each other in the context of the practitioners' feedback-governed interac-tions with the environment – again, I think, without relying on the prior assumption that the (substitution) inferential feature is also the key semantic and rational feature of the practices described. Brandom's pragmatism, I would argue on behalf of Brandom, is the attempt to reductively explain all the key semantic, epis-temic, and cognitive features of our discourse and reasoning in terms of social practices exhibiting *this* rich, normative pragmatic machinery.

Skeptics will have ample opportunity to object to this, that, or the other move Brandom makes in laying out this normative pragmatic machinery and to his attempt to reductively explain this, that, or the other semantic, epistemic, and cognitive feature of our discursive reasoning to aspects of this machinery. What the skeptic cannot plausibly do, however, is to both grant that the richly structured practices introduced in these normative pragmatic terms share all these features with our discursive practices, and also to insist that these practices are nevertheless not genuinely discursive but are merely social games. Or, anyway, the skeptic cannot do this any more than a skeptic of the Received View could grant that the social exchanges the Received View labels "linguistic communication" share important features with genuine linguistic communication and also insist that these exchanges nonetheless are merely social games. Because the practices Brandom describes in these normative pragmatic terms have precisely the features of discourse that discourse has according to the Received View: syntactic and anaphoric structure, singular and general terms, and representational purport to an Aristotelian world of states of affairs.

Notes

Chapter 1

1   I borrow the term from Gauker (2003, Ch. 1).
2   Following Brandom's convention, I use underlined sentences or words to represent the corresponding sentence meanings/propositional contents or word meanings/concepts.
3   For an important commentary on this, see Shapiro 2004: 142–44.
4   MIE 20–1, 23–5. Cf. Wittgenstein 2001: §§ 197–202, Sellars 1991: 321.
5   Wittgenstein 2001: § 185; Kripke 1982: chap. 2.
6   See Horrwich 1998, 2005 for an attempt to work out such a dispositionalist regularity theory of discursive practice. For commentary see Loeffler 2009: 201–5.
7   See Adams and Aizawa 2010, Sect. 4; Neander 2012, Sect. 4 for overviews of problems for naturalistic theories of mental representation within the Received View.
8   See e.g. Rorty 1979, Ch. 4; Gauker 2003, chap. 2 for attempts to make this case.
9   Wittgenstein 2001: §§ 199–202, 269–75; Davidson 2001.

Chapter 2

1   Kant 2000: 10. See RP 33, 39, MIE 8.

Chapter 3

1 Most readers interpret Brandom as pursuing this explanatory strategy, and I shall follow this interpretation. For critical discussion of this interpretation cf. MacFarlane 2010: 88–94, and for an alternative, nonreductive reading cf. Wanderer 2008, chap. 4: 89–93. Cf. the Conclusion for discussion.

2 This view has been challenged by Kukla and Lance (2009) and Wanderer (2010). For brief defenses cf. Brandom 2010d and 2010e.

3 Moreover, deductive inferences are usually regarded as monotonic, yet Brandom regards both the committive and the permissive consequence relation as non-monotonic (chapter 4).

4 MIE 193, 2010e: 315; 2010f: 27. For a detailed critique of this claim see Wanderer 2010.

5 For an attempt to botanize other type of speech acts within a broadly Brandomian framework, cf. Kukla and Lance 2009.

6 For a nuanced discussion of the epistemology of testimony underlying this picture, see Wanderer 2010: 107–11.

7 See chapters 7 and 8 for more discussion of this point.

Chapter 4

1 Grover et al. 1975. Cf. MIE 275–305.

2 See in particular SOT chap. 6: 75–91; EE chaps. 3, 5, 6.

3 For an important qualification see n. 6.

4 This aspect of Brandom's work is strongly influenced by Frege's and Dummett's work in the philosophy of language (e.g. MIE 347–50).

5 This is Brandom's example. However, the example raises far-reaching issues concerning names vs. definite descriptions, familiar from the literature initiated by Kripke (1972). Brandom could sidestep these issues without theoretical cost, I think, by limiting the following discussion to the substitution of *logically proper names* (such as "Cicero" and "Tully", or "Hesperus" and "Phosphorus") for each other, setting aside *definite descriptions* (such as "The first Postmaster General of the US").

6 Brandom explains the contrast between primary and (what might be called) secondary substitution-semantic occurrences of terms – extensional vs. intensional contexts – in terms of the substitution of component sentences into larger compound sentences

containing logical (or other explicitating) vocabulary (MIE 346–52). I cannot discuss the surrounding technical issues in this limited space.

7   Corresponding to the three species of substitution inferential norms, we thus may speak of committive SMSICs, permissive SMSICs, and incompatibility SMSICs.

8   This does not mean that Brandom does not share the common view that some referring expressions, paradigmatically deictical ones, refer with particular strength (MIE 567–73).

9   I follow Brandom's convention to use the slashes "/" as quotation marks for *token* expressions (MIE 314, 452).

Chapter 5

1   For usage of the slashes "/" see chap. 4, n. 9.
2   Compare Gettier 1963.

Chapter 6

1   Compare MacFarlane 2008: 59–60.
2   Brandom explicitly argues that it is impossible to algorithmically elaborate the abilities PV-sufficient to participate in autonomous discursive practices from non-discursive abilities (BSD 79–83).
3   See also BSD 46, n. 6, and EE 139–43. This passage is in the context of a discussion of modal vocabulary, but the point applies to conditionals as well.
4   Unfortunately, Brandom has not so far extended this theory to conditionals – his paradigm piece of logical vocabulary.
5   MIE 125, BSD 147–55. For an argument that the requirement of conservativeness is on second glance less urgent, and that it is in tension with Brandom's vision of the purpose of logic, see Weiss 2010: 248–9, 253–5.
6   In accordance with Brandom's claim that the "is" of identity is logical vocabulary that allows speakers to make explicit symmetric SMSICs (MIE 416–26).
7   See, e.g., BSD 101, 181; EE 140–1, 186–7.
8   "Concept $\underline{P}$ is *sense dependent* on concept $\underline{Q}$ just in case one cannot count as having grasped $\underline{P}$ unless one counts as grasping $\underline{Q}$. ... Concept $\underline{P}$ is *reference dependent* on concept $\underline{Q}$ just in case

P cannot apply to something unless Q applies to something" (TMD 194–5).

9 See EE 178, BSD 97.

Chapter 7

1 Brandom's theory of technical truth and reference talk, not thematized in this book, complicates this picture of ubiquitous representation *relations* (MIE chap. 5, especially 310–13).

2 Kant 1997: B137 (cited from RP 45). See also BSD 187.

3 Here and in the following, I use such capitalization to indicate talk about properties and relations.

4 The quote attributes this view to Hegel. But it is clear that it is also Brandom's own.

5 For the treatment of definite descriptions as singular terms here compare chap. 4, n. 5. For symmetric SMSICs and identity compare chap. 6, n. 6.

6 This does not, however, imply that the inferential commitment from 1 to 5 will contribute to C's linguistic understanding of "The inventor of bifocals" and "George Washington," since terms occurring in that-clauses of belief ascriptions do not have primary substitution-semantic occurrence (see chap. 4).

7 For a critique of this view see Loeffler 2014.

8 MIE 481–4. For a good discussion cf. Wanderer 2008: 147–51.

Chapter 8

1 MIE 592–7, 626–44. For skeptical responses, see, e.g., Rosen 1997, Hattiangadi 2003, Rödl 2010, Laurier 2008. Wanderer (2008: 206–8) argues that MIE should not be regarded as an attempt to explain semantic norms at all (see conclusion below). For a defense of phenomenalism in accordance with Brandom's core theoretical commitments, see Loeffler 2005.

2 See TMD 13–15, 230–3; RP Chap. 3; SOT chaps. 9 and 10.

3 Compare Quine 1960, chap. 2; 1980; and various essays in Davidson (2001).

Conclusion

1 For the various approaches see Davies and Stone 1995(a), 1995(b); Carruthers and Smith (1995).

2   For a philosophical argument that autonomous discourse must include explicit belief ascriptions, see Lauer 2012.

3   Relatedly, Sharp has challenged that, on pain of paradox, Brandom's theory of meaning cannot explain the meaning of the sentences in which this theory is formulated, and that, therefore, Brandom's semantic theory is not *expressively complete*. See Sharp (2010) for discussion.

4   The case is different for non-autonomous discursive practices involving truth talk, according to Brandom's prosentential theory of truth. (MIE Ch. 5, in particular 301–5.)

Glossary

These are not meant to be precise definitions but rather brief glosses, intended to facilitate the reading of the main text. Unless indicated otherwise, all glosses aim to capture the meaning of these terms as Brandom uses them, and they may thus deviate from other prominent uses of these terms in the literature.

Algorithmic elaboration Generating a complex ability by applying a set of simpler abilities in a specific order. For example, the ability to long-divide is algorithmically elaborated from the skills to multiply and to subtract.

Anaphora Mechanism of cross-reference determining which term-tokens in discourse count as recurrences of which other term-tokens, and thus as instances of the same term. Modeled on anaphoric uses of pronouns, such as in "Tom is sad because *his* dog died."

Anaphoric commitment A speaker's commitment, regarding two term-tokens in discourse, that one is *anaphorically* related to the other and that both thus are instances of the same term.

Aristotelian world The world of actual and possible states of affairs, that is, of individuals as having certain properties and as standing in certain relations to each other. In virtue of the structure of their reasoning and discourse, speakers represent the world as Aristotelian.

Assertional commitment A speaker's commitment to an assertion or declarative sentence <u>that p</u>. Roughly, his or her obligation to assert <u>that p</u> when asked whether <u>p</u>.

Assertional entitlement A speaker's entitlement to assert <u>that p</u>. Roughly, his or her justification to assert or believe <u>that p</u>.

Autonomous discursive practice The simplest possible kinds of *discursive practices*. They exclude any use of *universal LX-vocabulary*, and assertion is their only speech act.

Autonomy The view, defended in different ways by Kant and Hegel, that rational beings are self-legislating (autonomous) in that they give the norms of reasoning to themselves.

Auxiliary moves Speech acts such as queries, challenges, disavowals, or withdrawals, which, by contrast to the speech act of assertion, are strictly speaking not part of *autonomous discursive practices*.

Belief An acknowledged *assertional commitment* (empirical psychological sense of belief) or an assertional commitment one is bound to acknowledge in consequence of acknowledging certain other assertional commitments (normative sense of belief).

Conservativism/conservative extension Adding new vocabulary V to a stock of old vocabulary V' is a conservative extension of V' just in case adding V does not alter the meaning of V'. Brandom thinks that adding new *logical* (or, more generally *universal LX*) vocabulary to any old ordinary empirical vocabulary must be conservative in this sense.

***De dicto* belief ascription** Ascription of a belief to someone that fully specifies the belief's propositional content. For example, "Aristotle believes <u>that the earth is the center of the universe</u>."

Deflationism (about truth) The view that the predicate "is true" is not a philosophically explanatory notion, and that, accordingly, meaning, knowledge, justification, reasoning, logical validity, etc., cannot properly be philosophically explained in terms of truth, truth conditions, likelihood of truth, preservation of truth, and the like.

Deontic attitude An acknowledgment (for oneself) or attribution (to someone else) of a commitment or entitlement to something. (See also *deontic status*.)

Deontic practice Norm-governed social interaction between two or more participants.

Deontic status A commitment or entitlement (roughly, an obligation or permission) a deontic practitioner has at a given stage of the *deontic practice* he or she engages in.

***De re* belief ascription** An ascription of a belief to someone that involves reference to an item and ascribing a belief *about it*. For example, "Aristotle believes of the earth <u>that it is the center of</u>

the universe." Here the earth is referred to, and a belief *about it* is ascribed to Aristotle.

Discursive intentionality The ability to use concepts in theoretical and practical judgments, that is, to reason, to evaluate propositions, and to take things thus and so.

Discursive practice Linguistic communication. A species of deontic practice.

Expressive completeness A semantic theory is expressively complete just in case it can explain the meaning of the very sentences in which the theory is formulated.

Externalism (epistemic) The view that one can be justified in believing that p although one is in no position to ascertain, through reflection and introspection alone, *that* one is so justified.

Externalism (semantic) The view that "meanings are not in the head," that is, that the meaning of many words is partially constituted by social or natural factors outside a speaker's head or skin.

Game of giving and asking for reasons Any instance of *discursive practice.*

General term A predicate. Any term representing a property or relation.

Holism (semantic) The view that certain relations between the sentences of a language constitute the meaning of each sentence of the language. Brandom's *inferential role semantics* is a holistic semantics.

Inferential commitment A speaker's commitment to treat two sentences as *materially inferentially* related, in accordance with the norms of inference governing discourse.

Inferential role semantics View that the *inferential role* of a sentence S, that is, the norms of *material inference* and incompatibility relating S to other sentences of the language, constitute the meaning of S.

Inferential role The inferential role of a sentence is its role in reasoning – its location in the space of reasons – and it consists in the sum of the norms of inference and incompatibility (norms of reasoning) relating S to other sentences of the language.

Intention A *practical commitment* to act in a certain way. *Practical commitments* may be acknowledged (empirical psychological sense of *intention)* or inherited in consequence of acknowledging certain other *assertional* or *practical commitments* (more normative sense of *intention).*

Intentionality (discursive) The propositional contentfulness of speech and of the cognitive mental states of rational beings.

Intentionality (practical) The ability to engage in feedback-governed ways with features of one's environment; many non-rational beings are practically intentional systems. *Discursive intentionality* is a species of practical intentionality.

I-thou sociality (of norms) The view, held by Brandom, that while each rational being's perspective is a basis for evaluating other such perspectives and while not all such perspectives are equally meritorious, there are no ultimate, fixed, perspective-transcendent standards determining which rational perspective is really correct.

I-we sociality (of norms) The view, rejected by Brandom, that some feature of the community of rational beings as such (perhaps the opinions or reasoning patterns of the majority) ultimately sets the standard for correct reasoning.

Language entries/exits *Observational beliefs/observation reports*, that is, discursive commitments that are formed in immediate response to (non-linguistic) perception; and *practical commitments* that immediately lead to non-linguistic actions.

Linguistic understanding A speaker's linguistic understanding of a sentence S consists in his or her acknowledged *inferential commitments* regarding S. A speaker's linguistic understanding of a term T consists in his or her acknowledged *SMSICs* regarding T.

Logical vocabulary *Universal LX-vocabulary* that makes explicit semantic aspects of discourse, that is, aspects of the inferential and incompatibility relations between sentences.

Material inference An inference that is valid independently of any *logical vocabulary* (formal vocabulary). For example, the inference from "Fido is crimson" to "Fido is red" is materially valid as it stands, independently of the conditional "If Fido is crimson then Fido is red." The material inferential and incompatibility relations between the sentences of a language constitute the meaning (propositional contentfulness) of the sentences of the language.

Meaning The meaning of a sentence is its *inferential role* – its role in reasoning, aka its position in the *space of reasons*. The meaning of a *singular* or *general term* is its *substitution-inferential* role, that is, its contribution to the inferential role of the sentences in which it occurs.

Meaning-use analysis Analysis that correlates specific *pragmatic* abilities with the specific meaning of sentences or terms of a language.

Modality (alethic) Causal and metaphysical necessities and possibilities, built into the largely non-linguistic, objective world.

Modality (deontic) Normative necessities and possibilities (obligations and permissions, commitments and entitlements) governing and constraining rational subjects.

Modal realism The view that the non-linguistic world includes objective modal facts – facts about what is causally or metaphysically possible and necessary – independently of any discursive or rational activity.

Modal expressivism the view that use of modal vocabulary – the vocabulary of (alethic) possibility and necessity – makes explicit aspects of the inferential role (hence the semantics) of the ordinary empirical vocabulary in use.

Mutual social recognition Our recognition of others as rational beings – as bound by certain shared norms of reason and as more or less living up to these standards – and of others as creatures recognizing us as rational beings as well.

Mutual social recognition model (Hegel) Hegel's (and Brandom's) idea that rational beings institute or create the norms of reason through their *mutual social recognition* in their social interactions. See *Phenomenalism about norms*.

Naturalism The view, rejected by Brandom, that all norms can ultimately be explained in purely non-normative, descriptive terms, such as statistic regularities. See *regularism*.

Normative status See *Deontic status*

Normative attitude See *Deontic attitude*

Normative pragmatics A *pragmatic theory* that describes the use of language in discourse in part in normative terms, that is, in terms of how the language should or may be used.

Observational belief A belief that p formed in immediate response to perceptual input, unmediated by intermediary beliefs from which the belief that p would be formed inferentially.

Observation report An assertion or declarative sentence expressing an *observational belief*.

Original synthetic unity of apperception A speaker's system of theoretical and practical judgments (acknowledged *assertional* and *practical commitments*). It is a unity created through the speaker's ongoing rational, inferential activity, through which he or she integrates his or her judgments into a more or less coherent and comprehensive whole.

Phenomenalism about norms The view that the *scorekeeping* activity of acknowledging and attributing commitments and entitlements, distributed over participants in *deontic practices*, creates or institutes the norms governing the practices. See *Mutual social recognition model (Hegel)*.

Practical commitment An intention to act, that is, a practical judgment. A speaker's commitment to a certain course of action. To be expressed via a *shall-statement* that p.

Practical intentionality The ability to engage with features of one's environment in feedback-governed ways, by mapping, tracking, or – for rational beings – conceptually representing those features and by adjusting one's behavior to detected changes in those features. See *TOTE cycle*.

Pragmatic meta-vocabulary A vocabulary describing, for a certain vocabulary V, the norms and abilities speakers need to follow and to employ if they are to say anything using V.

Pragmatics Discipline concerned with the use of a language in discourse, that is, with the skills employed and the norms followed in using the language.

Pragmatic Theory See *Pragmatics*.

Pragmatism The view that the central semantic, epistemic, and cognitive feature of discourse and reasoning (propositional meaning and content, justification, knowledge, truth, etc.) are to be explained in *pragmatic* terms, that is, in terms of the use of language in discourse.

Propositional content The content of a cognitive mental state (belief, intention, etc.). It consists in the *inferential role* of the sentence by which the cognizer would express the cognitive state.

Rationalism The view that the role in reasoning of a concept or term constitutes the content of the concept or the meaning of the term.

Received View Approach to linguistic meaning and communication in terms of the speakers' prior ability to reason, and to the conceptual contents employed in such reasoning in terms of (non-linguistic) mental representations. Brandom opposes this view.

Reference class The class of items with respect to which the degree of *reliability* with which a speaker forms an *observational belief* is assessed. Picking the appropriate reference class is an irreducibly normative affair.

Reference dependence A concept P is reference-dependent on a concept Q just in case P successfully refers to some item only if Q successfully refers to some item.

Referential purport The objects, properties, or relations a speaker purportedly picks out by engaging in discursive reasoning, that is, by acknowledging a system of *assertional* and *inferential commitments*. See *Original synthetic unity of apperception*.

Regulism The view, rejected by Brandom, that, in general, the ability to follow a norm n requires explicit, propositional knowledge of the norm, viz. of the corresponding *rule*.

Regularism The view, rejected by Brandom, that, in general, regularities of behavior in a community set the standard of correct behavior.

Reliability (epistemic) Paradigmatically, a speaker's propensity to form predominantly correct *observational beliefs* about a certain topic. Processes of reliably forming *observational beliefs* are neither inferential nor naturalistic, and they justify the beliefs formed.

Reliability inference Move from attributing to someone else a belief <u>that p</u> (an acknowledged assertional commitment <u>that p</u>) as reliably formed to forming on that basis the belief <u>that p</u> oneself.

Rule A norm made explicit in the form of a propositionally contentful thought or claim.

Scorekeeping The cognitive activity of tracking one's own and one's peers' *deontic statuses* and *deontic attitudes* while engaging with them in *deontic practice*, by acknowledging (for oneself) and attributing (to others, both as acknowledged and as to be acknowledged) constellations of commitments and entitlements, in accordance with what one takes to be the norms governing the practice.

Sense dependence A concept P is sense-dependent on a concept Q just in case one cannot understand P unless one also understands Q.

Singular term Any term referring to an individual object. Proper names and indexicals are paradigmatic singular terms.

Shall-Statement A statement expressing a *practical commitment*.

SMSIC Simple material substitution inferential commitment. A speaker's commitment, concerning a pair of terms <T1, T2>, that substituting T2 for T1 into a sentence ...T1... (where T1 occurs in extensional context) will yield a valid *substitution inference*. The SMSICs a speaker has regarding a term T determine how the speaker should understand T; the SMSICs the speaker acknowledges regarding T constitute the speaker's linguistic understanding of T.

Space of reasons The normative space of *material inferential* and incompatibility relations between sentences. Reasoning is the activity of navigating this space more or less properly, in accordance with what one takes the norms of reason (norms of inference and incompatibility) to be.

Substitution inference A valid one-premise inference, generated by substituting for some term in the premise another term of the same syntactic category, thereby reaching the conclusion. The meaning of a term T consists in its substitution inferential role, that is, in the sum total of proper ways to generate substitution inferences by substituting T for certain other terms, or certain other terms for T.

Substitution inferential commitment See *SMSIC*.

Substitution semantic commitment See *SMSIC*.

Synthesizing The ongoing rational, inferential activity of integrating one's theoretical and practical judgments into a unified system. See *Original synthetic unity of apperception*.

TOTE cycle Test-Operate-Test-Exit cycle. The cycle characterizing the feedback-governed engagement of a *practically intentional* system with its environment.

Universal LX-vocabulary Universally elaborated explicating vocabulary. Any vocabulary *algorithmically elaborated* from, and expressing, structural features or pragmatic abilities that any discourse or speaker at all must exhibit. Paradigmatically, *logical vocabulary*.

References

Works by Robert Brandom

This is a list of Brandom's writings that are referred to in this book.

(1976) "Freedom and Constraint by Norms," *American Philosophical Quarterly* 16: 187–96

(1983) "Asserting," *Noûs* 17: 637–50

(1987) "Singular Terms and Sentential Sign Design," *Philosophical Topics* 15: 125–67.

(1994) *Making it Explicit. Reasoning, Representing, and Discursive Commitment*. Cambridge, MA: Harvard University Press.

(1995a) "Knowledge and the Social Articulation of the Space of Reasons," *Philosophy and Phenomenological Research* 60: 895–908.

(1995b) "Perception and Rational Constraint," *Philosophical Issues* 7: 241–259.

(1997) "Study Guide," in W. Sellars, *Empiricism and the Philosophy of Mind. With an Introduction by Richard Rorty and a Study Guide by Robert Brandom*. Cambridge, MA: Harvard University Press, 119–81.

(1999) "Interview of Robert Brandom, by Susanna Schellenberg, for the *Deutsche Zeitschrift für Philosophie*." Manuscript in the author's possession. (The interview appeared in German as "Interview. Von der Begriffsanalyse zu einer systematischen Metaphysik," *Deutsche Zeitschrift für Philosophie* 47: 1005–20)

(2000a) *Articulating Reasons. An Introduction to Inferentialism*. Cambridge, MA: Harvard University Press.

(2000b) "Facts, Norms, and Normative Facts: A Reply to Habermas," *European Journal of Philosophy* 8: 356–74.

(2002a) *Tales of the Mighty Dead. Historical Essays in the Metaphysics of Intentionality.* Cambridge, MA: Harvard University Press.

(2002b) "Analyzing Pragmatism. Pragmatics and Pragmatisms," in J. Conant and U. Zeglen (eds.), *Hilary Putnam: Pragmatism and Realism.* London, UK: Routledge, 40–59. Reprinted in *PP*. (All text references are to this reprint.)

(2002c) "Non-Inferential Knowledge, Perceptual Experience, and Secondary Qualities," in N. H. Smith (ed.), *Reading McDowell On Mind and World.* London, UK: Routledge, 92–105.

(2007) "Inferentialism and Some of Its Challenges," *Philosophy and Phenomenological Research* 74, 651–76. Reprinted in B. Weiss and J. Wanderer (eds.), *Reading Brandom: On Making It Explicit.* New York: Routledge, 159–80. (All text references are to this reprint.)

(2008a) *Between Saying and Doing: Towards an Analytic Pragmatism.* New York: Oxford University Press.

(2008b) "Responses," in P. Stekeler-Weithofer (ed.), *The Pragmatics of Making It Explicit.* Amsterdam, Philadelphia: John Benjamins Publishing Company, 209–29.

(2008c) "Responses," *Philosophical Topics* 36: 135–55.

(2009) *Reason in Philosophy. Animating Ideas.* Cambridge, MA: Belknap Press of Harvard University Press.

(2010a) "Reply to Jerry Fodor and Ernest Lepore's 'Brandom Beleaguered'," in B. Weiss and J. Wanderer (eds.), *Reading Brandom: On Making It Explicit.* New York: Routledge, 332–37.

(2010b) "Reply to Michael Kremer's 'Representation or Inference: Must We Choose? Should We?'," in B. Weiss and J. Wanderer (eds.), *Reading Brandom: On Making It Explicit.* New York: Routledge, 347–52.

(2010c) "Reply to John MacFarlane's 'Pragmatism and Inferentialism'," in B. Weiss and J. Wanderer (eds.), *Reading Brandom: On Making It Explicit.* New York: Routledge, 313–14.

(2010d) "Reply to Mark Lance and Rebecca Kukla's 'Perception, Language, and the First Person'," in B. Weiss and J. Wanderer (eds.), *Reading Brandom: On Making It Explicit.* New York: Routledge, 316–19.

(2010e) "Reply to Jeremy Wanderer's 'Brandom's Challenges'," in B. Weiss and J. Wanderer (eds.), *Reading Brandom: On Making It Explicit.* New York: Routledge, 315.

(2010f) "Conceptual Content and Discursive Practice," *Grazer Philosophische Studien* 81, 13–35.

(2011) *Perspectives on Pragmatism. Classical, Recent, and Contemporary.* Cambridge, MA: Harvard University Press.
(2015) *From Empiricism to Expressivism: Brandom Reads Sellars.* Cambridge, MA: Harvard University Press.
(forthcoming) *A Spirit of Trust. A Semantic Reading of Hegel's Phenomenology.* 2014 draft, http://www.pitt.edu/~brandom/spirit_of_trust_2014.html. Accessed 04/02/2014.

Works by other authors

Adams, Fred and Ken Aizawa (2010) "Causal Theories of Mental Content," Stanford Encyclopedia of Philosophy, https://plato.stanford.edu/entries/content-causal/. Accessed 02/03/2017.
Carruthers, Peter and Peter K. Smith (eds.) (1995) *Theories of Theories of Mind.* Cambridge, UK: Cambridge University Press.
Davidson, Donald (2001) *Inquiries into Truth and Interpretation.* New York: Oxford University Press.
Davies, Martin and Tony Stone (eds.) (1995a) *Folk Psychology: The Theory of Mind Debate.* Oxford: Blackwell.
Davies, Martin and Tony Stone (eds.) (1995b) *Mental Simulation: Evaluations and Applications.* Oxford: Blackwell.
Dretske, Fred (1981) *Knowledge and the Flow of Information*, Cambridge, MA: MIT/Bradford Press.
Dretske, Fred (1988) *Explaining Behavior: Reasons in a World of Causes.* Cambridge, MA: MIT/Bradford.
Fodor, Jerry (1987) *Psychosemantics: The Problem of Meaning in the Philosophy of Mind.* Cambridge, MA: MIT/Bradford.
Fodor, Jerry A. and Ernest Lepore (1992) *Holism: A Shopper's Guide.* Oxford: Blackwell Publishing.
Fodor, Jerry A. and Ernest Lepore (1993) "Why Meaning (Probably) Isn't Conceptual Role," *Philosophical Issues* 3: 15–35.
Frege, Gottlob (1960) "On Sense and Reference," in P. Geach and M. Black (eds.), *Translations from the Philosophical Writings of Gottlob Frege.* 2nd ed. Oxford: Basil Blackwell, 56–78.
Gallagher, Shaun (2001) "The Practice of Mind: Theory, Simulation or Primary Interaction?" *Journal of Consciousness Studies* 8 (5–7): 83–108.
Gauker, Christopher (2003) *Words Without Meaning.* Cambridge, MA: Bradford Book, MIT Press.
Gettier, Edmund L. (1963) "Is Justified True Belief Knowledge?" *Analysis* 23: 121–23.

Goldman, Alvin (1976) "Discrimination and Perceptual Knowledge," *Journal of Philosophy* 73, 771–91.

Grice, Paul (1989a) "Meaning," in Paul Grice, *Studies in the Way of Words.* Cambridge, MA: Harvard University Press, 213–23.

Grice, Paul (1989b) "Meaning Revisited," in Paul Grice, *Studies in the Way of Words.* Cambridge, MA: Harvard University Press, 283–303.

Grover, D., J. Camp, and N. Belnap (1975) "A Prosentential Theory of Truth," *Philosophical Studies* 27, 73–125.

Hattiangadi, Anandi (2003) "Making It Implicit: Brandom on Rule Following," *Philosophy and Phenomenological Research* 66: 419–31.

Horrwich, Paul (1998) *Meaning.* New York: Oxford University Press.

Horrwich, Paul (2005) *Reflections on Meaning.* New York: Oxford University Press.

Hume, David (1975) [1748] *An Enquiry Concerning Human Understanding.* In D. Hume, *Enquiries Concerning Human Understanding and Concerning the Principles of Morals. Reprinted from the 1777 edition with Introduction and Analytical Index by L. A. Selby-Bigge.* Ed. by P. H. Nidditch. 3rd ed. New York: Oxford University Press.

Kant, Immanuel (1997) *Critique of Practical Reason.* Trans. and ed. by M. Gregor. Cambridge, UK: Cambridge University Press.

Kant, Immanuel (1998) *Groundwork of the Metaphysics of Morals.* Trans. and ed. by M. Gregor. Cambridge, UK: Cambridge University Press.

Kant, Immanuel (2000) *Critique of the Power of Judgment.* Trans. by Paul Guyer and Eric Matthews. Cambridge, UK: Cambridge University Press.

Kremer, Michael (2010) "Representation or Inference: Must We Choose? Should We?" In B. Weiss and J. Wanderer (eds.), *Reading Brandom: On Making It Explicit.* New York: Routledge, 227–46.

Kripke, Saul (1972) "Naming and Necessity," in G. Harman and D. Davidson (eds.), *Semantics of Natural Languages.* Dordrecht: D. Reidel Publishing Co. Reprinted as Saul Kripke, *Naming and Necessity.* Oxford: Blackwell. (All text references are to this reprint.)

Kripke, Saul (1982) *Wittgenstein on Rules and Private Language.* Cambridge, MA: Harvard University Press.

Kukla, Rebecca and Mark, Lance (2009) *"Yo" and "Lo!": The Pragmatic Topography of the Space of Reasons.* Cambridge, MA: Harvard University Press.

Lauer, David (2012) "Expressivism and the Layer Cake Picture of Discursive Practice," *Philosophia: Philosophical Quarterly of Israel* 40: 55–73.

Laurier, Daniel (2008) "Pragmatics, Pittsburgh Style," in P. Stekeler-Weithofer (ed.), *The Pragmatics of Making It Explicit*. Amsterdam, Philadelphia: John Benjamins Publishing Company, 127–46.

Loeffler, Ronald (2005) "Normative Phenomenalism: On Robert Brandom's Practice-Based Explanation of Meaning," *European Journal of Philosophy* 13: 32–69.

Loeffler, Ronald (2009) "Neo-Pragmatist (Practice-Based) Theories of Meaning," *Philosophy Compass* 4/1: 197–218.

Loeffler, Ronald (2014) "Belief Ascriptions and Social Externalism," *Philosophical Studies* 167: 211–39.

MacFarlane, John (2008) "Brandom's Demarcation of Logic," *Philosophical Topics* 36/2: 55–62.

MacFarlane, John (2010) "Pragmatism and Inferentialism," in B. Weiss and J. Wanderer (eds.), *Reading Brandom: On Making It Explicit*. New York: Routledge, 81–95.

McDowell, John (2008) "Motivating Inferentialism: Comments on *Making It Explicit* (chap. 2)," in P. Stekeler-Weithofer (ed.), *The Pragmatics of Making It Explicit*. Amsterdam, Philadelphia: John Benjamins Publishing Company, 109–26.

Millikan, Ruth (1984) *Language, Thought and Other Biological Categories*. Cambridge, MA: MIT Press.

Millikan, Ruth (1989) "Biosemantics," *Journal of Philosophy*, 86: 281–97.

Neander, Karen (2012) "Teleological Theories of Mental Content." Stanford Encyclopedia of Philosophy, https://plato.stanford.edu/entries/content-teleological/#4. Accessed 02/03/2017.

Papineau, David (1984) "Representation and Explanation," *Philosophy of Science* 51: 550–72.

Papineau, David (1998) "Teleosemantics and Indeterminacy," *Australasian Journal of Philosophy* 76: 1–14.

Peregrin, Jaroslav (2005) "The Nature of Meaning: Brandom versus Chomsky," *Pragmatics and Cognition* 13: 39–57. Reprinted in P. Stekeler-Weithofer (ed.), *The Pragmatics of Making It Explicit*. Amsterdam, Philadelphia: John Benjamins Publishing, 35–52. (All text references to this reprint.)

Putnam, Hilary (1975) "The Meaning of Meaning," in Keith Gunderson (ed.), *Language, Mind, and Knowledge*. Minneapolis: University of Minnesota Press, 131–93.

Quine, Willard Van Orman (1960) *Word and Object*. Cambridge, MA: MIT Press.

Quine, Willard Van Orman (1980) "Two Dogmas of Empiricism," in W. V. O. Quine, *From a Logical Point of View: Nine Logico-Philosophical Essays*. 2nd ed. Cambridge, MA: Harvard University Press, 20–46. [Originally published 1951.]

Rödl, Sebastian (2010) "Normativity of Mind versus Philosophy as Explanation," in B. Weiss and J. Wanderer (eds.), *Reading Brandom: On Making It Explicit*. New York: Routledge, 63–80. [Modified translation of: Rödl, Sebastian (2010) "Normativität des Geistes versus Philosophie als Erklärung," *Deutsche Zeitschrift für Philosophie* 48: 762–79.]

Rorty, Richard (1979) *Philosophy and the Mirror of Nature*, Princeton, NJ: Princeton University Press.

Rosen, Gideon (1997) "Who Makes the Rules Around Here?," *Philosophy and Phenomenological Research*, 57/1: 163–71.

Rosenberg, Jay (1975) *Linguistic Representation*. Dordrecht: Reidel.

Sellars, Wilfrid (1957) "Counterfactuals, Dispositions, and the Causal Modalities," in H. Feigl, M. Scriven, and G. Maxwell (eds.), *Minnesota Studies in the Philosophy of Science*, 2. Minneapolis: University of Minnesota Press, 225–308.

Sellars, Wilfrid (1980) [1948] "Concepts as Involving Law and Inconceivable Without Them," in W. Sellars, *Pure Pragmatics and Possible Worlds: The Early Essays of Wilfrid Sellars*. Ed. by J. Sicha. Reseda, CA: Ridgeview Publishing, 95–123.

Sellars, Wilfrid (1991) [1954] "Some Reflections on Language Games," in W. Sellars, *Science, Perception and Reality*. Atascadero, CA: Ridgeview Publishing, 321–58.

Sellars, Wilfrid (1992) [1967] *Science and Metaphysics: Variations on Kantian Themes*. Atascadero, CA: Ridgeview Publishing.

Sellars, Wilfrid (1997) [1956] *Empiricism and the Philosophy of Mind: With an Introduction by Richard Rorty and a Study Guide by Robert Brandom*. Cambridge, MA: Harvard University Press.

Sellars, Wilfrid (2007) [1953] "Inference and Meaning," in K. Sharp and R. Brandom (eds.), *In the Space of Reasons. Selected Essays of Wilfrid Sellars*. Cambridge, MA: Harvard University Press, 3–27.

Shapiro, Lionel (2004) "Brandom on the Normativity of Meaning," in *Philosophy and Phenomenological Research* 68/1: 141–60.

Sharp, Kevin (2010) "Truth and Expressive Completeness," in B. Weiss and J. Wanderer (eds.), *Reading Brandom: On Making It Explicit*. New York: Routledge, 262–75.

Stampe, Dennis (1977) "Toward a Causal Theory of Linguistic Representation," in P. French, H. K. Wettstein, and T. E. Uehling (eds.), *Midwest Studies in Philosophy* 2, Minneapolis: University of Minnesota Press, 42–63.

Stout, Rowland (2010) "Being Subject to the Rule to Do What the Rules Tell You to Do," in B. Weiss and J. Wanderer (eds.), *Reading Brandom: On Making It Explicit*. New York: Routledge, 145–56.

Strawson, Peter F. (1964) "Intention and Convention in Speech Acts," *Philosophical Review* 73: 439–60.

Wanderer, Jeremy (2008) *Robert Brandom*. Montreal and Kingston: McGill-Queen's University Press.

Wanderer, Jeremy (2010) "Brandom's Challenges," in B. Weiss and J. Wanderer (eds.), *Reading Brandom: On Making It Explicit*. New York: Routledge, 96–114.

Weiss, Bernhard (2010) "What Is Logic?" In B. Weiss and J. Wanderer (eds.), *Reading Brandom: On Making It Explicit*. New York: Routledge, 247–61.

Williams, Michael (1996) *Unnatural Doubts: Epistemological Realism and the Basis of Scepticism*. Princeton, NJ: Princeton University Press.

Wittgenstein, Ludwig (2001) *Philosophical Investigations. The German Text with a Revised English Translation*. Trans. by G. E. M. Anscombe. 3rd ed. Malden, MA: Blackwell Publishing.

Index